The Life of Russian Business

The Life of Russian Business

(Re)cognizing, (Re)activating and (Re)configuring Institutions

edited by

Tomas Casas i Klett

University of St. Gallen (FIM-HSG)
SKOLKOVO Moscow School of Management

Yuliya Ponomareva

SKOLKOVO Moscow School of Management
ESADE Business School, Ramon Llull University

IAP

INFORMATION AGE PUBLISHING, INC.
Charlotte, NC • www.infoagepub.com

This edited work is derived from a research project by the SKOLKOVO Moscow School of Management and its Academic Office.

Library of Congress Cataloging-in-Publication Data

A CIP record for this book is available from the Library of Congress
http://www.loc.gov

ISBN: 978-1-64113-450-7 (Paperback)
978-1-64113-451-4 (Hardcover)
978-1-64113-452-1 (ebook)

Printed and bound by CPI Group (UK) Ltd, Croydon, CR0 4YY

Contents

SECTION IV

Internationalization, Outbound, and Inbound

SECTION V

Leadership

Introduction

This Time It's a Business Revolution

Tomas Casas i Klett
Yuliya Ponomareva

The understanding of Russian business in the world today is still anchored to 1990s images of wild capitalism and a Dutch-diseased, resource-dependent economy with poorly functioning rules. Despite the continued relevance of these issues in the current environment, readers of this book will discover that business in Russia has undergone a remarkable transformation. Unknown to many outsiders, this process is still unfolding in parallel with the reconfiguration of the institutions that shape the business environment. It is still unclear where these developments are leading. Yet, as one would expect from an emergent market that has suffered more than its fair share of shocks, on the frontlines of business there is resilience, an uncanny ability to handle uncertainty, and the strong will to create new wealth. The distinctive, agile, and creative business practices appearing to be more and more prevalent in Russia provide inspiration and maybe lessons for managers, entrepreneurs and policy-makers elsewhere.

The Life of Russian Business, pages xiii–xviii

So, What Will I Find in this Book?

The rich and diverse content has been edited to provide a narrative about an ongoing economic transition. One resembling a punctuated equilibrium, characterized by relatively short periods of rapid crises subsequently followed by longer periods of political and economic stabilization and attempted reforms. Despite the unevenness of these reforms, a renewed transformational impetus has emerged since the double whammy that hit Russia in 2014. It is well known that the imposition of economic sanctions by the West coincided with the sharp fall in oil prices and affected the stability of budgets, the currency, and inflation, all seriously compromising growth. The resulting anti-crisis mobilization seems to have crossed a qualitative threshold and has led to changes in how Russian companies and economic agents operate. The dynamic of these changes constitutes a phenomenon in itself: The fascinating institutional interplay between Soviet legacy state capitalism and the dynamism and freewheeling entrepreneurship of emerging market capitalism. At the same time, Western scholarship and media have disengaged from many aspects of Russian economic life and comparatively little is known about how these change dynamics are working themselves out on the ground.

What is different about this book is that it combines a plethora of voices from contemporary Russian businesspeople, politicians, economists, and other professionals. We believe that there is real value in bringing together such a wide set of voices in one place and thereby offering managers, entrepreneurs and policy makers from Russia and beyond a wealth of insights—both positive and critical—into the life of Russian business today. The aim is to broaden the understanding of Russia, its economy, culture, and people and to outline the unique and abundant opportunities the country offers, while being fully aware of the challenges and risks that these bring. The reader will hear the beating heart of business life in Russia, with contributions that address a wide array of both macro and micro topics.

The perspectives collected here highlight the multifaceted nature of Russian business that is subsumed in the proverbial VUCA environment. Genuine volatility, uncertainty, complexity, and ambiguity are present throughout, often in a very raw form. Hence, nearly every contribution depicts original, curious, and even amusing business responses to crises and VUCA challenges, as well as how these responses are relentlessly tested and evolve. Beyond the overall context, we, as editors, had to find other frames of reference to make this work a consistent whole, especially in view of having 50 participating authors and 55 contributions.

How the Book Is Organized

We provide structure for the book in two ways. First, there is the framing indicated in the title and subtitle of this book. Second, contributions have been organized into five sections that group the contributions thematically.

Institutions can be *de jure* and *de facto* rule sets, visible and enshrined or invisible and tacit. Both are powerful and condition the behavior of actors in the economy. The book's contributions bring formal and informal institutions to the foreground, especially the latter that are often ignored as they are shaped by culture and the dynamics of social relationships. To organize the institutional transformations described, we use the framework enunciated in the subtitle of the book: (Re)cognizing, (Re)activating, and (Re)configuring Institutions.

The real world cases depicted in the book bring to life and allow us to *re-cognize* emerging institutions. For example, the cultural shifts of middle-class families in Siberia in terms of their social relationships with neighbors affect the opportunities available to real estate developers (see Chapter II.3). Likewise, the massive state-sponsored business accelerator that is transforming venturing in second and third tier cities allows us to recognize a high-impact emerging formal institution (see Chapter III.12). We also focus on institutional arrangements now being *re-activated* after decades of neglect and even decay. One example is Russia's great expertise in science and its attendant innovation system. A modest but vibrant and growing entrepreneurial scene has been activated while more effective innovation processes at large firms are undergoing a re-activation of sorts. Some readers may judge some of the entrepreneurial projects described as one-offs with little chance to scale, while others will assess these start-ups as well managed and able to leverage Russian inventiveness into international expansion and profitability. Lastly, there are institutions that need *re-configuring* such as Russian healthcare, the fiscal and legal systems, and Russian steel. We examine re-configuration as it is literally happening right now with, for example, a newly minted Russian credit rating agency that is developing methodologies to assess risk in the financial areas of emerging markets left uncovered by the big three rating agencies (see Chapter II.10). In another analysis piece, some readers will be surprised by how effective the re-configuration of the Russian coal sector has been (see Chapter I.12).

The second structural framework that we use is to theme the content of the book into five sections. The themes attempt to cluster diverse experiences and analyses of Russian business in terms of: (1) markets and macro perspectives, (2) strategy and governance, (3) innovation and entrepreneurship, (4) internationalization inbound and outbound, and (5) leadership. Each section has 10 to 12 short contributions. Thematic patterns emerge as the reader navigates each section, leading to a deeper understanding of Russia's economic system, its players and the nature of doing business in Russia and/or with Russians.

An important caveat that we must make is that this book is *not intended to be comprehensive account of Russian business,* nor has it the ambition to make outright generalizations. As editors, we focused on selecting work from the frontlines of business experience, on aspects that explain the functioning of the system, and that bring forward the subjective voices of many participants in the Russian business environment. The book does not make claims on new conceptualizations of Russian business, but instead presents a range of vignettes around its themes.

How to Present the Multifaceted Nature of Russian Business?

The diversity of contributions in the book often uncovers *creative tension.* For example, when reality meets vision in partial or unintended ways. One instance is the much-hailed Sino-Russian relationship, with the supporting institutional framework of the Belt and Road Initiative (BRI), as it contends with the facts on the ground. Mindset, educational, vocational, and other challenges need addressing. One contributor contends that a pivot to the East starts via the West, while another explains the gritty details of Sino-Russian business ventures. How to reconcile such different views? That is left to the reader. As are the answers to long-term questions on Russia, some of which hark back to earlier eras.

How Westernized has Russian business become, how Asian is it becoming, and how essentially Russian do its business practices remain? This leads to reflections on the *differences* between Russia and other emerging economies. Then, the nature of the unique features of Russian business elicits questions on whether these are advantages or disadvantages. As we reflect through the prism of transformation we will see that paradox, surprise, and opposites live side by side. One such irony is that transformations in the business arena are not immediately paralleled by changes in other areas, such as relations with the West or the implementation of decisive new models to bring the country out of economic stagnation.

Another *paradox* is that Russia's management models, ways of governance, innovation system, and approaches to internationalization seem to defy easy classification. There is a dearth of academic research and related theoretical discussions about the ongoing transformation of Russian businesses; consequently, there is scant normative insight for practitioners. This book's purpose is not to fill this academic gap, but its contributions bridge the dichotomies between both the "essentialist vs. indigenous" management models and the "advanced vs. transition" economies. This, again, illustrates the multifaceted nature of Russian business.

If one word characterizes Russia it is "diversity." We aim to bring to the reader the multiplicity of configurations and behaviors of Russia's institutions, entrepreneurs, and executives. Accordingly, and in addition to the five themes, there is a *diversity* of sources, situation, and methods. Case studies and opinion pieces figure prominently and these are complemented by industry reports, expert analyses, practitioner experiences, and even summaries of research papers. Traversing the book might at times feel like travelling across a *geographically dispersed* reality with cases and analyses covering both Moscow and Russia's many far flung locations. The reader will travel to Tula, the Russian Arctic, the Urals, and the Far East. The connections to places such as China, Israel, Switzerland, or Central Asia place Russia's international business relationships in a global context.

The wide range of contributors adds to the richness of this book. Insights from practice, academia, thought leaders, financiers, and educators are combined. While these were edited for style, we gave the contributors full independence in terms of what they wished to say. The reader will find Russian pessimism at its best while also hearing from optimistic and enthusiastic new voices. The heterogeneity means that after each piece, the reader may need a mental rest. The editors have provided a degree of order, but the reader will sense the chaos of mixture. This is not uncommon in the Russian context and we hope that it will be a delight for some readers. In any event, the chapters can either be read in order or the reader can capriciously select the sequence that befits their particular interests.

Despite the variety of contributions, some relevant aspects of doing business in Russia are *not covered*. These include important tracts of the state sector, the political economy of the geopolitical crisis or the high profile business cases that one might read about in the pages of leading global media outlets like *Financial Times* or the *Wall Street Journal*. At the same time, many of the management, strategy, innovation, leadership, or governance insights found here are not covered at all in the pages of mainstream media. Views into facets of the ordinary life of business in Russia can be, well, extraordinary.

What Comes Next?

The contributors to the book provide fresh insights on decision-makers and institutions, ultimately enabling more informed participation in Russia's economy. However, they avoid direct prescriptions and present opinion, along with facts. It is for the reader to reach his or her own conclusion.

This does not take away from the fact that one major aim of this book is that businesspeople, investors, and managers will find that it has *practical value,* providing new ideas and inspiration. The stories collected here interconnect, linked as much by the readers own views as by the structural frameworks we have imposed. In that respect, institutions, both through their formal and informal sides, are critical for practical work in Russia. So is culture, which both limits and extends the reach of institutions and rules.

The overall aspiration that we have for the book is that the readers will come to relish the motivations of the protagonists in the business cases, the metaphors and mental shortcuts suggested by the various authors, and the articulation of particular worldviews or unexpected outcomes. Here is where this book also becomes relevant for the non-businessperson. For those generally interested in Russian affairs we believe that the book can be valuable and stimulating as "the life of business" is in many ways the "business of life."

Acknowledgments

This book would not be possible without the support from numerous people. We are grateful to the president of SKOLKOVO School of Management,[1] Andrei Sharonov, whose commitment to institution-building has informed and inspired many of this book's authors and its editors. The dean of SKOLKOVO, Marat Atnashev, provided essential support for this work from its very inception and even contributed three fundamental pieces. Steven DeKrey, who is developing the relationship between the Hong Kong University of Science and Technology (HKUST) and SKOKOVO as well as driving academic excellence at the institution as chairman of SKOLKOVO's Academic Council, strongly backed the book. The academic dean, Denis Konanchuk, and director, Violetta Grigorieva, at SKOLKOVO's Academic Office have created an environment that promotes and supports the dissemination of knowledge and research initiatives. We would like to thank our colleague Alexey Kalinin, director of SKOLKOVO's IEMS, for his generous allocation of researchers and resources. Regina Mamykina and her team have helped with managing the publication process. We thank Julia Tkach who has provided administrative support together with the team of designers who helped to visually convey key ideas in the book sections.

We would also like to express our sincere gratitude to John Stuart from John Stuart Editorial, who patiently and committedly stood by the editors throughout the editorial process. We also thank our publisher, George F. Johnson at Information Age Publishing, for his belief in the project.

Note

1. This institution will subsequently be referred throughout this book as SKOLKOVO.

The Life of Russian Business, page xix

I

Markets and Macro Perspectives

SECTION I

Introduction

The development of market institutions has been a perennial challenge for the Russian economy. The fall of the Soviet system and the rapid transition to a capitalistic open economy was largely problematic because markets needed proper institutions to work effectively. At the same time, some incumbents saw a business opportunity in such institutional voids and used these to create competitive advantage. With the advent of the new century, Russia has made substantial progress in creating and developing functioning markets. The results of these changes have included the consolidation of a business elite, a growing middle class, higher standards of living, and a gradual integration into global knowledge flows. Yet Russia did not become an emerging tiger in the Asian mold, nor did it reach European levels of social welfare. The development suffered from path dependency and the persistence of parts of the Soviet system and culture. A weak legal system, the Dutch disease[1] (in Russia caused by massive oil and gas exports), a large state-owned economy and shrinking demographics were all major impediments for growth that have an institutional component. At the same time, Russia's increased integration in the European and global economy came both with advantages and costs, such as vulnerability to events in the international arena. The changed geopolitical environment—with the imposition of Western sanctions and the fall in oil prices—has made economic transformation at home more critical than ever for Russian markets to reach full potential.

The Life of Russian Business, pages 3–4

This section opens with a broad discussion on the distinguishing characteristics of emerging markets, outlining the key factors facilitating economic development and growth (Chapter I.1). The discussion then turns to the domestic economy with a review of the challenges the country is facing as we ask: "Quo Vadis Russian economy?" (Chapter I.2), and continues at the macro level, with Russia's engagement in China's much discussed Belt and Road Initiative (BRI) (Chapter I.3). One answer to this question is "import substitution," which is covered from a practical perspective by Lorenz Widmer, Director of the Swiss Business Hub (SBH) Russia (Chapter I.4).

The subsequent three articles delve into some of the key challenges to successful economic development. These include demographics and the aging labor force (Chapter I.5); the health care system, critically reviewed by a team of researchers (Chapter I.6); and financial management at the city level, namely how city administrations can implement budgets without "federal crutches" (Chapter I.7). This section also includes unique insights into four Russian markets tightly linked with the international economy but determined by domestic institutional dynamics. The first examined is agribusiness and centers on unrealized potential and hidden opportunities (Chapters I.8 and I.9). Then, we discuss three of the country's main economic drivers—steel, oil, and coal (Chapters I.10, I.11, and I.12). Here, Marat Atnashev, Dean of SKOLKOVO, provides a fascinating insider view on where markets meet institutions; both successes and failures are candidly articulated and some of the ideas will surely surprise foreign pundits globally operating in these high-impact industries.

The first section of the book, then, is a top-down, macro look at the critical questions facing the Russian economy and its business sectors. It is an apt starting point to reflect on the nature of the economic transformations taking place, as well as on the work ahead. We also aim to build a practice-oriented awareness of the idiosyncratic characteristics of key industries in Russia.

Note

1. The Dutch disease attacks a country's economy when large currency inflows result in an appreciation of the currency. Currency outflows are due to large export volumes caused by one sector, usually in the natural resources. This increase in the value of the domestic currency makes other industries less price competitive thus causing an array of economic distortions and imbalances.

1

No Size Fits All

The Diversity of Emerging Market Opportunities[1]

Andrey Shapenko
Vladimir Korovkin

Emerging markets are shaping the economic history of the twenty-first century. In recent years we have witnessed dramatic transformations of their role in the global economy; from being attractive export markets or investment destinations to becoming the birthplace of rising multinationals and other actors impacting political, economic, social, and technological developments worldwide. In the last decade there have been years where the top seven emerging markets outgrew the G7.[2] Moreover, the total population in the emerging world is five times as large as that of the advanced economies. Transformations in these markets, including what their consumers buy and their producers' sell, will have dramatic implications. Economies that we now call "emerging" will be "shaping" the global economy in the coming decades.

The Life of Russian Business, pages 5–10

However, the emerging markets phenomenon is best understood not in terms of statistics. Rather, it is a combination of risks and opportunities for trade and investment defined by a complex interplay of economic, political, geographical, social, and other developmental factors. As such, emerging markets are very diverse and moving targets. Thus, it is crucially important for international business decision makers to develop the frameworks and competencies to both grasp these dynamics and differentiate across different types of markets. In this regard, the *Brave New World Index* developed by SKOLKOVO Institute of Emerging Markets (SKOLKOVO IEMS), sees three distinct categories of emerging markets: the advanced stage to which Russia belongs, the intermediate stage, and the early stage.

Advanced stage emerging markets are entering a period when, on the one hand, they need to restructure almost their entire economy to boost productivity and maintain competitiveness in light of their growing cost base. On the other hand, they are opening new opportunities by moving from global manufacturing hubs into increasingly attractive and sophisticated post-industrial markets. This group includes Russia, China, Turkey, Malaysia, Saudi Arabia, Costa Rica, Chile, Qatar, Thailand, and United Arab Emirates.

The *Intermediate stage* group benefit from the slowdown of advanced emerging markets while the bigger countries in this group, such as Brazil and India, are also attractive markets due to the vast size of their middle classes. This group includes Azerbaijan, Argentina, Belarus, Brazil, Colombia, India, Indonesia, Kazakhstan, Kuwait, Lebanon, Dominican Republic, Peru, Philippines, Serbia, South Africa, Sri Lanka, Mexico, Vietnam, Ukraine, Uruguay, and Tunisia.

Early stage emerging markets are growing from very low-income levels and need to first build infrastructure foundations. Many economists see the highest business potential lying in such markets. The group includes Algeria, Angola, Bangladesh, Ecuador, Egypt, Ethiopia, Ghana, Guatemala, Iran, Iraq, Kenya, Morocco, Myanmar, Nigeria, Pakistan, Oman, Sudan, Tanzania, Uzbekistan, and Venezuela.

Growth is a key attribute of emerging markets and it is this that makes them attractive to international business. Yet maintaining the high growth rates witnessed in the 2000s will be increasingly difficult. Thus, for a successful business operation it is important to understand the different types of growth, because they define the developmental responses to the key global challenges emerging markets face: growing populations, increasing urbanization with a breakdown in many traditional habits and patterns, subsequent

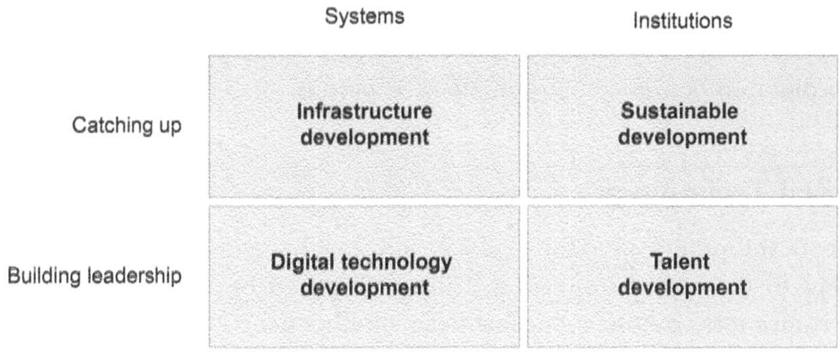

Figure I.1.1 Four key development areas for emerging markets.

social tensions, increasing geopolitical tensions, climate change; depletion of some key resources, and deterioration of the environment.

There are four key areas where emerging markets can respond to these challenges: (a) infrastructure development, (b) sustainable development, (c) digital technology development, and (d) talent development (See Figure I.1.1). These domains are defined by the necessity to develop systems alongside institutions in order to catch up with advanced economies. The strategies and policies pursued in these areas will define the growth and development of each specific market over the next two decades.

Infrastructure Development

Projects focusing on core forms of infrastructure—transport, power, utilities, and communications—vary greatly in quality and scope among different types of emerging markets. While advanced stage emerging markets are increasingly investing in "superpower" projects, such as building high-speed railways and world-class power generation stations, early stage markets are often only striving to achieve basic levels of access to electricity, water, and paved roads. Yet, communications networks often develop at a quicker pace than basic infrastructure. In some areas of Africa, for example, one can get online with a mobile phone while at the same time having no access to running water. Between these extremes, in the intermediate group, there is a huge amount of modernization to be accomplished, especially when it comes to transport infrastructure and electricity generation.

Major emerging economies need to find ways to mobilize both public and private resources and build appropriate institutions to manage projects in a way that combines development priorities with operational effectiveness. A revolutionary new development in the execution of infrastructure projects is "emerging to emerging" cooperation, which involves coordination between emerging market nations.

Digital Technology

This development gradually pushes advanced stage emerging countries closer to the global innovation frontier, typified by achievements in supercomputers, robotics, and artificial intelligence. The countries of the intermediate group face the dual tasks of maintaining competitiveness in the use of digital technologies in their industrial sectors along with striving for the digital inclusion of their populations. In these markets, international business champions often emerge which rely on solid operational models and leverage approaches tested on their sizeable customer base. The early stage group, meanwhile, tend to develop innovative "bottom of the pyramid" solutions. In this way, "digital" has become the new form of basic literacy, especially for younger people, and digital accounts, not bank accounts, have become the norm for families and businesses. The phenomenon of "leapfrogging"—overcoming the deficiencies of traditional infrastructure through digital systems—creates diverse business opportunities across the early stage group.

Generally speaking, the scale of the market opportunities in digital technology is huge for all three groups. Overall, they invest approximately 2–5% of their GDP in this area. China alone is the world's biggest market for industrial robotics, while India is moving tens of millions of people online every year.

Sustainable Development

Advanced emerging markets are usually stronger on the social dimensions of sustainable development than intermediate or early stage markets. They boast good education systems, have reduced abject poverty, and tend to embrace both diversity in the workplace and the inclusion of minorities. Yet, rapid industrialization has also had significant environmental impacts, especially in countries such as China or Russia, and the consequences of the past disregard for ecological protection need to be addressed. The countries from the intermediate group often have a better understanding of environmental issues, but face pressing social issues, while those in the early stage group have extensive basic human development work ahead.

It is hard to estimate the size of forthcoming investment in sustainable development, as it often involves "soft" issues such as improving educational standards and employment practices. Through these investments, advanced emerging markets need to focus on mitigating the environmental damage done in the past, as well as upgrading their industrial base to reduce their future ecological footprint. This emerging trend of a greater emphasis on sustainability is no longer the prerogative of large multinationals, as leading local companies follow their examples.

Intermediate group countries need to ensure that the process of industrial growth is both environmentally friendly and socially inclusive and pay special attention to the inclusion of minorities. The main challenge for early stage countries lies in the development of an all-encompassing and balanced sustainability strategy that focuses on designing and enforcing national policies and regulations related to sustainable development, while at the same time leveraging competencies transferred from global business.

Talent Development

This is an area of vast opportunity, as 90% of global youth live in emerging markets, though less than half of global GDP is produced there. The lack of educational, social, economic, and institutional opportunities prevents demographic capital from being transformed into human capital and gainfully employed talent. As a result, human capital is more of a liability than an asset for many emerging markets.

In a globally interconnected economy built on knowledge, talent is the key to the global competitiveness of a nation. Emerging markets need to make investments to attract, integrate and retain talent as their key priority. Encouragingly, some emerging economies such as Moldova, Solomon Islands, Cuba, Namibia, and Swaziland are already among the global leaders in the proportion of GDP they spend on education.

Advanced emerging economies face the dual challenge of both assimilating low-skilled immigration while retaining the well-educated and skilled part of the native population, which often seeks to migrate to the "advanced world." A combination of greater economic opportunities and a higher quality of life is required to avoid the brain drain.

Intermediate group countries need to focus on developing local technical, engineering, research, and managerial personnel required for industrial growth, with the help of imported knowledge and competencies from the more advanced economies of the West and the East. Achieving a better gender balance in professional occupations will tap into a powerful underutilized resource.

Early stage countries face very basic challenges such as achieving 100% literacy (including digital literacy), developing a competitive working class, and nurturing national "elites" capable of integration into global markets.

Summary

In summary, the world of emerging markets is diverse and has outgrown anything that one might have thought possible just two decades ago. Each of the important markets will pursue their own approaches and agendas in the four domains that we have outlined. Russia and other emerging markets will move forward in their own ways. For global firms, such diversity calls for sophisticated business strategies when handling their portfolio of emerging market activities.

Notes

1. This contribution has been derived from the report *Emerging markets decoded: The four domains of development for growth* by A. Kalinin, A. Shapenko, V. Korovkin, N. Zaitseva, O. Remyga, K. Novak, & B. Michael, published in June 2016 by SKOLKOVO IEMS.
2. G7 refers to the seven largest economies in the world including Canada, France, Germany, Italy, Japan, the United Kingdom and the United States.

2

Quo Vadis Russian Economy?

On Trials and Challenges[1]

Andrey Shapenko
Tomas Casas i Klett

In 2014 the continuous solid growth of the Russian economy since 1999, its only setback the aftermath of the 2008 global crisis, came to an end. Fifteen years of reforms and high oil prices led to a doubling in Russian GDP, Russia joining the G8[2] and the World Trade Organization (WTO), accumulating formidable currency reserves, as well as seeing a steady rise in real incomes. By 2017, many economists both in Russia and around the world still argued that the country's economic crisis was due to the collapse of oil prices and geopolitical tensions resulting in sanctions being placed on Russia. We believe that is incorrect: Russia's economic stagnation started in 2013 ahead of the introduction of economic sanctions in mid-2014. But before looking at where Russia is heading, we will first examine from where it came. Over the last 25 years, Russia has undergone three distinct economic periods.

The Life of Russian Business, pages 11–20

The first period, also known as "Shock Therapy," was instigated by the economic team of President Boris Yeltsin—headed by Yegor Gaidar, under the auspices of Western advisers—on January 2, 1992, immediately after the collapse of the Soviet Union. This economic approach was based on the ultra-liberalization of markets, withdrawals of price controls and mass privatization. Although conditions were dire, they did not prevent the incipient formation of the basic institutions of a market economy: liberalized prices, free trade, and free flows of capital. Nonetheless, this shock therapy created serious problems: the initial collapse of the financial system; hyperinflation; factory closures causing millions of people to lose their jobs; followed by a mass of acute social problems, from worsening crime to the "brain drain" and even to an increased mortality rate. It took about seven years to develop even a modicum of private initiative, to establish relatively efficient market institutions and to accumulate the initial capital to support self-sustaining growth. Then, Russia was hit by the financial crisis in 1998. That crisis, which was in turn the result of the financial crisis in East Asia, caused foreign investors to panic resulting in unrestricted flows of capital being directed away from *all* emerging markets. The upshot was a threefold devaluation of the Russian ruble.

The second economic stage, or "Golden Period," started in 1999, when Vladimir Putin came to power and oil prices started to climb, eventually reaching US$ 140 per barrel, a significant increase from the US$ 20–25 level seen in the 1990s. In addition, as the ruble lost 75% of its value against the dollar after the crisis of 1998, industrial production surged on lower costs and higher demand for cheaper domestic goods. Oil prices continued to rise at an almost uninterrupted rate until 2014. Russia's revenue surged, but oil hijacked the economy, "contaminating" it with the Dutch disease as other sectors suffered. A newly created Stabilization Fund, later divided into a Reserve Fund and National Wealth Fund, absorbed some of the oil revenues. This rainy-day fund helped Russia glide through the global economic crisis of 2008–2009 relatively smoothly. By the early 2000s, Russia's major industrial and resource assets were in private hands. The new owners started to invest in order to boost the value of their companies. At the same time, a set of institutional and fiscal laws (the so-called Gref Program, named after Herman Gref, the Minister of Economic Development at that time) were introduced to ease the business tax burden and to improve the investment climate. This marked the beginning of a long phase of investment activity and capital inflow, which lasted until 2008. Russia became one of the world's Top 10 economies, joined the G8 and the G20, and lent its "R" to the BRICS (Brazil, Russia, India, China, South Africa) acronym. It seemed that growth and rising wealth were here to stay.

However, the third stage had been simmering in the background and fully and dramatically came to the forefront in 2016. The Russian economy had begun to slow down in late 2013, and within just six months, stagnation had manifested itself. The key causes were not the drop in oil prices and economic sanctions, since these events occurred only towards the middle of 2014. These external economic factors only added to the severity of the underlying middle-income trap, which Russia was now fully caught up in. When the oil price collapsed in 2014, state reserve levels fell by 30%. Russia ended 2015 with a 3.7% GDP contraction, the ruble down by 50%, 12.9% inflation and a budget deficit of 3%. Domestic consumption decreased for the first time in 13 years, while real income fell to 2011–2012 levels. Anemic growth is expected to last until 2019.

What are the appropriate responses to reverse the recent recession and ultimately foster economic growth? Any policy effort must start with a candid assessment of the trials and tribulations that Russia's economic and financial system has had to face.

Trial #1: Low Rates of Investment and Capital Formation

Russia's US$ 9,000 GDP per capita in 2015 was low compared to advanced Western nations, which stood at between US$ 30,000 and US$ 45,000. Was the country a potentially good investment destination? Absolutely, according to catch-up theory; with all other things equal, it is easier for a lower income—hence low capital—country to grow fast(er) thanks to higher marginal returns on capital. However, the share of investment spending as a percentage of Russia's GDP was just 18%—similar to much more mature economies—while other emerging, fast growing countries, had ratios of at least 25%, with China exceeding 40% for many years. In addition, Russian capital and labor utilization capacity was close to maximum levels—the need to invest in new capacity was pressing.

Trial #2: Capital Outflow

In the 2000s the growth of the Russian economy was accompanied by capital inflows, primarily in the form of foreign direct investment (FDI). Amounting to US$ 2.7 billion in 1999, FDI increased to US$ 74.8 billion in 2008, but by 2015 it had declined to US$ 6.5 billion—a level not seen since 2003. It must be noted that the bulk of the foreign direct investment came from offshore jurisdictions (such as Cyprus, the Bahamas, the Bermuda Islands, the British Virgin Islands, etc.), and was de facto not foreign, as Russian companies and high net worth individuals preferred to park their cash savings abroad. As for the foreign players, they saw the country risks mitigated by high profit margins and growth prospects. As soon as the market began to shrink and the profits fell, the risks outweighed the benefits. The mood quickly reversed and was followed by capital flight.

Trial #3: Weak Institutions

Development of effective institutions has always been the cornerstone challenge for Russian economic development. The general consensus in the West was that Russia's institutions were weak and did not adequately protect investors' capital from expropriation by the state and other actors in the economy. Hence, the investment in the economy was low despite the need to add new capacity. Low rewards, often due to costs associated with weak institutions, could not compensate for such high risks. The feeling was that if the institutions that support the financial system, such as the legal and court systems, were more effective, the ability to distribute capital efficiently would increase greatly.

Paradoxically, during the past four years Russia has shown significant progress in improving its business environment: From 2013 to 2016 the country made a spectacular leap in the World Bank's Doing Business Index, rising by 72 positions (from 112th to 40th place). It ranked higher than any other BRICS country and almost made it into the world's top 20% nations. This result seems contradictory because of the widely held assumptions of obstacles associated with doing business in Russia. At the same time, many former Soviet states were ranked above Russia—Armenia ranked 38th, Belarus 37th, Kazakhstan 35th, and Georgia 16th. Moreover, in the 2016 World Competitiveness Report released by the World Economic Forum, Russia ranked only 97th, out of 140 in institutional development, 110th in financial market development, and 92nd in commodity market effectiveness. If one added to these Russia's 131st position in Transparency International's Global Corruption Perceptions Index in 2016, then one can see that the problem of falling oil prices was only one among many problems facing the Russian business climate.

Trial #4: Looking for the Small Guys

Compared with the majority of developed and even developing countries, Russia has a very low share of small- and medium-sized enterprises (SMEs) in the economy. The SME sector accounts for only around 15–20% of GDP, about 25% of employment, and only 0.5% of exports. In contrast, in the United States, Germany, and China, where SMEs greatly contributed to the development and diversification of the economy, these indicators easily account for a 50% share. According to the U.S. National Centre for the Middle Market, the growth of medium-sized companies (from US$ 10 million to US$ 1 billion in revenues) exceeded that of the overall economy by 4.4% on average. While representing only 3% of all registered enterprises they employed a third of the workforce. It is evident that Russia is missing this backbone mid-market segment in its economy.

Trial #5: Stability vs. Inflation

With the beginning of the economic crisis and the enactment of sanctions, a jump in inflation at the end of 2014 threatened to destabilize the country and even brought back memories of the difficult 1990s. The Central Bank of Russia (CBR) intervened and stabilized the situation in December 2014 by radically raising the key interest rate from 9.5% to 17% overnight—earlier in the year it had stood at 5.75%.

During 2016, the situation stabilized and by mid-September of 2016 the CBR lowered its benchmark one-week REPO[3] rate to 10%. Inflation was under control at 7%. Given the economic slowdown, tight monetary policy has been a valiant, responsible, and successful move.

Trial #6: Sanctions and Resilience

Economic sanctions imposed by the West have turned out to be not as destructive as once feared. Their impact was rather limited, as they affected only some private individuals, as well as areas such as technology transfer (for example, offshore oil and gas and the military). Of course, there was also a significant "image" impact as foreign investors started to evaluate any decisions with regards to Russia with increased caution. At the same time, sanctions and the counter-sanctions that Russia imposed led to the inflation discussed above. The ban on imported food initially led to shortages and was followed by an inevitable increase in prices. By 2016, however, Russian agribusiness had managed to increase both the quantity and quality of food production. Agriculture has been one of the few sectors that has demonstrated growth.

Where sanctions hurt most was clearly in the area of finance. The strength and sophistication of Western financial services became apparent in areas such as leasing (planes), insurance (to finance pipelines), or investment banking (complex deals or foreign listings). There was a sense in the business community that the sanctions proved that the Russian financial system was not as efficient in allocating capital as it had once seemed to be, and that there were many knowledge gaps that could only be plugged by international financial firms.

The trials and tribulations facing Russia's economy have meant that policy-makers are seeking solutions to a variety of challenges:

Challenge #1: Is Non-Oil-Powered Growth Possible?

From 1999 to 2012 the average annual price of Brent crude oil increased six-fold, while its production in Russia approximately doubled. There was no denying that the natural resource sector, particularly the oil and gas industry has been the key contributor to the economic development of Russia over the past 15 years.

According to the World Bank, between 2001 and 2010, poverty rates in Russia dramatically fell from 35% to 10% while the middle class boomed from 30% to 60% of the population. At the same time, the dependency on oil reached astonishing levels. According to various estimates, up to 80% of the state's budget income was derived from oil and gas, directly and indirectly (fees, taxes, import duties, etc.). That, despite the fact that oil and gas represented just 10% of GDP, and oil rent[4] 13–14% of the economy.

By 2014 it looked like the era of oil-fueled growth was over. Nobody harbored illusions that oil prices would return to US$ 100+ levels. Moreover, for energy to now drive growth in the economy, prices would have to climb to impossible levels of over US$ 200 per barrel. Russia needs to find new drivers for growth outside the natural resource sector. Yet discussion of diversification is an old and unresolved one. Nevertheless, the need for action has become increasingly urgent as the country's economic diversity has continued to fall and few industries remain competitive in international markets. Russia's economy clearly needs to find new avenues of growth.

Challenge #2: Can Devaluation Help Exports?

The Russian ruble devaluation in 2014 was more related to the decrease in the value of oil and gas exports than to the imposition of sanctions. Devaluation was seen as potentially beneficial, particularly to Russia's domestic producers, just as had been the case following the 1998 economic crisis. At the end of the day, however, these expectations remained largely unmet—though there were some notable exceptions, including the aforementioned agricultural sector. The economy was, after all, operating at capacity and was not investing in potential projects meaning that there was scant new capacity for an export push. In addition, many components necessary for production were imported, further increasing inflationary pressure.

Challenge #3: How to Raise Productivity?

Russia has consistently lagged behind developed countries in terms of labor efficiency. Over the past 25 years the gap has remained practically unchanged: different sources indicate that Russia was 2–3 times less productive than most of the Organization for Economic Co-operation and Development (OECD) countries. This lag was structural in many ways, due to the geographical and industrial heritage of the Soviet Union. Given the demographic challenge and a relatively low unemployment rate (5.6% in 2015), improving labor efficiency became paramount for growth. At the same time, the working age population is expected to decline by anything from 5 to 32 million by 2050.

One of the factors that hindered productivity growth in Russia is the share of the government's ownership in the economy. According to the Federal Antimonopoly Service, in 2015 almost 70% of GDP was directly or indirectly related to the public sector (compared to 35% in 2005). State-owned enterprises are far from being the most efficient market participants. The most successful companies of the last decade in Russia are those operating in sectors with minimum government regulation, such as information technology (IT), fast moving consumer goods (FMCG), telecommunications, services, and the retail trade. In contrast, state monopolies have regularly applied for government subsidies or subsidized loans. Many experts agree that to improve productivity, Russia needs to eliminate state monopolies in many sectors, promote competition and actively encourage the development of private initiatives.

Increasing productivity does not necessarily mean large-scale investments in facilities. Many have argued that a quick solution would be the elimination of non-productive state entities, coupled with deregulation and the reduction of supervisory pressures. However, a significant reduction in non-productive jobs could lead to an increase in social tension as was the case in Pikalyovo in 2009.[5] These protests resulted in the town's large and unprofitable plant remaining operational.

Challenge #4: Can Demographic Trends be Reversed?

After the shock therapy of the "dark 1990s," Russia was finally enjoying a modicum of positive demographic dynamics: In 2012, population growth finally turned into the black. But, at the same time, the population was aging and the proportion of the working age population was decreasing, while the ratio of dependents (pensioners and minors) was growing. Thus, in order to maintain growth, the Russian economy needs to either increase productivity or the size of its labor force—according to some pundits by a huge 4.6 million people. The question has become whether an economic growth breakthrough can be made with an ageing population.

Another serious challenge was the decrease in the quality of human capital and talent due to migration and the "brain drain." According to various estimates, emigration in 2015 was close to the record levels of the 1990s. While Russia's net migration was still positive, it was the quality of the migration balance that was worrisome. Russia ranked second only to the United States in terms of migrant influx. However, most of the immigrants were low-skilled workers, while many of those who were leaving were the better educated—sorely needed if quality economic growth was desired. How can Russia retain its better-educated population and compete for skills and talent?

Challenge #5: How to Raise Wages and Household Consumption?

Household consumption has fueled growth in many sectors of the economy and contributed significantly to the expansion of GDP. It was domestic consumption that allowed the economy to recover after the crisis of 2008–2009. However, in 2015 the situation changed. Consumption began to decrease and dropped sharply by 5%, as the recession loomed. By late 2016 there was still no reason to hope for consumer demand to return to growth, as a significant proportion of households were directly or indirectly dependent on the public sector and the shrinking budgetary spending.

The burgeoning growth in household consumption between 1999 and 2014 was fueled by a steady rise both of real wages and real disposable incomes. Russia's average real wages increased fourfold over 15 years. Oil revenues had trickled down to the masses. Yet, as oil prices fell, prosperity fell along with them. Real wages dropped to the levels of five years earlier. This made labor costs in Russia lower than those in China for the first time ever in modern history. However, the average Russian was still much better off than he or she was in 1999. The question was how to stimulate demand when the 2016 average salary was now at 2011 levels, with many experts in agreement that that there was still scope for further drops in the coming 2–3 years.

Challenge #6: How to "Pivot East"?

In 2014, in the wake of Western sanctions, Russia adopted the "Pivot to the East" strategy, aiming at new export markets in Asia and at closer economic ties with China. Three years later the results of this strategy are not encouraging. Trade turnover between the two countries has dropped by more than a fifth, reflecting lower prices for commodities exported to China and a lower appetite for Russian imports. Moreover, Russia has dropped out of China's ten most important trading partners. The structure of Russia's trade with China was extremely uneven. Russia appeared to have little to offer to its eastern partner apart from commodities, arms, space and nuclear technologies. On the other hand, Russia was hungry for Chinese machinery, electronics and consumer goods. This misbalance suggests that Russia needs China rather more than China needs Russia.

In order to successfully implement the "Pivot to the East" strategy, Russia needs human resources able to deliver innovation. However, Russia's Far East lacks economic momentum—its scattered 6.3 million inhabitants have gravitated towards its gargantuan neighbor despite the obvious cultural differences.

Within Russia's economic and policy-making circles there is an acute understanding of these facts and the challenges ahead. There are two main competing approaches in addressing them: liberal and interventionist. There is vigorous debate both in the media and the top echelons of government between their respective proponents. The liberal program revolves around the Centre for Strategic Research led by Alexey Kudrin, a long-serving Russian Minister of Finance (2000–2011). Those supporting interventionist policies are known as the Stolypin Club, and reference Pyotr Stolypin (1862–1911), Prime Minister from 1906 to 1911 and considered to be one of the last major statesmen of Imperial Russia and much admired for his public policies and major reforms.

How the liberal and interventionist tendencies play out over the next few years will determine the future prospects for growth and economic development in Russia.

Notes

1. This contribution has been derived from the case study *Quo Vadis Russian Economy? Liberal vs interventionist policy debate on finance reform out of stagnation* by Andrey Shapenko and Tomas Casas i Klett, published at the Case Centre (Reference no. 217-0057-1) in 2017.

2. G8 refers to World's biggest industrial nations including Canada, France, Germany, Italy, Japan, Russia, the United Kingdom, and the United States.
3. Term REPO (from repurchase agreement) refers to short term government securities.
4. Oil rent is calculated as the difference between the value of crude oil production at world prices and total costs of production (*Source:* World Bank).
5. Pikalyovo is a town 246 km from St. Petersburg, where a large cement factory was located. Most of the towns inhabitants were economically linked to the plant. In 2009, in the midst of the financial crisis, about three hundred inhabitants blocked the highway between St. Petersburg and Vologda to protest late payment of their wages. Vladimir Putin, the then Prime Minister of Russia, flew to Pikalyovo and, skipping the legal process, ordered Oleg Deripaska, the plant's owner, to pay out the wages and debts immediately.

3

Russia, Perfect Partner?

China's Bold Belt and Road Initiative (BRI)

Oleg Remyga

It's no secret that China is facing the challenge of declining growth rates. After many years of double-digit growth, annual increases in GDP have fallen to the 6–7% range and will further decline. In order to keep inclusive growth and achieve its main development goal (that is, a "moderately prosperous society") by 2021, China must tackle several challenges. Some could be addressed in the context of its ambitious Belt and Road Initiative (BRI) that focuses on connectivity and cooperation across Eurasian countries (See Figure I.3.1).

For instance, there is a striking contrast between the degree of development of the Eastern (coastal and globally integrated) and Western (inland and not globally integrated) regions. Infrastructure deficiencies in neighboring countries hinder the export and import potential of the Western regions. China needs expanded access to new export markets, in part

The Life of Russian Business, pages 21–26

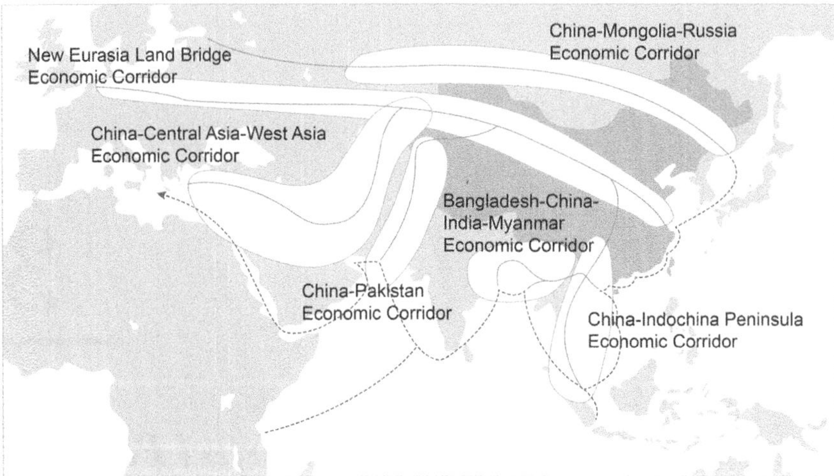

Figure I.3.1 Routes and economic corridors along the Belt and Road Initiative (BRI). *Source:* Derived rendition from HKTDC Research (2017).[1]

because it is facing overcapacity problems in various key industries such as metallurgy and machinery. With regards to sustainability, the cost of environmental degradation in China has been calculated at about 3.5% of GDP; the environments of many BRI countries are in far better shape and could supply China with clean agricultural products.

Yet perhaps the greatest challenge for China's continued economic growth lies in the field of human capital and innovation. The country is now facing the problem of the middle-income trap where growth stalls as it reaches the trap's glass ceiling of US$ 17,000 GDP per capita. In essence, as China's GDP rises, it might be losing its competitive advantage, as the average cost of labor increases faster than productivity. To escape the trap, the Chinese economy must transform to an innovation driven economy. How could the BRI initiative address these challenges?

Announced by Chinese President, Xi Jinping, in September 2013 during his state visit to Kazakhstan, the BRI initiative has two major elements: The Silk Sea Road and the Silk Road Economic Belt (SREB). SREB aims to develop a powerful Eurasian transportation "belt" that links the Eastern part of China with Western Europe (the port of Rotterdam), along six economic corridors. Two of these corridors are especially relevant to Russia: the China-Mongolia-Russia (from North to Eastern Russia) and the China-Central Asia-West Asia (from Western China to Turkey).

The Silk Sea Road, meanwhile, includes both a traditional route to the Indian Ocean through the Malacca Strait and a daring attempt to link to Northern Europe along the Russian polar coast. The latter project was primarily initiated by Russia and received support from Beijing. This is now known as the "Ice Silk Road" or, in Western media, as the "Polar Silk Road." COSCO (China Ocean Shipping Company), the country's largest and the world's number two integrated shipping company, has already launched a northern route which starts from the Chinese port of Dalian and ends in Rotterdam. Cargo is delivered in 30 days, against 45 days via traditional routes. Now Russia and China are busy developing the related infrastructure, including an icebreaker fleet, which boasts nuclear icebreaker ships.

These ideas, at least, reflect the initial "connectivity" concept. Yet, as is often the case in China, ambitious strategies tend to be amorphous at the initial stage, and BRI is no exception. As a result, policymakers and economists all over the world have been engaged in guesswork while China is revising and adding to the BRI strategy. Nevertheless, the status of BRI was upgraded in 2017 during the 19th Chinese Communist Party (CPC) Congress when a reference to the initiative was added to the Constitution of the CPC.

Initially, BRI was a collection of projects. At the infrastructure level, the budget was once estimated at a whopping US$ 890 billion. It was intended to cover over 900 separate projects touching more than 65 countries with a total population over 4.4 billion people and about 30% of world economic output. The Asian Infrastructure and Investment Bank (AIIB), had planned to spend US$ 100 billion and the Silk Road Fund earmarked US$ 40 billion to support BRI. During the BRI Summit in May 2017, an expansion of the Silk Road Fund was announced taking it to US$ 55 billion. Chinese "policy" banks including The China Development Bank, the Export-Import Bank of China and the Agricultural Development Bank were also eager to contribute. The People's Bank of China (the central bank), allocated close to another US$ 100 billion. In addition, a special BRI multi-currency lending scheme was adopted totaling US$ 56 billion. Even the New Development Bank (informally known as the BRICS Bank) is being steered towards BRI.

BRI can also be relevant in the institutional sense. In the global context, the two new main trading blocs of the twenty-first century were stillborn: The Trans-Pacific Partnership (TPP) and Transatlantic Trade and Investment Partnership (TTIP). Neither of them planned to have China as a member state. Yet, with the TPP reborn as the Japan-lead CPTPP (Comprehensive and Progressive Agreement for Trans-Pacific Partnership) and the TTIP now dead, the BRI strategy is still actively being promoted, reflecting an alternative economic model of cooperation which could eventually connect Asia and Europe into a single economic space.

We already see notable results from BRI activity. According to the statistics from China Railway Corporation in 2017, a total of 57 China-Europe rail lines were launched from 35 Chinese cities to 34 cities in 12 European countries. More than 6,000 China-Europe express trains were dispatched in total. Trade volume between China and countries along BRI amounted to US$ 1.2 trillion in 2017, surging 17.8% on an annual basis. China's exports to BRI countries climbed 12.1%, while imports grew by 26.8%, which in times of growing market protectionism is a good sign for win-win cooperation. Mergers and acquisitions deals with BRI countries increased by 15% in 2017, exceeding US$ 40 billion.

Russia appears to be a natural ally for China in realizing the aims of BRI. Besides its unique geographical position at the crossroads of Europe and Asia, there is an institutional basis for economic cooperation. Mutual diplomatic and geopolitical reliance to address international problems of sovereignty, security and development are laid out in the Russian-Chinese Treaty of Good Neighborliness and Friendly Cooperation (2001). As a result, Russia and China often have similar positions on key international issues from the Korean Peninsula crisis to the Syrian war against ISIS. Bilateral trade and investment cooperation also grew at a rapid pace, the limiting factor being the Russian economic climate. Here, the crisis of 2014 and subsequent devaluation of ruble badly hit the overall trade volumes. As a result both the cost of labor and Russian assets became cheaper. China then made strategic investments like the purchase of a 9.9% stake in the Russian liquefied natural gas (LNG) Yamal LNG project, via the Silk Road Fund.

Historically, China has been amongst the key trading and economic partners of Russia. In 2017, bilateral trade turnover between Russia and China hit US$ 80 billion. Yet this dependency is not reciprocal. Unfortunately, Russia is not among China's top 10 economic partners. Russian exports to China consist mainly of petroleum oils, minerals, wood and turbojets. Chinese imports to Russia are mainly manufactured goods and electronics. The structure of trade turnover is in line with China's needs and the BRI strategy. This is despite the fact that both sides are trying to increase the share of manufactured goods and high-tech products in bilateral trade turnover.

Investment cooperation is also robust. From 2010 until 2016 Russia was the seventh largest destination for Chinese Overseas Direct Investment (ODI), hitting US$ 22 billion. According to different estimates between 14% and 20% of these investments were BRI related. The five most important industries for Chinese investments in Russia were energy, infrastructure, minerals and metals, agriculture and real estate. This is in line with the industries in which Chinese companies invest globally with the exception of the technology sector. Russia's high-tech and technology sector hasn't attracted much attention from Chinese investors yet. Still, Russia might be the perfect example of realizing the BRI investment strategy that is believed to consist of two major phases. First, the focus is on hard infrastructure development, more precisely transport, logistics, power, and communications. The second phase is on the financial sector, education, tourism, healthcare, and e-commerce. Russia and China have ongoing mutual investment projects in each of above-mentioned industries.

Moreover, BRI is important in complementing Russia's regional integration initiative, the Eurasian Economic union (EEU). An official agreement on coordinating the development of the EEU and the Silk Road Economic Belt (SREB) was signed in May 2015. However, detailed work is still ongoing due to structural differences (the EEU is an integrated and institutionalized union, while SREB is still a conceptual strategy) and the large number of states involved. Nevertheless, a big step forward was made in October 2017, when negotiations on the Agreement on Trade and Economic Cooperation between the EEU and the People's Republic of China were finalized and the document was signed. The document focuses mainly on liberalizing custom duties, supporting multilateral trade, defining intellectual property rights, interdepartmental collaboration, formalizing state contract procedures and e-commerce.

Despite the progress made we are still at the very beginning. There are several areas for further development and synergies:

- United trade and investment space (free trade areas as a long-term goal)
- Infrastructure (creating a multiregional transport infrastructure)
- Finance (the use of national currencies in bilateral and multilateral trade to establish unified bond and equity markets)
- Innovation (targeting specific industries, developing multinational production facilities and global R&D centers).

BRI can be a crucial international trade and investment stimuli for every country along the modern Silk Road, and it is potentially particularly relevant for Russia. Russia is a key provider of connectivity and public goods (such as security). It could participate in the establishment of the Chinese-lead cooperation framework in both the economic and political domains, which will shape Eurasia for several decades to come. However, when Russians think about how the cooperation framework will look like in practice, China's interests need to be considered.

There is no doubt that China will focus first and foremost on its own internal economic development and national strategic objectives. That means, infrastructure (in the broadest sense, including transport, energy, and telecommunications), high-end digital sectors (such as cross-border e-commerce and the "Internet of Things"), talent development (including education services and R&D facilities), and possibly sustainable development (including the environmental industry and clean energy). Yet if the initiative is to have any chance of success, it is critical that BRI, still ambiguous and not clearly articulated, is properly conceptualized—especially with a view to robust rule and norm building. It also needs to be a multilateral initiative, even if it is China-led.

BRI will not suffer the same fate as the TTIP or TPP, but without the establishment of clear rules of cooperation and business models in the broader sense, it might in time just fade away. The potential benefits of an economically unified new Silk Road region are immense for Eurasia. Moreover, in a world where new trade barriers are now being erected it is essential that BRI becomes a success. To do so, BRI will have to produce world-class multilateral institutions in areas such as project finance rules, security arrangements and free trade agreements—institutions that are effectively norm-based. Even for a country as prosperous and powerful as China this is an immense challenge. Russia has a clear and present opportunity to make a significant contribution in many of these fields.

Note

1. HKTDC Research (2017). *The Belt and Road Initiative.* http://china-trade-research.hktdc.com/business-news/article/The-Belt-and-Road-Initiative/The-Belt-and-Road-Initiative/obor/en/1/1X000000/1X0A36B7.htm

4

Import Substitution

Russia's Unrealized Business Opportunities for Foreign SMEs

Lorenz Widmer

It is well known that in recent years, the Russian Government's national industrial policy has increasingly promoted Russian products and services with the aim of decreasing the country's reliance on imports (import substitution). The expected results involve increased domestic production (production localization). The government pursues this goal through three types of policies: incentives in the form of subsidies or tax breaks; restrictions on the sale of foreign-made goods to Russian government and state-owned companies; and political instruments such as counter-sanctions and sanitary measures, mainly targeting the food sectors of specific countries.[1]

Foreign SMEs largely view this trend as a threat to doing business in Russia. They typically work in small niches and lack the critical mass of revenues that would economically justify the localization of their production

The Life of Russian Business, pages 27–29

to Russia. Moreover, SMEs typically lack the reserves and capacity to take the risks needed for larger investment projects.

However, it is less well known that import substitution has also led to a multitude of export opportunities for foreign SMEs. The government allocates significant financial resources for the development and the expansion of entire industries. Indeed, Russia's plans to increase its production capacity require large investments to build-up and modernize local production facilities. Moreover, the trend towards localization also generates a demand for modern management, marketing, sales and distribution structures. In all these sectors, foreign SMEs have technologies and competencies that are interesting to Russian players.

We can illustrate these opportunities by providing additional detail on two sectors of particular relevance where the Swiss Business Hub Russia has conducted market studies.

The machine tool industry is one of the central sectors in the scope of the import substitution plans. The Russian authorities are putting considerable effort into incentivizing domestic and foreign manufacturers to invest in the modernization and expansion of production. Our research[2] reveals 13 major ongoing investment projects implemented by domestic companies, which offer opportunities for foreign suppliers, specifying the types of equipment prioritized for import substitution. These types of equipment have currently, and for the most part, been supplied by foreign firms, even as Russian manufacturers are, in principle, capable of producing similar equipment (the study in question identifies these companies as potential partners for foreign suppliers). The types of equipment identified include equipment for turning, boring, milling, grinding, thread grinding, tool grinding, gear processing, electroerosive treatment, pressing, blanking, welding as well as metrological equipment, foundry equipment, means of automation in production, additive equipment, thermal equipment, tool products, and accessories for machines.

Increasing productivity and creating additional capacity in food processing and agriculture is another special focus of the Russian authorities. It is expected that billions of dollars will need to be invested in machines and equipment to achieve Russia's ambitious goals in this area. Another study[3] has identified the following opportunity areas for foreign suppliers:

- food processing industry (meat, milk, cheese, vegetables, fruits, canning)—technology and infrastructure (e.g., greenhouses) for modernization;
- food processing ingredients;

- agro-industrial breeding and cultivation: animal husbandry, animal feed; and
- crop production and farming: fertilization, storage.

How can foreign SMEs benefit from these opportunities as a new market entrant? We recommend a gradual approach. Experience shows that starting with export operations based on a streamlined local presence is crucial for gaining experience in the market and for testing partners. In order to be successful in the Russian market, the following competencies are particularly important:

- a local presence either with a subsidiary, a representative office, or through a reliable partner;
- good functioning logistics, which are generally more important than in Western markets;
- consulting support capabilities for projects in order to win tenders; and
- customer training and development of professional service staff.

In conclusion, Russia's import substitution policies are clearly a threat for foreign exporters. However, import substitution policies also offer new opportunities. This contribution has provided a number of hints of where these opportunities might lie. Needless to say, before taking the decision to enter the Russian market, one is advised to do the proper research or to engage a third party to do so. The objective is to understand the market and to find a reliable business partner. Lastly, and in terms of the business model, foreign SMEs are best served with a gradual market entry approach. That is, in the initial phase, they should dip their feet into the water and test the Russian market and their chosen local partners.

Notes

1. Heidemann, T. (2016). Practical Guide: Import Substitution in Russia. Swiss Business Hub Russia. Retrieved from https://www.s-ge.com/sites/default/files/cserver/mig/sites/default/files/censhare_files/swiss-business-hub-russia-practical-guide-import-substitution-russia_14.pdf
2. Swiss Business Hub Russia (2017). Russia: Opportunities for Machine Tool Suppliers. https://www.s-ge.com/sites/default/files/cserver/article/downloads/201706_e_machine_tool_sector_russia.pdf
3. Slavina, K., and D. Rehmann (2015). Business Opportunities for Swiss companies in the Agricultural and Food Processing Industry in Russia, Swiss Business Hub Russia. https://www.s-ge.com/sites/default/files/cserver/publication/free/market-study-russia-food-processing-s-ge-20150826.pdf

5

Human Capital or Encumbrance?

How to Create an Economic Miracle with Russia's Aging Population[1]

Andrey Shapenko

Russia entered the 21st Century with a complicated demographic legacy. The wars, revolutions, repressions, and socioeconomic shocks of the past century had cost the country tens of millions of lives. Taking into account all of the unborn children and grandchildren, instead of the current population of 146 million, Russia today could easily be a country of over 300 million people. While at the beginning of the 20th century Russia had the fourth largest population in the world, equal to the United States, today it ranks only ninth, below countries such as Nigeria and Bangladesh. By 2030, Russia will have been surpassed by Ethiopia, the Philippines and the Congo, but the United States will still remain in the top three. Globally, the country is already quite small in numbers—less than 2% of the world's population, accounting for less than 2% of the world's GDP.

The Life of Russian Business, pages 31–34

"Demography is destiny," wrote Auguste Comte, the father of modern sociology, back in the 19th century. Many economists have noted that one of the key engines of the global economy in the second half of the 20th century was population growth. It is extremely difficult to ensure economic growth without concomitant increases in demographic capital. What fate awaits Russia in view of its aging population and related trends?

It is generally assumed that the increase in birth rates in Russia that began in 2012 is the result of the government's efforts (for example, by the provision of maternity benefits). However, a simple look at the population pyramid shows that the increase in the birth rate was caused to a greater extent by the fact that the generation born in the 1980s had reached child-bearing age, as well as by previously delayed parenthood due to difficult economic conditions associated with the early post-Soviet era. Consequently, we can expect another decrease in the birth rate in the near future. Already it is clear that by 2025, the number of working-age people in Russia will decrease by about 5–10 million, even after taking into account immigration. Children and senior citizens over 60 will then make up almost 50% of the population (compared to 41% today). Russia has left the cohort of countries with a "demographic dividend," and its population is gradually ageing. Not surprisingly, the government intends to try and mitigate the effects of what could become a demographic time bomb by considering a raise in the retirement age. This implies that as in other European countries, retirement benefits are by no means guaranteed.

World War II ended more than 70 years ago, but its impact lasted for decades afterwards. Russia's "Lost Generation" of 1923–1935 left deep gaps in the population pyramid, which today resembles more a Christmas tree. Even the dramatic drop in the birth rate in the 1990s was the result not so much of the collapse of the USSR and the ensuing difficulties, as a reflection of the unborn grandchildren of the generation of men and women lost to the war. In Russia, the number of people aged 10–25 and 40–55 is very small, but there are millions of baby boomers aged 50–65 and "Children of Perestroika" who are about 30 years old. The former possess much of the power and money, while the latter will be building the country's future. The outlook of the former was shaped back in the times of the Soviet Union, and they made their fortunes or careers in the turbulent 1990s, while the latter have seen almost nothing in their adult lives except stable economic growth fueled by rising energy prices.

Paradoxically, the current demographic situation resembles the one that existed during the decline of the USSR. At that time, society was divided into "old communists" who had won the war and sought to preserve the status quo, and young reformers who wanted change. In 1988, the average

age of Communist Party of the Soviet Union (CPSU) Politburo members was 60. The average age of today's "Politburo 2.0" members (in the terminology of the political analyst Yevgeny Minchenko) is also 60. Over one third of Russian citizens included on the Forbes billionaires list are over 55 years of age, while only one-tenth are less than 45. At some point in the near future—perhaps the next 5–10 years—the elites will definitely be replaced and wealth, influence and power will be transferred to a new generation, most likely the "Children of Perestroika." In the 1990s, the 35-year-olds, who grew up in the era of stagnation, had to quickly adjust to a market economy. In the 2020s, the new 35-year-olds, who grew up in the era of oil wealth, will have to find new ways to rebuild the economy and restart growth at a time when the population is shrinking, the intellectual capital of the nation is slipping away due to emigration, consumption is stagnant, and geopolitical tensions seem to be on the rise.

The scale of the problem is much larger than it appears to be at first glance. A rough calculation shows that even if Russia's annual economic growth reaches 4%, as the Ministry of Economic Development boldly states in its projections, and the growth of the U.S. economy remains at 2.5% per year, it will take Russia 60 years of stable growth to catch up with the United States in terms of GDP per capita at purchasing power parity (PPP). At the same time, we must not forget that the population of the United States, unlike that of Russia, is growing slowly but steadily, including via highly qualified immigration. Russia will have to bear the burden of worsening demographics with rapidly increasing productivity. To do this, it is necessary to address many complex challenges that have been left off the agenda for too long.

First of all, the Russian social security system needs to be reformed, no matter how difficult this may be. The Pension Fund is already running a deficit, while the average pension is only 38% of the average wage (for comparison, in developed countries the ratio is 60–70%). Since the proportion of pensioners will certainly grow, the fund will not be able to provide them with pension benefits using only rent and taxes paid by the working population. Is the social welfare state doomed? We saw that the government is considering a rise in the retirement age, but this is not sufficient in the long run. What other alternatives could be considered?

If the population is shrinking and we want growth, the only option is to increase productivity, which today is merely a fraction—one fifth to one quarter—of the productivity of advanced economies. This issue has already been discussed at length, but advances in digitalization and automation now offer opportunities to make it happen. However, if inefficient human capital is simply replaced by machines and artificial intelligence, a number of moral dilemmas and social tensions will emerge. On the other hand, if productivity remains at its present level, Russia may have to follow the example of Asian countries, most of which do not provide their retirees with any significant pension benefits. This solution is also fraught with uncertainties and potential social crises.

The problem with improving productivity to compensate for demographic stagnation is that such investments alone are not sufficient. For example, installing a document management or accounting system does not improve efficiency by itself. It is also necessary to have good rules, to manage and measure the process. Yet process optimization and regulatory change could leave millions of people who have clearly redundant jobs out of work in Russia. It has been estimated that only one in five workers in all Russian companies is directly involved in creating a product or adds new value. Moreover, although the labor force as a whole is shrinking, there is still unemployment in certain sectors and regions because of another productivity-depressing feature of our society: low geographic and social mobility.

People can be both demographic capital and demographic encumbrances. Demographic capital is nurtured through offering relevant and high-quality education, the presence of business sector demand for talent, and economic conditions that encourage intellectual and entrepreneurial self-realization. An economic miracle is impossible if one considers population solely as a labor force, or as a liability that must be paid pensions and salaries. In Russia, the demographic window of opportunity in terms of the quantity of working-age people is, unfortunately, closing. It is high time for Russia to bet on quality.

Note

1. This contribution has been derived from the article Капитал или обременение: Как совершить экономическое чудо со стареющим населением [Capital or Encumbrance: How to Create an Economic Miracle with Aging Population?] by Andrey Shapenko available at https://republic.ru/posts/68858, June 3, 2016.

6

Russian Healthcare

The Pharmaceutical Industry in Transition?

Alena Soboleva, Yury Krestinskiy, Irina Svyato,
Oleg Svyato, and Elena Dumnova

Russia has been striving to become a developed and innovative economy for many years, but a number of key areas remain problematic: Healthcare is among them. According to the World Health Organization report from 2015,[1] Russia lags far behind in key healthcare indicators such as life expectancy (ranked 110th out of 189 countries) and mortality rates. Some of the causes of high mortality rates are diseases with a social component. The high incidence rates for cancer (ranked 3rd out of 172 countries surveyed)[2] and alcoholism (ranked 4th out of 172 countries)[3] are revealing.

The goal of our project at the SKOLKOVO Healthcare Management Center is to understand what lies behind this state of affairs. Our main research methods included: interviewing leading experts representing the healthcare and pharmaceutical industry, an analysis of domestic and

The Life of Russian Business, pages 35–38

foreign publications, and an analysis of the available statistics. The ultimate objective is to identify the core problems in Russian healthcare in order to suggest possible solutions.

The Constitution of the Russian Federation stipulates and protects the right to receive free medical care. According to international norms and Russian legislation, this right also includes the provision of medicines. However, at the moment, this right is only implemented in hospital care. In the case of outpatient treatment, the majority of Russians must pay for medicines from their own pockets. This situation is dangerous as it both undermines a key foundation of our constitutional system and negatively impacts public health.

Moreover, this also leads to a limited and irrational public health system. State expenditures on drugs for outpatient treatment in Russia are considerably lower than in the majority of OECD countries. The vast majority (69%) of medicines consumed in Russia are not provided by the state but purchased by citizens. Consequently, those without the means to buy medicine (regular outpatients) have an incentive to push for inpatient treatment in order to access medicines (which are then provided free). Hospital occupancy raises, and healthcare provision costs inflate. Insufficient outpatient spending on medicines leads to increased spending at the hospital level.

The public procurement system for medicines is also imperfect. The procedures and the criteria for the establishment of restrictive lists (medicines eligible for reimbursement) are not always justified and transparent. For instance, the current criteria for the interchangeability of pharmaceuticals are simply inconsistent. Moreover, some medicines on the list have unproven therapeutic efficacy, and lack medical evidence-based data.

In addition to the above mentioned issues, Russia has an unequal distribution of healthcare system resources. Per capita state expenditure on medicine varies by a factor of up to 8.3 across different regions. Such inequality increases the risks of "social disintegration" in our country.

Another pain point is the lack of coordination between the development programs of the pharmaceutical industry and the healthcare system in terms of objectives, activities, and key performance indicators (KPIs). An important issue that needs to be addressed is the absence of sustainable and effective communication channels for the interaction between regulatory authorities, pharma firms, and the medical profession. As a result, it is hard to reach a satisfactory consensus on matters such as regulation.

Regulation is a challenge at all levels of the industry's value chain including preclinical and clinical trials, drug registration, listing, and pricing regulation. What are the authorities doing to improve the rules? Well, they have their own challenges, as there are several key stakeholders and related administrative bodies overseeing healthcare. It does not come as a surprise that all of them have different objectives and that these are not aligned with one another. There is a fundamental communication problem at the very heart of this inconsistent management of policy.

Another problem, often mentioned in the interviews we conducted, is the low level of investment into research and development in the Russian pharmaceutical industry. The Russian pharmaceutical industry has a focus on the production of generics. The resources required for developing new molecules are scarce both in the private and public sectors. This problem is being additionally aggravated by customs regulation, limiting international cooperation, and access to reagents and appropriate technology.

A parallel issue is that the government is interested in drugs manufactured locally. Production localization policies and protectionism constitute a trend that is hard to reconcile with international competitiveness. Science is further discouraged in Russian pharma due to the focus on increasing the share of generics that reduces incentives for the development of innovative medicines.

Those firms able to leverage Russia's scientific talent need to go abroad to test their mettle. Some are trying to build partnerships with Japanese and Chinese firms. An innovative private pharma company complained about the lack of support and, referring to official policy noted: "If you do not help us going abroad, at least do not create impediments for our development at home."

To conclude, the problems in Russia's healthcare system and pharma industry are significant. In a private discussion, a high-level government official had no qualms in stating that the elderly are a burden for the economy. When we looked for leadership in healthcare we found a shortage of leaders with a professional background. The transition towards favoring local firms over foreign ones has further reduced the supply of talent and ideas. The core challenge is one of institutional and managerial quality. Improvements will require complex solutions, including identifying new sources of financing, new management approaches, and more effective communication across all stakeholders in the value chain.

Notes

1. World Health Organization (2016). World Health Statistics 2016: Monitoring Health for the SDGs Annex B: Tables of Health Statistics by Country, WHO

Region and Globally. http://www.who.int/gho/publications/world_health_statistics/2016/en/
2. World Health Organization (2012). GLOBOCAN 2012: Estimated Cancer Incidence, Mortality and Prevalence Worldwide in 2012. http://publications.iarc.fr/Databases/Iarc-Cancerbases/GLOBOCAN-2012-Estimated-Cancer-Incidence-Mortality-And-Prevalence-Worldwide-In-2012-V1.0-2012
3. World Health Organization (2011). Global Status Report on Alcohol and Health—WHO. http://www.who.int/substance_abuse/publications/global_alcohol_report/msbgsruprofiles.pdf.

7

Russian Cities

Is There Life Without Federal "Crutches"?[1]

Elena Korotkova

It is no secret that the budgets of Russian cities rely heavily on federal funds. At present, with the tense economic situation in the country and a rapidly shrinking federal budget, there is a risk that cities will end up seriously underfunded.

Since the breakup of the Soviet Union, cities have relied mainly on money disbursed to them by the federal government. On the one hand, this money constitutes taxes transferred to the federal budget by cities in the first place. On the other, the federal treasury is used to cover deficits and organize major events such as the 2018 World Cup, build large infrastructure projects such as dams, bridges, and embankments, or restore urban areas. In this system, a city is like a child that is not allowed to walk by itself (translated into the language of taxes, it means that the municipal share of personal income tax revenues has been reduced from 50% to 15% over the

The Life of Russian Business, pages 39–43

past 10 years), but is instead given crutches (in some Russian cities, grants reach up to 80% of total budget revenues). In addition, cities receive bonuses in the form of significant investments in infrastructure such as new bridges or dams.

When federal money gets scarce, as is now happening, cities have to tighten their belts and also consider ways to increase their income generation and galvanize their own resources. Based on the study "Urban Economic Development and Spatial Planning. Hidden Resources" conducted by SKOLKOVO Centre of Urban Studies, we see indications that some cities have started to think about how to tackle this problem before others, and this has helped them to be in a far better position as the economic crisis has deepened. Among these forward-thinking cities are Kazan, Samara, and Novosibirsk—all cities boasting independent sources of income. Thus, during 2010–2014, Samara's receipts from the federal budget made up only 25% of the city budget. In Novosibirsk, the figure was 35% for the same period, while in Khabarovsk, Ufa, and Kazan it was well over 40%. A large number of other cities, which for a variety of reasons have not tried to stand on their own feet, now need to develop their own resources.

On average, a quarter of total city budgets in Russia are now made up of the income generated by the city. Most of these revenues originate from so-called "hard currency." That is, revenue from municipal land and real estate. Each city controls, to a considerable extent, revenues from land tax, land rental, personal property tax, and the sale of real estate. This means that cities can increase their independence from federal subsidies by developing and generating income from municipal land. The problem is that often these revenues are insignificant when compared with receipts from the federal and regional budget, which disincentivizes generating local revenue. For example, if 77% of the budget comes from the federal budget, as in Kyzyl, why should the city worry about the remaining 23%? However, as federal revenues decrease it is essential for cities to identify new revenue opportunities and learn how to manage them.

Taxes on Property

Using the "child" metaphor again, even in the limited space where cities are allowed to walk on their own—setting land and personal property taxes—they are still not allowed to walk as freely they would wish. Let's examine how far cities can walk on their own in the current system and how far they would ideally like to.

Cadastral value can only be reappraised every 3 years, which is consistent with other countries in Europe. In the Netherlands, cadastral values are reappraised once every 4 years; in Germany, once every 6 years; while in Denmark, it is once every 2 years. However, cities can make the most of the cadastral value by adjusting tax rates. For example, when the cadastral value of commercial land fell by 14%, the Russian city of Ufa increased the tax rate by 375%. The appraisal of land for office real estate did not fluctuate as much—the cadastral value dropped by 8% and the city raised the tax rate by "only" 42%. By offering differential taxes rates to owners and developers of real estate, the city influences its development direction.

A different approach with a similar goal is used in Khabarovsk, where tax rates are determined by appraisal zones rather than by land use type. There are 50 such zones in the city. By changing the rates for land, the city encourages or discourages construction in certain districts.

Another source of revenue for the municipal budget is leasing out land, which can be very profitable, since no limitations on leasing prices are imposed on cities. In this respect, the best system has been developed in Ufa, where the land has been divided into a number of categories and subcategories, assigning different rates for each of them. The pricing for the system is recalculated annually, which proves that this resource is of great importance to the city. This is an example where municipalities can build an effective system to monetize available space.

Another significant potential resource that currently brings almost no income to cities is personal property tax. At present, it accounts for only 1% to 2% of total city revenue. The amounts are so small because the formula used to calculate the taxable value includes a large number of parameters, and results in ridiculously small final values. As a result, the owner of a luxury flat in an old apartment building in the center of Moscow pays taxes that are several times less than the owner of a flat in a new building on the outskirts of the city. A new system recently introduced remedies this mistake and now calculates taxes based on market prices. Municipalities now expect that the amount of revenues from personal property tax will increase considerably.

One of the traditional problems in Russia is "legislative nihilism." A city that has shown a willingness to govern is Ufa, which for instance has developed best practices by investing considerable resources in creating an "orthophotomap"—a detailed, high-resolution image of all buildings within the city limits. This map was combined with the ownership information and the cadastral divisions of the land, which enabled the city to see all buildings and their locations in detail, and to get information about the owners and whether or not they paid taxes. This system allows the city to identify each tax evader, and has helped increase revenues to the local budget by tens of percentage points. Of course, tax evasion through the deliberate non-registration of taxable items (houses, land, real estate) is only one of the causes of low tax collection. There are also a number of purely technical problems. For example, cadastral registration data may be inaccurate, incorrect, or outdated.

Data Vitamins for Cities

The above tools can be seen as fast-acting drugs. It is also important to understand that a city also needs a longer-term and more strategic "treatment"—comparable to something like a course of vitamins. Territorial planning documents are exactly the management tools that can be used for this purpose, although they are not the most obvious instruments. These tools have a significant positive effect on the development of the whole system. The important thing is that cities are free to choose this "treatment" for themselves.

For example, if a city needs to stimulate the development of business and economic activity in a particular area. What can it do? First, it should revise the rules of land usage and development, and permit land to be utilized for either social or business functions. A city may allow temporary trade in a particular area, or allow the ground floors of buildings to be used for commercial purposes. It may lower land taxes and rental rates, and support small businesses through special programs. These are local tools with immediate effect that can stimulate a neighborhood by encouraging shops, cafés, bank branches, and other services to appear. The area will be completely transformed, adding color to the cityscape, and attracting residents to spend their leisure time there.

In Russia, there are few such examples as yet. A classic international example is the SoHo district in New York. Since the beginning of the 1970s, New York City systematically changed the way it approached zoning to encourage the nascent energy of shops, galleries, and other small entrepreneurs.

To plan and apply the proper "treatment," cities have to know themselves, and Russian cities, unfortunately, do not know enough to effectively self-diagnose and self-medicate. They obtain their scant knowledge from statistics that are generated at a special department of the Federal State Statistics Service. In reality, this means that the knowledge the city desperately needs is hidden behind seven seals, and it is incredibly difficult for the local administration to access it. In addition, the cities have to pay for most of this information. For example, every year Samara spends a million rubles just to find the answers to such questions as how many square meters of housing have been built and in which areas and how much hazardous housing there is in the city. In the United States, anyone can visit the Open New York Data website and view well-organized statistical data that can serve as a basis for any similar calculations. In Russia, cities have to spend money to receive even the minimal amount of data, and they are lucky if they get the information they really need. Most statistics are presented in such a format and quality that they are practically unusable. Clearly, budgets are tight, and cities have to economize and use only the meager data they can afford to help them get through another year using the same model, without changing anything.

It is a great irony that Russian cities are better informed about abstract plans and objectives than about the details of what is happening in the here and now. How can a doctor diagnose an illness and prescribe treatment unless he knows the patient's vital signs?

In fact, the provision of new data to a city could constitute a huge resource for its development. When you finally discover how many children actually go to each school in your city, and from which part of the city (as was the case in Ufa), you get a better idea of how to plan your city's future growth. When you have accurate data on the state of the transport network of the city at any time of the day (as does the Centre for Traffic Organization in Moscow), it becomes possible to plan the future development of the transport system. Such information would also save the city billions of rubles!

Planning and developing new revenue sources is essential. After all, in order to walk, you have to first get on your feet, not just throw away your crutches. The bigger objective is, of course, to dance. When Russian cities stand firmly on their feet, and are data enabled, they will have less need to worry about next year's federal government funds—they will know exactly which way to walk and which dance to dance.

Note

1. This contribution has been derived from the article "Российские города: есть ли жизнь без федеральных "костылей"?" [Russian Cities: Is There Life without Federal "Crutches"?] by Elena Korotkova published in SKOLKOVO BeInTrend in Spring 2016.

8

Russia as an Agrifood Superpower?

Seizing Opportunity From Key Trends

Anastasia Belostotskaya

The agrifood sector remains one of the few bright spots in the global economy. Investors are looking for new opportunities to capitalize on changing consumer behavior, technological innovation, demographic trends, and inefficiencies across markets. While in some countries such opportunities are recognized and successfully exploited, in Russia these are only partially realized. At the same time, few doubt that Russia is potentially an agrifood superpower. That is, on condition that it seizes on a number of promising trends which will shape the future of the industry. Let us consider some of these potential opportunities in more detail.

The Life of Russian Business, pages 45–48

China Growth[1]

It is projected that by 2020 almost half of the global population will reside in the Asia-Pacific region, and China will remain the fastest growing consumer market in the world. The rise of a Chinese middle class with a level of spending power comparable to advanced economies provides high-potential opportunities for its neighbors. Although today Russia accounts for only 1.5% of Chinese global agriculture imports, its advantageous strategic position that includes the availability of resources, increasing agricultural production and a large land border of 4,200 km, has to be leveraged more effectively.

"Made in Russia" Brands

Today, most iconic "local" brands in Russia are actually manufactured abroad or foreign owned. At the same time, there are a number of specialty product categories where Russian regional brands offer prime quality and value. For example, premium oral care producer R.O.C.S. has for a long time positioned itself as a foreign brand despite being founded and developed in Russia. Moreover, compared with their national and multinational competitors, local small- and medium-sized producers are more attuned to customers' needs and market trends. Smaller local firms must gain brand recognition in domestic and foreign markets and start their paths to growth.

Halal Food Gains Momentum

Muslim populations are projected to become 35% of the world's population over the next two decades, and Russia will continue to host the largest absolute numbers in Europe. More specifically, the number of Muslims in Russia is projected to rise to 18.6 million in 2030, or the equivalent to more than 60% of Saudi Arabia's population by that time. This trend drives current demand for Halal products, and not only among Muslims, but also among other cultural and religious communities. Today the share of sales of Halal food in Moscow is about 5–10% of retail sales, while Halal products are virtually absent in many other regions. A growing number of companies will capitalize on this opportunity.

The Sustainability Imperative

Across the globe, more and more consumers have started to adopt sustainable behaviors. Nielsen Data found that 66% of global respondents are willing to pay more for products produced from sustainable sources.[2] Agriculture and food companies that embrace more rigorous environmental and social standards will be able to better position themselves in the face of evolving consumer habits and to take advantage of this trend. Although there are examples of companies in Russia that have already turned to sustainable practices, they are still exceptions.

Precision Farming

Technological advances are driving the development of smart agriculture. According to a Roland Berger report, precision farming technologies are expected to hit an average 12% growth rate over the next years, compared to just 4% for traditional agricultural equipment.[3] Advanced economies have been steadily expanding the application of smart technology solutions in agriculture. Precision farming brings together various technological applications such as automation, sensors for geo-mapping, and big data analysis that can improve evaluations of climate and soil data and thereby increase crop productivity and the efficiency of resource use. Unfortunately, while precision farming sees wide applications in emerging markets like Argentina, Brazil, and China, its adoption in Russia is still at a very low level and limited to large agricultural companies.

Food of the Future

According to the World Wildlife Fund (WWF) we currently use 50% more natural resources than the planet can generate, while, based on United Nations (UN) predictions, it will be necessary to increase global food production by as much as 70% to fully meet global demand by 2050.[4] While Russia and many other countries are focusing on conventional approaches to agriculture, the future of food security will depend largely on finding and developing alternative sources. Sustainable protein, meat substitution, edible insects, and jellyfish are just a few examples of unconventional sources of food supply where many international startups have already emerged. According to a recent AgFunder report, despite the decline in global venture capital (VC) investments, 2017 was Agtech's busiest with deals increasing by 10%.[5] Clearly, investors continue to place big bets on those that promise to innovate and disrupt the future of food industry.

To summarize, the agrifood sector in Russia must transform itself to take advantage of a number of emerging trends. In order to realize its unfulfilled potential, a multifaceted approach is required including the development of infrastructure, the improvement of the business environment, and the creation of favorable investment conditions. The success of these endeavors will depend on effective cooperation between the Russian state, business sectors, scientists, non-governmental organizations (NGOs), academia, investors, and other market players. The quality of coordination among these key stakeholders will determine whether Russian agriculture remains competitive only at home, or whether it can become a player in international markets and realize its superpower potential.

Notes

1. Nielsen (2015). *The Sustainability Imperative: New Insights on Consumer Expectations.* https://www.nielsen.com/content/dam/nielsenglobal/co/docs/Reports/2015/global-sustainability-report.pdf
2. Roland Berger Strategy Consultants (2015). *Business Opportunities in Precision Farming. Will Big Data Feed the World in the Future?* https://www.rolandberger.com/en/Publications/pub_precision_farming.html
3. The Guardian (2014). *Earth Has Lost Half of Its Wildlife in the Past 40 Years, Says WWF.* https://www.theguardian.com/environment/2014/sep/29/earth-lost-50-wildlife-in-40-years-wwf
4. The Guardian (2011). *UN: Farmers Must Produce 70% More Food by 2050 to Feed Population.* https://www.theguardian.com/environment/2011/nov/28/un-farmers-produce-food-population
5. AgFunder (2017). *Investing Report: Year in Review.* https://research.agfunder.com/2017/AgFunder-Agrifood-Tech-Investing-Report-2017.pdf

9

Bumper Harvests Beat Soviet Production Records

Where Are the Profits?

Michail Mishchenko
Tomas Casas i Klett

Russia's first Dutch disease was not about oil but about grain. In the early 20th century the legendary Czarist Prime Minister, Pyotr Stolypin, implemented agrarian reforms that included land redistribution to smallholders. By the time of his assassination in 1911, the Russian Empire had become the world's main producer of grain, selling more abroad than all the exports of North and South America together.

The Soviet experience in agriculture with its collectivization drive was painful and inconsistent. Rapid modernization was punctuated by horrible famines. Paradoxically, by the early 1970s as the Soviet Union's grain output hit record heights, the country went from being a net exporter of grain to

The Life of Russian Business, pages 49–51

becoming a net importer. This was because the Politburo had decided in the 1960s to set higher meat consumption targets which shifted production to fodder and animal feed. In the 1980s management problems accumulated and grain imports became responsible for the large increase in Soviet debt. Despite President Jimmy Carter's short-lived partial grain embargo, the USSR became the largest foreign buyer of American grain.

The difficult 1990s saw underinvestment in agriculture, but also a halving of livestock. It was only in 2016 that Russia beat the maximum grain production levels achieved in 1978. Is Russia today set to regain its role as the world's bread-basket?

The rounds of sanctions and counter-sanctions, along with the import substitution strategy, have spurred investment in agricultural production. As a result, the 2016 production record was exceeded in 2017 by an incredible 40%. Such large-scale production of grain and cereals, however, has met the laws of supply and demand: Domestic prices have gone down tumbling. More worryingly, of the additional grain output, only 30% was exported. That is despite the fact that while at present, global price levels are modest by historical standards, they are substantially higher than those in the home market. Yet, most of Russian grain does not manage to travel aboard—and the problem is domestically made.

Russian infrastructure bottlenecks are severe. First, there is a lack of grain elevators and storage facilities, which incidentally means that the import of agricultural equipment from the West to Russia is a thriving business. At the same time, Russia has not enough grain terminals in its ports. If that were not enough, the rail network is overloaded and many producers are unable to reach the export grain terminals at ports in the first place. Logistic limitations result in higher costs and there are also other causes that erode competitiveness.

Many farmers and agribusiness are still not optimizing their production costs, despite the vast stretches of high quality soils and suitable climates in the Black Earth region, the Krasnodar bread-basket or the Republic of Tatarstan. Agribusinesses are simply not using the latest productivity enhancing approaches like liquid fertilizer, advanced irrigation systems or site-specific crop management. To transform the mindset and management techniques of the Russian farmer implies disturbing cultural inertia, a herculean task.

Where do those agricultural products that Russia does manage to export go? To the Middle East, Turkey, India, or Egypt. The latter is the world's number one grain importer and Russia has been its main supplier. Russia is also starting to export grain to China indirectly via meat products.

Grain feeds animals that are often raised in ventures with Chinese partners. This model of selling higher value-added products appears to be supported by government policy.

However, the meat export model is not necessarily in the farmers' best interests. Inexpensive grain that feeds livestock is necessary to keep meat cheap. The Russian state refrained from stocking grain last year which would have contributed to keeping prices stable, to the delight of meat producers and the chagrin of grain producers.

Without decisive investments in technical and management skills, as well as in the logistics and infrastructure to move produce abroad, Russia's recent agricultural boom will not be as profitable as it ought to be. The industry's over-capacity depresses prices while costs are not optimized. Profits have not materialized to the extent once expected and long-term sustainable returns may remain elusive. Sanctions spurred Russia's commitment to become a superpower food producer. In an impressively short period this vision has become a reality—at least partially. The answer one gets from agribusiness, teeth clenched, is still: "Stay calm, all will be well."

10

Russian Steel

The Urgent Need for Reform

Marat Atnashev

Since the first 5-Year Plan in 1928, the steel industry has been a major engine of the Russian economy. Steel was also a symbol of its modernization drive. It is no coincidence that Stalin—né Joseph Dzhugashvili—chose a nom de guerre that means "man of steel." Today, and despite being privatized and having become relatively competitive, the industry is burdened with a variety of structural problems.

The steel industry accounts for 20% of the country's industrial production and employs around 1 million people. Since being privatized in the 1990s, steel has become one of the country's most market-oriented industries. The state is minimally involved in steel, making it more efficient and competitive than other industries. Competition and private ownership have optimized production capacity and introduced important technological innovations. However, despite the successful post-Soviet reforms in

The Life of Russian Business, pages 53–55

steel, there are signs of trouble. The industry is gradually depleting its investment capital—some of it hailing from the Soviet era—but it is not able to generate enough revenue to renovate dilapidated facilities. The steel business can only survive as long as its physical plants last.

Revenue has fallen, largely because of the global economic downturn. Moreover, falling demand has led to excess production capacity, driving down prices and forcing producers to work at or below variable cost. The present low demand might last for decades, meaning that profit margins in the steel industry will be small for quite some time.

The industry's woes are also related to its experience with privatization in the 1990s, which coincided with the rapid growth of the Chinese economy. Emboldened by seemingly limitless demand and easy access to financing, the leaders of the Russian steel industry quickly set their sights on foreign assets. However, none of the companies' major investments abroad have paid off. Instead, they have become burdened with large amounts of debt, much of which is now owned by the Russian government. Thus, while steel is reformed and market-oriented, it remains highly dependent on the state.

The current surplus of global production capacity, much of it driven by China, means that Russian steel companies will have to search for new ways to remain profitable. Could the U.S. steel industry be a model for Russia?

Unlike Russian steel, which is produced in massive, remote "mono-cities" (cities in which a single industry comprises most of the economy), U.S. steel is produced in small, compact plants. These plants provide a significant advantage, as they are geographically well distributed. They enable low freight costs and often produce niche products that are difficult to substitute. Moreover, complicated marketing schemes and regional and national protectionism mean that international competitors face considerable barriers when entering the U.S. market.

If the Russian government continues to take a hands-off approach to the steel industry, the U.S. alternative may be a viable way forward. It would entail a further reduction and restructuring of production facilities, closing inefficient enterprises, and abandoning some unprofitable export business. These steps would cut off fat from an industry that is stuck in the past. Given Russia's tight labor market it would also free up several hundred thousand people for more productive employment, and increase the efficiency of the workers that remain. Understandably, the government is unlikely to support such restructuring, as it would also create profound shifts, some with negative social consequences in the immediate term.

In the future, Russia may also consider re-nationalizing the steel industry. This could be done easily enough. Currently, the total capitalization of all steel companies is many times less than their total debt, most of which belongs to state-owned banks. In other words, the state is already the main investor in the industry.

However, the state isn't looking to add to its problems. Mechel, one of Russia's largest metallurgic companies, has been on the verge of bankruptcy for 3 years. Yet shutting Mechel down would imply to take on responsibilities. The state avoids them by extending debt. The shareholders of Mechel, and those of other such companies, hire managers to deal with the problems. For their part, shareholders see their assets as relatively inexpensive stock options—their losses are capped by low capitalization, and they get to keep any gains.

In the long run, the Russian economy may pay a high price for the creeping nationalization of the industry through increased state debt and the avoidance of painful reform. Besides the cost of debt forgiveness, government support allows inefficient enterprises to stay in business, maintain low operational efficiency, and increases corruption. This nudges the industry towards gradual monopolization.

In summary, even though Russian steel is currently a market-oriented industry with little government participation, it must continue to reform itself. If it does not, it is headed for greater government involvement and the host of maladies that such a move will entail.

11

The End of Oil Rent, Not of the Oil Age

How Technology Has Ushered in Commoditization

Marat Atnashev

On May 25, 2017, the Organization of Petroleum Exporting Countries (OPEC) and Russia agreed to retain restrictions on oil output. A mere decade ago, the news about Russia agreeing to OPEC restrictions would have guaranteed a shock price increase. Today, such decisions have a limited impact on price.

Oil has been a unique commodity in the global market for over a hundred years. In the past, the world became accustomed to high prices and worried about shortages. OPEC restrictions, wars and political instability in the Middle East, along with environmental disasters like the Gulf of Mexico oil spill, all resulted in sudden contractions of supply. Producers needed years and multi-billion dollar investments to increase supply, while oil consumers (especially, in the transport industry) had almost no alternatives. On the other hand, during periods of excessive supply, it was hard to

The Life of Russian Business, pages 57–60

reduce production as the operating costs of most producers were so low, and a significant price drop was not a disincentive to stop production in existing fields. In addition, natural depletion is a fairly slow process in traditional fields. As a result, when there was a sudden shortage of oil, the price rocketed; when there was excess, the price dropped sharply. It took years to restore balance in the market.

Global demand for oil has been growing steadily for decades and continues to increase by an average of 1% to 2% a year. The number of geopolitical risks remains unchanged. Today, some of the most important oil producing countries such as Iraq, Libya, Syria, Iran, and Venezuela, face civil wars, sanctions, and political instability.

However, the oil market has undergone a drastic change and the main reason for this is the emergence of new technologies. A long period of high oil prices resulted in an investment boom into new production technologies (above all, the shale revolution), improvement of internal combustion engine performance, and alternative technologies for energy generation and storage.

Shale gas production in the United States has a short investment cycle and implies a constantly decreasing production cost. The period from an initial investment decision to the start of product marketing is just several months—a massive contrast to the 5 to 10 years this takes for traditional oil fields. U.S. shale oil dampens price fluctuations in the oil market. When the price drops below operating costs (currently, about US$ 40 to US$ 50 per barrel), the number of drilling rigs decreases rapidly. When the price rises above US$ 50 to US$ 60 per barrel, the number of drilling rigs sharply increases. Thus, the United States had more than 1,500 drilling rigs operational at a price peak in 2014. In May 2016, after a price drop to US$ 40, only about 300 were operating. By May 2017, with prices slightly above US$ 50 (thanks to OPEC and Russia's restrictions on production, which stabilized prices), their number again exceeded 900. An oil excess or shortage of up to 2 to 3 million barrels per day, that is, 2%–3% of global demand, can now be absorbed within 6–12 months rather than the years this would have previously taken. There is now no need to be an expert to forecast market trends; one can simply Google the number of operating drilling rigs[1] in the United States, Canada, or the world.

Moreover, the advance in production technologies has resulted in an increase in proven reserves by transforming previously discovered noncommercial reserves into commercially viable ones. Thus, shale gas fields, viscous oil fields and tar sand fields in Canada have now become commercially viable. Since the 1980s, global proven reserves have almost tripled, gradually diffusing the fears of shortages or the depletion of available reserves in the near future. Rather, the challenge is now to forecast whether there will be sufficient demand for these increased reserves in the foreseeable future.

Technological developments have also affected the demand side. The continuous improvement of traditional automobile engine performance has absorbed a significant part of huge demand increases related to the growth of population and mobility. These performance increases and the cost reductions of electric batteries have gradually turned electric cars into real economical alternatives. However, large fleet replacement will probably take a long time and most forecasts predict that even 20 years from now electric car fleets will play a minor role in the grand mobility picture. That said, the growth of electric cars disrupts one of the fundamental tenets of high oil rents: Oil ceases to be the only source of fuel.

As a result, the role of OPEC and its influence in the oil market will continue to decrease. Tactically, Russia and OPEC will benefit in the short-term through their joint efforts to add a couple of additional dollars in the current oil price. The price per barrel will go up a little for a limited period before U.S. shale gas manufacturers step in and compensate for OPEC production cuts over the year. It is their decreasing production costs—thanks to the improvement of technological and operational performance—that will drive global oil prices going forward.

An economic bogeyman has entered the story. Who today knows the price per ton of coal apart from dedicated industry experts? Yet coal was the main fuel and a critical strategic resource from the industrial revolution until the early 20th century. Then, the invention of the internal combustion engine, along with the development of oil production and refining technologies destroyed coal's monopoly. By the latter half of the 20th century, all nonprofitable coal mines ceased to produce rents, with large-scale economic, social, and political consequences. Currently, coal has been relegated to an ordinary commodity with tough production cost competition. Meanwhile, global coal demand has never ceased to grow, and it still grows today.

Fights to gain access to new reserves will no longer be the focus of the oil industry. The greater emphasis of competition is now in the domain of new technologies and operating performance. The role of alternative fuels is growing.

All of these signs signal an oil market recovery. But, in this recovery, oil is being transformed, like coal, into an ordinary trading commodity with its price determined by production costs and the price of available alternatives, rather than by consumer fear or price fixing by producers.

Oil demand may continue to grow for a good many years. Producers, including Russia, will not stop producing oil, and the world will continue to buy it. But the rent element built into the price will steadily erode. The age of oil will not end, but the age of oil rent certainly will.

Russia will slowly but surely give up its overreliance on oil.

For Russia, oil revenues are a key element in funding the budget as well as the basis for welfare payments to its citizens. Now, Russia has to think beyond how to efficiently and fairly collect oil revenues and combat the Dutch disease. Russia has to transform the oil industry to make it technologically competitive and focused on sustainable value creation rather than on pursuing ever more elusive oil rents. There is a precedent: The challenging transformation of the Russian coal industry.

Note

1. See the Baker Hughes Rig Counts at http://phx.corporate-ir.net/phoenix.zhtml?c=79687&p=irol-rigcountsoverview

12

Coal

The Russian Economy's Most Successful Reform[1]

Marat Atnashev
Sergey Stepanov

Today, in Russia, everyone is talking about the need for structural reforms. Without them, the economy will continue to stall. But what exactly needs to be done, and what form should the structural reforms take? Successful examples are few, not just in Russia, but for other countries as well. Yet, as is often the case, the best reform is the one that makes the least noise.

Coal has been mined for millennia, as far back as ancient Greece and Rome. In the 18th century, the invention of the steam engine turned coal into the main source of industrial energy. It was only at the beginning of the 20th century that coal ceded this strategic role to oil and gas, while nonetheless retaining a significant share in the energy equation as a cheap, low quality fuel and as a raw material for metallurgy (See Figure I.12.1).

The Life of Russian Business, pages 61–67

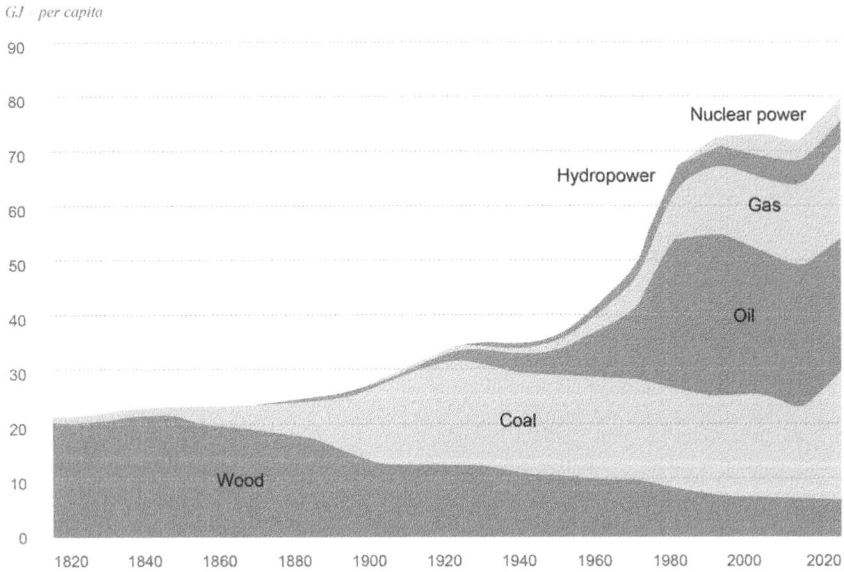

Figure I.12.1 Global energy consumption in gigajoules per capita. *Source:* Smil (2010)[2] and United Nations.

Over the past half century, the global coal mining industry has undergone a radical transformation. As a result of competition, production has shifted from industrialized countries (such as the United Kingdom, Germany, and the United States) to countries where production is cheaper, due to natural endowments or low-cost labor (such as Australia, China, or India). The main source of demand has also shifted to Asia. Today, two countries are of key importance for the global coal market (See Figure I.12.2).

China dominates both the production and consumption of coal. Since 2000, China has increased production from 1.4 to almost 4 billion tons—higher than the production capacity of the United States, India, and Australia combined. Today, the most modern and productive mines and open pits are being built in China. There are so many new projects that the country is closing thousands of old mines to improve safety. The growth of the Chinese industry was the main factor behind the high coal prices that started at the beginning of the 2000s and lasted until 2013–2014, when signs of a slowdown in the economy affected the prices of all commodities.

Australia plays a special role as the world's largest exporter of coking coals. Since the early 1990s, Australia has been continuously increasing production. Development continues despite falling prices, due to the implementation of advanced technology and the high quality of its reserves.

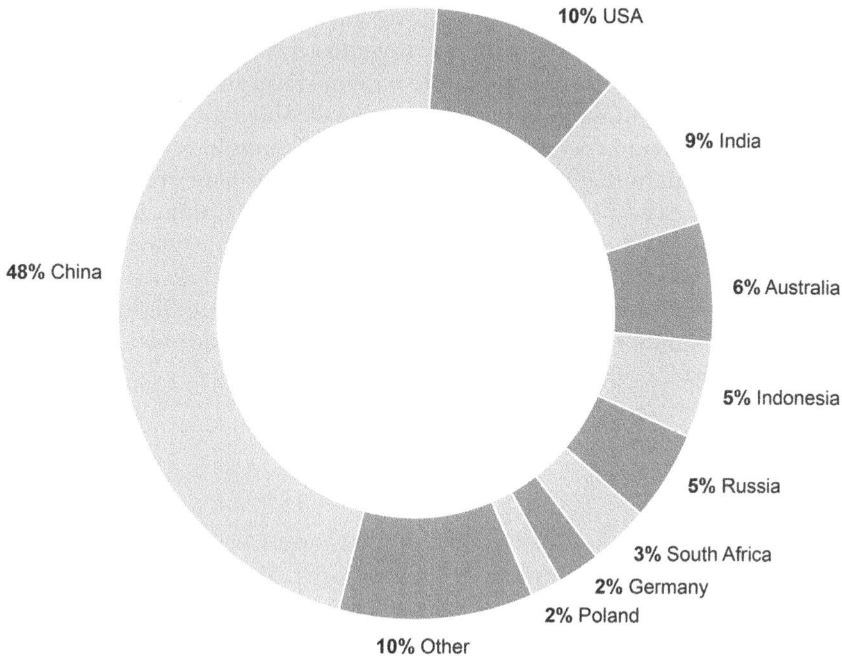

Figure I.12.2 Global coal-mining breakdown in 2015, by country.

While the export volumes continue to increase, the Australian coal industry is undergoing a major shake-out, shedding jobs and resetting its cost base.

The modern coal-mining industry is characterized by several key features:

1. A globalized market makes the industry extremely competitive, and prices are difficult to predict. This forces all participants in the market to continuously improve efficiency. A modern Australian mine produces 3–7 million tons of coal per year from one wall. To do so requires 350–500 people. In Russia, the average mine produces 1.5 million tons per year with a workforce of 900–1,000 people. The recent problems in Australian industry have however contributed to the production growth of Russian mines.
2. A loss of competitiveness inevitably leads to social and political complications, which force governments to become involved in regulating and supporting the industry. The United Kingdom, France, Germany, Poland, and even the United States have undergone difficult decades of transformation, government subsidies and miners' strikes and, as a result, an inevitable decrease in production.

3. Safety concerns and the significant environmental impacts of coal are the key negative factors of the industry, which probably explains why most players operate at the national level and the market share of multinationals is relatively small. Since the beginning of underground coal mining, methane explosions have been a major problem. In the 20th century, major accidents have occurred in the United States, United Kingdom, Australia, and China, and claimed the lives of thousands of miners. One of the main trends worldwide is the transition to opencast mining, which carries no risks of methane explosions. Still, Australia and the United States have retained high numbers of underground mines without major incidents for the last 20–30 years.

Russian Coal

By the early 1990s, the Russian coal mining industry was 80% dependent on subsidies, which amounted to 1.4% of GDP. Almost half of all mines and open pits were operating at a loss. The industry employed more than 900,000 workers. In the summer of 1989, a wave of miners' strikes swept through all the producing regions, and was one of the key factors in the political destabilization of the USSR. At the same time, miner mortality was one of the highest in the world, with more than one death per million tons of coal mined.

Under these conditions, in 1993–1994 reforms began, with the participation of the IMF, the World Bank and the IBRD (International Bank for Reconstruction and Development). Reform was aimed at reducing the size of the industry and eliminating subsidies, while avoiding social upheaval. According to the estimates of the IBRD, the 370 million tons produced in 1992, would need to be halved.

As a result of this structural reform, the coal mining industry was almost completely privatized—the privatization process being no better or more transparent than in other Russian industries. Yet the result was a high degree of competition in the market. Today, there is no dominant player in the Russian coal mining industry. The market leader, Siberian Coal Energy Company (SUEK), has slightly over 25% of the market share. Among coking coal brands, the competition is even higher (See Figure I.12.3).

Additionally, there are both vertically integrated players (related to metallurgy and energy) and a large number of independent producers, creating a truly competitive environment. A third category, of third-party investors, sees owners from finance or other industries. This category is the

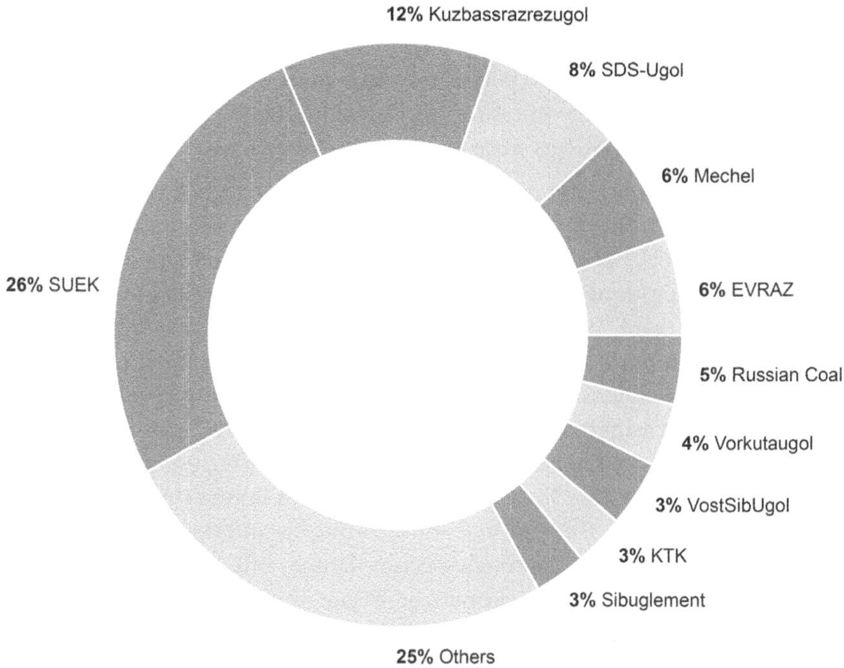

Figure I.12.3 Production breakdown in Russia in 2015, by company.

least stable as technical and geological complexities are often underestimated. As a result, third-party investors often leave the industry disappointed.

High competition has led to a continuous increase in the efficiency of the industry. The main areas of progress have been in technological improvements (modern equipment, new degassing methods, modern control systems), operational improvements, reorientation from absolute tonnage to meeting market demands, and in the professional management of new investment projects, with billions of new investment dollars flowing into the industry in the past 20 years. As a result, labor productivity has increased six-fold since the 1990s and doubled since the year 2000. At the same time, the number of employees in the coal mining industry has declined from 900,000 in 1992, to 400,000 in 2001, and to just 143,000 in 2015. The production level of 2015 amounted to 373 million tons, exceeding the volumes of 1992 (368 million tons). The 1990s saw huge falls in production, with a decrease to almost 200 million tones. This is an extraordinary result for a traditional, old industry.

What were the social and economic consequences in terminating 750,000 people (out of 900,000) from the coal industry? Coal mining towns saw rapid decreases in their populations: The population of Vorkuta decreased from 116,000 in 1992 to 59,000 in 2016; while Neryungri saw a reduction from 76,000 to 58,000 in the same period. Yet this colossal transformation went relatively smoothly and subsidies from the budget to cover the losses of coal producers were completely discontinued in 2002.

In terms of safety, the number of deaths has decreased from 1 person per million tons in the late 1980s, to less than 0.1 per million tons in recent years. Two factors have been key in this transformation: The adoption of international standards and technologies, as well as the consistent position of the Russian state. With the implementation of modern technology and operational standards, the work of a miner is gradually changing: It is becoming more mechanized and automated, with educational qualifications playing an increasingly important role and physical strength increasingly less. After a series of terrible accidents in the mid-2000s, all interested parties: Rostekhnadzor (the Federal Environmental, Engineering and Nuclear Supervision Agency), the regional administrations and the mine owners all agreed on a more strict approach to compliance, with regular monitoring of safety requirements. Rostekhnadzor began the practice of suspending work in unsafe areas and mines and demanding the punishment of guilty managers. At the same time, there was a dialogue with companies in which the state remained the arbitrator, which not only allowed the application of punitive sanctions, but also resulted in systematically fixing the situation.

Today, the Russian coal mining industry is quite adaptable, and can quickly react to changing conditions when necessary to successfully compete in the global market. Still, it faces further challenges, such as the gradual impoverishment of existing mining areas that will require the development of new coal basins. The Russian part of the Donbass is close to exhaustion, work in Vorkuta is already carried out at depths of 700–900 meters, and in Kuzbass, the reserves of the most valuable G and K brands are becoming ever smaller.

Also, in the past 3 years there has been a significant decline in global coal prices due to the slowing demand in China. Coal miners around the world survived due to the devaluation of local currencies and the closure of costly production facilities. The significant devaluation of the ruble allowed for the competitiveness of most Russian producers to be maintained. Then, at the end of 2015, China announced plans to close 2,000 mines, and from the beginning of 2016, a gradual decrease in production volumes has been registered, which, for the moment, is having a positive on prices.

The big picture is nonetheless clear. As a result of the reforms, the coal mining industry has completely relinquished subsidies which consumed up to 1.5% of Russian GDP, reduced the frequency of fatal accidents by a factor of 10, and become 6 times more efficient, releasing 750,000 workers while maintaining the same level of production. All of this has been achieved without significant social discord, and with a systemic reduction of social risks—at least in view of the reduced number of employed (and potentially dissatisfied) miners. If the entire Russian economy had undergone such a transformation, today our GDP would be similar to the level of Switzerland. The reforms proved to be much more successful than the IBRD plans and also more successful than reforms in neighboring Poland, where a series of social and political problems are still extant. Indeed, the reform was perhaps even more successful than the efforts of Margaret Thatcher in the United Kingdom, where the coal mining industry was, in fact, virtually eliminated.

Several factors contributed to this success. First, the reforms were dictated not by theoretical considerations but by the urgent need to assist the economic survival of industry participants as well as the political survival of the country's leadership. Second, the reform was prepared and implemented by people with very different views and experiences: regional governors and the heads of coal mining enterprises who had experience in mining work; a team of "young reformers," headed by Anatoly Chubais; and international consultants and representatives of business. The presence of international institutions brought great experience, and put pressure on the pace and direction of reforms. Participation from industrial and regional representatives grounded the reforms and created the prerequisites for on-site support.

The role of the state was also a unique one. In the absence of a natural resource rent, coal was seen more as a problem than a potential source of income. The state acted as a regulator and reformer, rather than as a rent distributor, and to this day it does not seek to have a role in an industry that conjures up a lot of unpleasant associations. The reform of the coal industry, virtuous for its pragmatism and outstanding results, deserves recognition as an important case study in how to prepare for the much needed and unavoidable structural reforms required in the rest of the Russian economy.

Note

1. This contribution has been derived from the article *"Даешь угля. Самая успешная реформа в российской экономике"* [Coal: Russia's Economy's Most Successful Reform] by M. Atnashev and S. Stepanov, published on republic .ru in 2016.
2. Smil, V. (2010). *Energy Transitions: History, Requirements, Prospects.* Praeger: Santa-Barbara, CA.

II

Strategy and Governance

SECTION II

Introduction

A decade and a half of rapid economic development, followed by the recent slowdown, illustrate how company strategies and governance practices in Russia differ substantially from those in the West. The unique Russian business environment has led to the emergence of astonishly agile executives who, while driven by mostly local demands, try to integrate best practices from both Western and Russian reality. With maturity and growth slowing, firms in both the state and private sectors are seeking new formulas to effectively balance global and indigenous approaches to strategy and governance.

This section starts off with two leading Russian businessmen, well-known philanthropists and opinion leaders, Mikhail Krushnirovich and Ruben Vardanyan, providing incisive comments on some of the burning questions faced by Russian businessmen (Chapter II.1). Subsequently we present the views of the chairman of Sberbank—Russia's largest bank—and the former reformist minister of economics and trade, Herman Gref, who provides personal insights into global trends (Chapter II.2). We then move from opinion to three specific cases, all showing different facets of the construction industry. Brusnika, a residential developer from Siberia, has a strategy based on carving out a new niche by capitalizing on fast-changing social norms and the new culture of the emerging middle class (Chapter II.3). Two follow-up cases exemplify the unorthodox and audacious business strategies of Russian founders. SmileMart details how young

The Life of Russian Business, pages 71–72

entrepreneurs launch a real estate project without equity and manage—in a couple of short years—to net millions in Russia's Far East (Chapter II.4). Velesstroy brings us to a remote location in Russia's Arctic, where a team of managers is running against the clock, and the Russian winter, to build a massive Liquid Natural Gas (LNG) tank on permafrost (Chapter II.5). The section then moves to corporate social responsibility where SKOLKOVO's Sustainability Lab outlines relevant approaches for foreign firms in Russia (Chapter II.6). To show how it is really done, we also provide the award-winning case of Unilever and its state-of-the-art waste management practices in Tula (Chapter II.7).

The final part of this section focuses on financial and corporate governance practices. A contribution by independent researcher, Dmitri Melkumov (Chapter II.8), dwells on the symbolic nature of Russian boards and the future prospects for corporate governance. This is followed by insights from leading academics Irina Ivashkovskaya and Irina Skvortsova from the Higher School of Economics (HSE) on the perennial question of whether and why firms diversify (Chapter II.9). The Analytical Credit Rating Agency (ACRA) case then illustrates how a venture addresses an institutional void—here in credit risk assessment—to improve the governance and development of domestic financial markets (Chapter II.10). An inside look at Russian wealth possessors poses an ultimate governance challenge: The transition of family assets to the next generation in the face of a partial wealth management infrastructure (Chapter II.11). We close this section with Troika Dialog's investment banking journey, one that encourages us to reflect whether upholding values is consistent with profit maximization goals (Chapter II.12).

This section combines hands-on cases with academic insight to describe scenes in strategy and governance across Russia. Readers will connect the dots with other emerging markets where strategic choice is uncertain and governance is conditioned by weak institutions.

II 1

Don't Swim With or Against the Current

Swim Anywhere You Like[1]

Ruben Vardanyan
Mikhail Kusnirovich

Comments are by Ruben Vardanyan (RV), founder of Troika Dialog, investment banker and philanthropist; and Mikhail Kusnirovich (MK), founder and chairman of the Supervisory Board of Bosco di Ciliegi Group, a luxury goods and services retail chain.

Trust and Partners

RV: When you start your business, the circle of people you can trust will be important. In the 1990s, I used to talk with a well-known professor, my mentor, on various topics. He shared with me a very interesting formula to measure success: "How much money can you borrow in relation to your monthly salary?" This is one criterion for measuring your success.

The Life of Russian Business, pages 73–77

It is important to understand that trust is binary, black or white. You either trust or don't. How many people do you trust? Are there any people that you trust to such an extent that you can share with them your house keys, money, or an idea you want to implement?

MK: First, you decide to do business with your partners but then might decide that it is better to do it alone. At different stages of your life, you make decisions that seem right at that time—you must always be responsible for your decisions. If you are alone, do everything alone! If you are ready to share investments, be ready to share the benefits and don't start to argue about them ("I stayed at work longer than you"). But if you do business with partners, choose those whom you like rather than those who foist themselves on you.

Mistakes

RV: I committed the most painful mistakes in my life when I departed from my inner principles and rules that I had set for myself. Every time I tried to find a compromise—say a certain transaction promised very large profits and was worth compromising some principles—I had to pay for it in a hard, painful, and troublesome way.

The investment company I found had many unpleasant chapters. People gave me money but later, when the crisis began, they asked me, "So everyone in the world but you knew that the market would fall? How could you not have known about this? You are a pro, we entrusted you with our money." In this sense, when you are working in the service industry, there are two important things: First, know your customers. Second, properly manage their expectations and at the same time be honest and understand what your customers can do and what they cannot do.

MK: I don't want to admit my mistakes. I even don't see them as mistakes. My dad used to say, "Don't regret anything because it's just life." Did I have a chance to write rough drafts? The periods that brought me a loss instead of a material gain are a part of my life, aren't they? I don't consider them mistakes. I like them. They were a path to some result or something else that is called life. Why do we need to worry if something has gone wrong? We should hope and make every effort to succeed.

Peace With Yourself

RV: No matter what you do, the most important thing is to be at peace with yourself and to receive satisfaction from what you do.

MK: Ruben (RV) says that you should be at peace with yourself. By no means do I agree with this. The most boring things in your life happen when you drowse in your harmony, when your desires match your capabilities, you are in a state of bliss wherever you are, when you are satisfied with yourself and your environment and when you are purring. I encourage you to create a potential difference—the difference between desires and capabilities—because this is the only driving force. Create a difference of temperature, concentration, pressure, anything. Any process is driven by a mismatch between desires and capabilities. And only a combination of all these mismatches can give you a sense of harmony, God willing. Rare happy moments occur when you are watching your kids, your loved ones—these are moments of happiness. Don't let yourself be calm the rest of the time. Otherwise, you will completely kill your qualities of leadership, your entrepreneurial spirit, and lively interest in life. When you are at peace with yourself, you are like a vegetable or a berry. Punish yourself for this boundless complacency.

It is very important to have a healthy sense of irony. If you take yourself too seriously, your success story will be very fragile. Our business is not a matter of life and death. A really important thing is, for example, to work with the Vera Hospice Charity Fund. This is when something irrevocable happens in your life. Everything that we do in our business is only a part of our life.

This is the only life; this is how it is. I live it my way and enjoy it. Don't beat yourself up because of stupid things. You should be well aware that you cannot win all the time. I personally don't like lottery tickets, especially when I win, because I haven't done anything for it. But when I have succeeded due to my own work, my own efforts, and at the same time my friends, relatives, and even strangers have received enjoyment, everything is fine, especially if you find a minute to relish your success.

What's Next

MK: Developing the next generation is much more important than any other achievements, which are transitory in comparison.

When experienced climbers who have made it to the summit are many times asked, "How is it up there?"; they usually answer, "You know, it's cold." A person who has arrived somewhere, reached a certain goal, is always asked, "And what does it feel like?" And the worst thing is feeling that you are alone at the top. You reached it alone, nobody is applauding you, the only way forward is down, and only then comes the next peak.

RV: You can achieve success in Russia only if you are aware of what's going on in the world, but at the same time you must learn, live, and work within Russia's environment.

Entrepreneurs

RV: I would identify two qualities of modern entrepreneurs. The first thing is that they are not afraid to fail. Historically in Russia we don't like those who fail, and I find it very important not to be afraid of failing, making mistakes, doing something wrong and then rising again. The second thing is adaptability. Everything around you is changing. On the one hand, you should have a strong backbone, but on the other hand you need to remain open to the changing world and quickly adapt to it. This is not easy.

MK: There are two things that are important in any time and place for a leader: To be able (and like) to make decisions. Then, the leader must be accountable for them. This is both a necessary and a sufficient condition, as in mathematics. This applies to any leaders, whether they are employees or entrepreneurs.

Scaling

MK: The transition from quality to quantity leads not only upwards, but downwards as well. If you are willing to be responsible for the satisfaction of your customers, reflect on the maximum scale you can sustain. When we scale a business up, it will lose its charm. Moreover, when there was one shop, one store, I knew exactly what to do. When there were 21 stores, I also knew. And when there are 211 of them, I still know what to do but nobody wants to hear me. And this is a problem. Even though the gross profit is fine, the rate of return, of course, falls.

Interestingly, the desire to scale up is also an attempt to avoid real responsibility. Because if you are alone and everything is on you, you personally have to answer—whether the soup is delicious, whether the floor is clean, whether a waiter is polite.

RV: I know a delicious little restaurant in Italy, but its owner is not going to open another ten restaurants. He is absolutely happy to make money from only one. Sometimes we want to become the biggest player, create a network, and have a giant business. However, there are very big opportunities and niches for small- and medium-sized businesses that should not be scaled up. There is nothing wrong with this. You don't need to become the owners of a McDonald's or a Walmart. You know, in the 15th century the

Chinese emperor gave an order to execute the captains and destroy all the ships that could potentially have reached America. He believed that his empire should not exceed a manageable size.

Choices

RV: Each of us has choices. Decision-making is a great source of happiness and a great responsibility. I advise you to read a few books, especially *Escape from Freedom* by Erich Fromm. It shows that people are reluctant to make decisions and take responsibility; they want someone to do it for them. So the right to have a choice is a huge responsibility. We all have choices—to compare, to believe, to not to believe, to assess new horizons.

There is no single right model in our life, no single model that tells you whether it's good or bad to do business with partners, whether you should or should not study in America or go to China. Ultimately, these are all but tools to help you be complete, fulfilled, successful, and happy. It doesn't matter where in the world you are; it's important that you don't lose touch with yourself, that you make, create, change something—bring something to the challenging and ever-changing world around you. You should always be able to answer the question, "For what and why should I emigrate, or why should I stay?" If you stay, get the maximum here and achieve the best results.

You know, Jorge Luis Borges has a very good story, *The Garden of Forking Paths*. It's just an endless garden of forking paths where we need to walk and make continual choices. I hope all of you clearly understand that it's your own choice on how to live, and you should not swim with or against the current. Swim anywhere you like. Know where you want to swim.

Note

1. This contribution has been derived from the article "Надо плыть не по течению и не против течения, а туда, куда вы считаете нужным" [Do not swim along the current, neither against the current, but where you consider necessary], N.A., published in SKOLKOVO BeInTrend in Spring 2016.

2

Evolve or Become Extinct

Insights from CEO and Chairman of the Executive Board of Sberbank[1]

Herman Gref

Herman Gref came to prominence as an ambitious, goal-oriented leader during his tenure as Russia's minister of economic development and trade from 2000 to 2007. Since the end of 2007, Gref has been president of the state-owned savings bank Sberbank—Russia's largest—spearheading important transformations at the technological, operational, and corporate culture levels. Below, we have collected a number of his insights on current business and organizational issues as they relate to Russia.

On Evolution or Extinction

This applies to many of today's organizations. The average life span of a successful company used to be 50 years. Now it has dropped to 7. Consider

The Life of Russian Business, pages 79–82

the iPod—once an advanced gadget—now it's just an icon on your iPhone's screen. Given the rate at which the world is moving, even governments will find themselves at risk, if they stop evolving.

On Digitization

Mobility and participation in data generation will completely change the world. Now all processes are based on work with large arrays of digital data. Netflix is worth almost as much as Sberbank. But Sberbank has 330,000 employees, and Netflix has only 3,000. Data is the new oil, but Netflix doesn't have complete data, because people usually don't register under their own names. But their smart system deciphers user accounts using such criteria as the time of registration, transitions, login times, the selection of films or the order for watching them. We are creatures of habits that we bring with us to the Internet, allowing this system to read us perfectly. Netflix has built a global database with information for each client and thus has gained the ability to satisfy everyone's needs. And so, a company that was just a streaming service has decided to make something of its own. Their first product was "House of Cards." When I visited Netflix this year, I felt like a relic from another century.

On Changes as Contradictions

The core of competitiveness lies not in the ability to make a product, but in the ability to supply it regularly. There is always someone who wants to eat your lunch—in the banking sector they are already eating it. This is why we need serious changes. Interestingly, changes always come with their own contradictions. For instance, how do you achieve uninterrupted operations while continuously delivering new products? Investors want to see profitable and competitive companies, but to be profitable you need long-term investments. Generation X and Y have fundamentally different values; we must take both into account as employers if we wish to retain and develop young talent.

On Customer Convenience vs. Information Security

Everything that is convenient for customers is at odds with information security. When it comes to banks, the biggest expenses are cybersecurity and compliance with regulations and corporate standards. If we do not invest in cybersecurity today, tomorrow we will have to invest in law enforcement agencies, so that they unsuccessfully search for our customers' stolen money.

On Customer Focus vs. the Regulator's Demands

Here we have the example of blockchain, a technology for securely storing data. I believe this technology is comparable to the Internet in terms of its potential scale. The technology aims at modernizing services and products simultaneously boosting the security and transparency of transactions.

On Agility in a Horizontal Culture

The term agile has become popular in the 21st century. Its philosophy can be summarized as "Don't do what I say; do what I do." What is agile? When we talk about agile, we usually talk about the so-called "two pizza rule," according to which any team should be small enough that it could be fed with two pizzas. This system is built in such a way that all managers become members of a team, and products get made within weeks. Agile teams have a culture of collaboration. Nowadays you cannot be competitive without this approach. Transitioning into agile management is a massive challenge for all large organizations, as it requires them to rethink all management processes. The larger an organization is, the harder it is to rebuild it. It is especially difficult in our country Russia, where everything functions within a vertical culture. The agile approach implies a horizontal culture, and this poses a challenge not only to the management of our companies, but to our employees as well.

On Leaders

Today's world needs T leaders—people whose knowledge is both deep and wide. The key competence of a T leader is systematic thinking, or the ability to combine analytical and synthetic approaches. The main and the most important thing is to change yourself. A company grows only when and as far as its leaders grow. When we talk about a "company" we are talking about a legal fiction. The only real thing is people, and it is people that should get your undivided attention. You have seven times more chance to succeed if you invest in developing your employees' skills. This follows the J. Welch's famous quote "If the rate of change on the outside exceeds the rate of change on the inside, then the end is near."

Note

1. This contribution has been derived from the article "Эволюционируй или вымрешь: Герман Греф на Конвенте выпускников СКОЛКОВО" [Evolve

or become extinct: Insight from Herman Gref from SKOLKOVO Alumni Convent], N.A., published in SKOLKOVO BeInTrend in May 2016.

3

How Brusnika Is Reshaping Real Estate Development in Russia

From Square Meters to Standard of Living

Irina Kulikova

While the Russian construction market was not yet saturated, the norm for many years had been selling real estate by the square meter rather than selling homes. That business model, however, was not to last. By 2017, the first signs of maturation had already become visible—competition was steadily increasing, economic conditions had become more volatile and the consumer more demanding. Offering a low price per square meter is no longer enough. When entering Tyumen's construction business in 2004 Brusnika,[1] a Siberian developer, had a choice: to be like everyone else and sell by the square meter or to look further and offer a new standard of affordable urban living.

The Life of Russian Business, pages 83–86

The development business had shown strong growth for 20 years, but there was still scope for growth with an average of 25 square meters per capita in Russia compared to 55 square meters in Europe, and 75 square meters in the United States. A lot of property was in disrepair and needed to be demolished. A typical developer strategy would be to cut costs on everything possible to offer the lowest price. No thought was given to the environment or the convenience of those who would eventually live on the property.

However, Russians became more demanding. As they travelled the world they started appreciating comfortable entry halls, nice courtyards, big windows, cobble-stoned paved roads, sports facilities, cycle lanes, and so on. This made them begin to question the status quo of residential construction practices in Russia:

> Why are our home prices similar to those in Western Europe when we don't get the same quality? All we get is a box with four walls and not more. One might also call it a kennel.

From the beginning, Brusnika aimed to create a new standard of quality for the mass-market residential segment. Brusnika's team started off by travelling to Europe, mainly to the Netherlands and Finland, exploring the best examples of human-centric construction development. They knew, though, that what worked well in Europe might not be suitable for Russia. To survive and thrive in the context of different construction practices the company had to create its own model.

In the first stage of the project, Brusnika's staff conducted research in several Siberian cities to understand the drivers and mindsets of consumers. It appeared that the majority of residents were quite happy with the quality of property they lived in, as they simply didn't know any better. They liked their city and their quality of life; the only thing they missed was an IKEA and a water park. More profoundly, a key insight garnered in this region 2,500 kilometers east of Moscow was: "Nothing depends on me. And one person cannot change anything anyway." The price per square meter was still the key decision criteria. So was the reliability of the construction company and its ability to complete construction within the promised deadline.

But there were some respondents who were more critical: "Why do I need such a big corridor?"; "Why is the entrance to the building so inconvenient?"; "Why are there so many flats on one floor?"; and "Why is there no space for my children to walk outside?" Some consumers were starting to articulate aspirations beyond square meters. In the end, however, price was still the key issue.

Another factor to consider was fierce competition from many developers eager to seize a slice of an expanding market. The construction market in Tyumen was highly fragmented with the biggest player having only a 5% share. This, however, left an opportunity for a company able to establish a strong brand and differentiating factors in their offering to consumers. Brusnika saw a chance to develop a different value proposition for homebuyers where price was not the only decision criterion. It therefore developed the concept of comfortable urban living in a block of flats, moving away from price-based competition and carving out a comfortable niche within the mid-price segment for consumers who valued their living environment over just square meters.

To deliver on this promise, Brusnika had to find innovative architectural and engineering solutions. That meant designing each apartment and the living environment based on three principles:

- reasonable sufficiency, that is, providing the optimum number of square meters, but no more space than necessary for comfortable living;
- ergonomic design; and
- a price only slightly higher (about 3%) than the competition.

Brusnika's first residential development, designed by Dutch architects, comprised the four buildings of the Sukhodolsky Quarters in Ekaterinburg. The buildings were placed in such a way that they created an enclosed area and gave residents a feeling of their own private space. The varied number of stories prevented the dark "effect of the well" and provided sufficient lighting. The courtyard had a sports ground, a special zone for children, and a relaxation area for grown-ups. The first floor was given over to shops, cafes, and other services.

The developer paid special attention to the design of the community spaces. The garden boasted evergreen plants to ensure color all year round. This is especially important for Northern Russia where winters can last up to 8 months. Garbage containers were placed two thirds underground, which conserved space and eliminated odor. This created an environment appealing to the five senses. The entrance to each building was on the ground level and was see-through and well lit, including a clear and simple navigation system. The facades of the building had a European look, which was also functional and preserved heat. Special places for air conditioners were designed on balconies so that the outward appearance of the façade was not spoiled.

Inside each apartment, Brusnika maximized the utility of each square meter. For example, it offered room for built-in wardrobes and divided the space between social and private zones. It also provided potential customers with a choice: a classic kitchen or a kitchen with a dining room.

Once the first residents moved in, Brusnika placed signs on the properties communicating the code of conduct: "Here we say Hello to each other"; "Thank you for parking the right way and thinking about your neighbor"; "Here are the bags for the dogs"; "Thank you for not smoking"; and "We try to keep our court-yard clean." Surprisingly, Brusnika had discovered via a survey of 150 residents from different buildings that the new environment led to a new kind of residential behavior. The fact that people felt part of a community stimulated politer and more respectful behavior towards each other. Residents call this "the Brusnika effect." Katya and Andrei, who recently moved into a Brusnika apartment describe it as follows:

> The environment here is different. We notice that people who move into the more "European" Brusnika properties do change. They park only in designated places, pick up after their dogs, don't leave their garbage in the building, don't walk on the grass, don't pluck the flowers from the flower gardens. Residents treat the common spaces as their own. They even take good care of the common property.

Note

1. Brusnika is a developer founded in Tyumen in 2004 and later expanded to Novosibirsk, Ekaterinburg, Surgut, Stavropol and subsequently to Moscow. It is now the 11th largest developer nationwide of residential property.

4

A Khabarovsk Shopping Mall Venture

Stepping Out of a Window[1]

Keith Goodall
Yuliya Ponomareva

It is January 2010, and two business partners and real estate developers, Denis Gros and Andrey Bezverhov, find themselves in a difficult situation. Their initial attempt to run a property leasing business has not been successful, and they are rapidly accumulating debt. Desperate times require desperate remedies and the partners decide to start a new project: building a shopping mall in Khabarovsk, in the Russian Far East, with no start-up capital.

> We asked ourselves how we could develop an entire building without any cash in hand? Where were we going to find an investor or land? We had plenty of questions.

The Life of Russian Business, pages 87–91

The partners began by looking at land for development but they didn't yet know what kind of project they wanted to develop. Andrey met a builder specializing in the development of large residential areas that were measured in city blocks rather than individual buildings. In between the residential blocks he was putting up, the developer had 3,500 square meters of land that was unsuitable for residential development. The nearby residential area could, however, provide Denis and Andrey with a customer base for any retail outlets they might develop. So it made sense to them to cooperate with the residential developer, particularly since they assumed that he wouldn't attach much value to this piece of land. The viability of a shopping center project clearly depended on Andrey and Denis finding early-stage investors who would buy "off plan," because they themselves had no capital to get the project started.

The partners' initial plan was to buy the land with a bank loan, and then sell 50% of the project in advance to investors (mainly businesses, including a chain of grocery stores that they thought may be interested). The money from the investors would then pay for the construction of the shopping center, which they had decided to call SmileMart. Once the center was complete, they planned to lease the half of the project they would own to generate an income against which they could secure financing for future projects. Operating as intermediaries between investors and the builders, Denis and Andrey planned to increase their profits through tight, direct control of the contractors and subcontractors. They would minimize construction costs by reducing bureaucracy, personally supervising the subcontractors rather than hiring agents, and through intense cost control processes. Once the project was completed, they also planned to increase their revenue by handling the management of the shopping center themselves.

This business model differed significantly from the industry norm in Russia where developers usually work for a fee, mostly taken from the difference between construction costs and invested funds, rather than investing themselves. While the usual fee for developers is about 20–30% of the value of the initial investment, Denis and Andrey planned to further increase this to 50% by retaining ownership of half of the center.

To keep their project moving, Denis and Andrey ran several stages in parallel with the land transfer process, including the search for investors and the building design. The deals with major investors, for example, were finalized while the building was still being designed. In the end the whole process of obtaining commercial building rights and a lease extension took almost 2 years. But progress had been made nonetheless thanks to the partners' willingness to take some risks.

At this point, the plan was to build a two-story center, but according to the regulations, the partners learned that buildings in the area had to have at least five stories. So, together with the builder, Denis and Andrey adjusted the plan to include the correct number of stories, and duly received approval for the changes. As a result of negotiating with, and listening to all the stakeholders, the size of the shopping center was tripled.

The original plan was to build a 3,000 square meter shopping center with the partners retaining 500 square meters. Now, this had grown to 9,000 square meters, with 6,000 square meters of this available for leasing (the rest of the space would be taken up with underground parking, corridors, and walkways). The partners' goal now became to retain 3,000 square meters (50% of the total area) in order to keep control of the property. The construction costs had obviously now increased.

The partners focused their efforts on the search for potential investors. The contract with the first investor, a business angel, was a big milestone but it didn't bring in enough cash to cover all of the building costs. They obviously needed to attract more investors, but this was a time of a great economic uncertainty in Russia and in a small city like Khabarovsk there weren't many people willing to invest in property. Looking back on this period, Denis and Andrey realized that during the whole project they were making decisions without a clear picture of where they would lead. For example, they started planning before paying for the land, so everything was very fragile and greatly depended on quickly finding investors and solving problems as they appeared. There was no Plan B. Success was also critical for their reputations since the few investors they had managed to attract to SmileMart so far were potential partners in future projects. The success of this first major project would determine whether they could stay in this business. Denis commented on this uncertainty:

> This is maybe a peculiarity of doing business in Russia: The feeling that when you take a step forward you don't know if there is solid ground to stand on. You have to believe that the solid ground will be there, but in reality, you step out of a window.

The partners then came across an entrepreneur who had a financial leasing company that acted as a middleman between banks and companies. The partners knew that he was interested in socially useful investments and approached him with a suggestion that he might set up a children's play center. This caught the entrepreneur's attention because a shopping center with a large grocery store would attract families living in the neighboring areas. In February 2012, he agreed to buy 2,000 square meters.

By April, after a three-way negotiation between the partners and two other major investors, 80% of the construction costs had been secured (180 million rubles, about US$ 6 million). The outstanding 50 million rubles (US$ 1.7 million) had to be covered by a bank loan but this turned out to be hard to get. In Russia it is always difficult to finance uncompleted projects and Denis and Andrey were rejected twice for loans, because they were at too early a stage of construction for the bank to mitigate its risk. Even though they personally knew the bankers and had a good credit rating, the bank was unwilling to release funds until the project was almost finished. There have been cases where a development company simply steals the down payment from the investors and the project is never finished. At the third attempt, in April 2013, however, the bank finally approved a loan request for 50 million rubles (US$ 1.7 million) at 20% interest. The collateral for the loan was the building, which was now closer to completion, and the land that the partners had secured on a long-term lease from the city. Effectively, the partners had now managed to generate almost two million dollars of capital on the back of a project they didn't yet own. The pressure on them to deliver results was now very intense.

By April 2012, all the pieces of the puzzle had come together. The partners got the final sign off from the city administration and by June, they had a permit to start construction. The land transfer had also come through meaning that Denis and Andrey were now the official owners of the lease. As Denis observed:

> The project did not seem to be interesting for me anymore. Now with the toughest part over, the only thing left was construction.

Fortunately for Denis, new challenges were waiting. The biggest of these was trying to squeeze the contractors on costs because the entire success of the project now depended on effective cost control. They had relied on their experience when searching for and negotiating with investors, but construction management and legal issues were entirely new areas for them. A specialist with experience of running large commercial building projects also joined the team to help prepare the budget and take responsibility for supervising construction. The cost of the 9,000 square meter project was estimated at 230 million rubles (about US$ 7.7 million) and the detail of this calculation was used as a reference point to quickly gauge if they were over or under budget.

There was also pressure from the investors. In their negotiations, the partners had promised to be completely transparent about how their investors' money was used. They also guaranteed to find lessees for them before trying to let their own space. In addition, the investor contract set out clear milestones, such as completion of the foundations and erection of the steel framework, and if the milestones were not reached, investors had the right to withhold their next stage payments. This level of transparency represented a very different approach to investors to that used in the partners' previous real estate company because, unusually for this industry, the contract worked in the interests of the investors not just the developers. For example, those parts of the building reserved for key investors were to be ready to be operated and leased as soon as the building was finished. Usually, investors would have to wait for principal construction to be finished before they could move into their own areas.

As a rule, this type of construction project included a developer, a general contractor, and various subcontractors providing labor and materials. Despite warnings from everyone, Denis and Andrey decided to do away with the general contractor. As a result, the project was sometimes more chaotic than they would have liked, but they nevertheless managed to save money. Altogether, the construction process took 12 months, 6 months less than planned, and the two partners, having started off with no capital, had built a 9,000 square meter building for what it normally cost to build 3,000 square meters.

The center opened on June 20, 2013 and, having found lessees for the principal investors as promised, the partners also managed to lease the rest of the facilities. The journey was finally over and Denis and Andrey decided to celebrate with a trip to Hawaii. There they visited the house on Maui that was described by Robert Kiyosaki, in his book with Sharon Lechter, *Rich Dad Poor Dad*, as one of his first entrepreneurial experiences.

Note

1. This contribution is based on the case by the authors "SmileMart: Stepping out of a Window" forthcoming at the CaseCenter.

II 5

Building an LNG Tank in the Russian Arctic

Scientific Management in the Snow[1]

Keith Goodall
Yuliya Ponomareva

Velesstroy is one of the three leading construction companies in the Russian Oil and Gas sector and employs around 13,000 people. At the end of 2014, the company was involved as a general contractor in over forty different projects, including work for Russian Transneft, Federal Electricity Grid Company, the Caspian Pipeline Consortium, Chevron, and Mobil. The company's annual income is over US$ 2 billion and it has grown at an average of over 20% per year since 2007. Velesstroy prides itself on completing all projects to the agreed deadline and will readily commit extra resources to compensate for delays.

The Life of Russian Business, pages 93–95

In January 2014, a contract was signed with one of the largest global EPC (Engineering, Procurement, Construction) companies, the French firm, Vinci Enterprise, to deliver four Liquefied Natural Gas (LNG) tanks, two to be completed in 2014 and two in 2015. The contract was part of the Yamal LNG project. With a total budget of US$ 27 billion it is one of the largest ever industrial undertakings in the Arctic, and is designed to ensure the production and distribution of the vast natural gas reserves in the Russian Arctic.

The scope of work included building the foundations, walls, and roofs of the tanks. Work was scheduled to begin on April 1, 2014, with the walls and foundations being finished by October 1st. The completion deadline was very important because in the Yamal region temperatures in October can fall as low as minus 20 degrees Celsius and concrete can only be poured up to minus ten degrees (and even then this requires special heating systems). So Velesstroy had a maximum of 6 months to pour 26,000 cubic meters of concrete and have 5,200 tons of reinforcement bars in place. There were other jobs to be completed in parallel but the concrete and reinforcement bars were on the critical path (i.e., the longest sequence of activities in a project plan which must be completed on time in order for the project to complete by its due date).

On the Yamal project, a subcontractor was responsible for the piles—the concrete or steel posts driven into the permafrost to support a structure. When the subcontractor finished this work over two months late it created a serious problem.

As a result, Velesstroy now had just 3 months to complete 5 or 6 months' worth of work before the temperatures dropped—at minus 20 degrees Celsius, concrete would freeze to the "formwork" and ruin the tanks. If the work had to wait to resume the following summer, then the project would be delayed by a year. The problem was substantial as the client had already signed contracts to sell the liquid gas and the tankers had already been scheduled to collect it. The costs of any delay would amount to hundreds of millions of dollars.

Velesstroy's project managers had planned to use "formwork" technology, which features support structures and moulds where concrete is poured. The "climbing form" is a relatively costly and complex process where the formwork rises with the building process. Its main advantage is a low risk of failure, as one can stop and redo the work at any point. However, formwork technology requires more time and was no longer suitable in light of the delay.

Velesstroy's engineers did some research and learned that LNG tanks could also be made using "sliding formwork" which can be faster but presented new technological challenges. The process works like an elevator, rising at a speed of 85 centimeters an hour for 24 hours a day with no stopping allowed. One needs to install reinforcement bars and pour concrete nonstop until the height of forty meters is reached. There is no room for error. Velesstroy decided to go ahead and use sliding formwork for the first time. How could they reduce the risk of failure with workers who were unfamiliar with the process?

- The engineers began by specifying the work process in great detail and dividing it into small operations, which were then assigned to specific workers who were given precise instructions.
- Every separate operation was measured and timed to make sure that the right resources and schedule were applied.
- Workers were assessed so that the most suitable person was allocated to each task.
- Workers were trained where necessary to make sure they could perform as planned.
- Progress was constantly monitored by supervisors and engineers.

In order to achieve a tight control over processes, the technology and materials needed to be tested. A team of engineers performed two mock up tests—one in a laboratory in Paris and another one on the construction site on the "sliding formwork" and all the elements of the production process. These tests allowed the engineers to spot any mistakes in the calculations and make necessary adjustments beforehand.

The first two tanks were duly completed by October 1st and the client was so pleased that they awarded Velesstroy another two contracts. The learning from this project was applied in other projects where work was again divided up into very small units and everything was measured and monitored. A time and motion department was created to measure the efficiency and quality of the work and develop a results-based compensation package tied to both individual and team performance.

Note

1. This contribution is based on the case by the authors "How to Build an LNG Tank in Twenty-One Days" forthcoming at the CaseCenter.

6

Sustainable Russia

A Guide for Multinational Corporations

Natalia Zaitseva
Kamila Novak

Leading multinational corporations (MNCs) are key agents driving sustainable development and promoting the sustainability agenda in the global economy. Many top corporations no longer view sustainable development as a bolted-on activity complementary to their core operations. Instead, sustainability has become an important component of shareholder and stakeholder value creation, as well as an integral part of global operations.

In each country, MNCs localize their global sustainability agenda differently depending on the distinct set of country-specific characteristics. In Western countries, characterized by developed legislative systems, strong markets, and advanced environmental and social norms, companies have significant natural opportunities for implementing corporate sustainability

The Life of Russian Business, pages 97–99

initiatives. On the other hand, in many developing countries the costs for investing in sustainability initiatives are lower while the return on social investments can be considerably higher than in developed economies. In addition, there are greater opportunities for scaling up social efforts while addressing the "bottom of the pyramid" and building a large customer base via community-based initiatives.

Between these two extremes, there is a group of emerging country markets, including Russia, where the notion of sustainability has not yet gained prominence and sustainability is not a straightforward concept. Russia is ranked 50th out of 142 constituent countries in the IEMS Sustainability Composite Index, which implies a "transitional" level of sustainable development characterized by a number of gaps. In particular, Russian consumers are largely passive when it comes to the issue of sustainability, "command-and-control" methods still prevail in the legislative and regulatory environment, and global multilateral institutions and international non-governmental organizations (NGOs) do not have such a strong influence as they do in other developing and emerging countries. Also, high impact initiatives targeting the "bottom of the pyramid" are often not applicable in the Russian context, as the demand for many services and products has been largely satisfied, usually through state intervention. The central question then becomes whether there are opportunities for MNCs to build the business case for sustainable development in Russia.

Research on the sustainability strategies of MNCs in Russia has led to the identification of a number of best practices.[1] Effective approaches revolve around the following building blocks: sustainable products, sustainable operations, communication with stakeholders, fundamental sustainability actions, and CSR activities.

Within this framework, some MNCs have found opportunities to capitalize on the lack of energy efficient products in Russia. Siemens' Sapsan trains on the Moscow-St. Petersburg high-speed rail line or Schneider Electric's solar power systems are such examples. Other global corporations have increased business value by reconfiguring their local operations and supply chains. Examples include Unilever's mission to eliminate landfill disposal of non-hazardous waste (see the next contribution for a detailed description) and McDonald's target to increase localized sourcing to 85%.

Based on the analysis of high-impact business practices, our sustainable business lab identified ten external barriers that impede the development of corporate sustainability in Russia. These are categorized into infrastructural, institutional, and informational barriers (See Figure II.6.1).

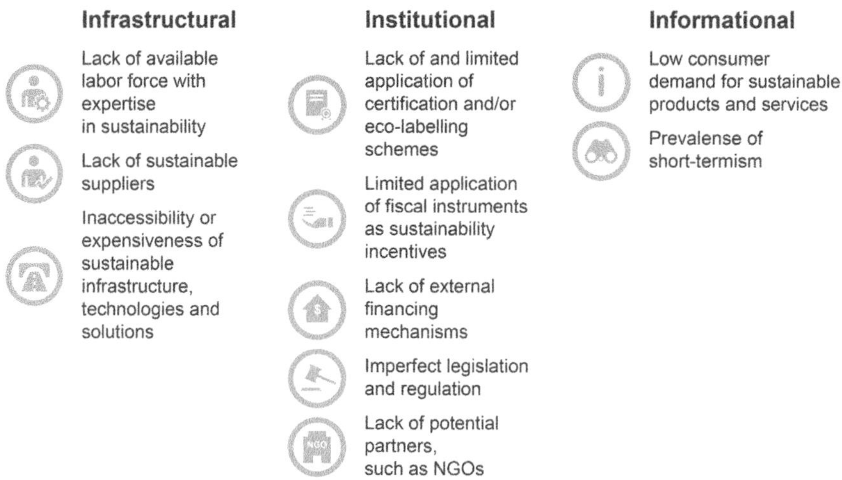

Figure II.6.1 Ten external barriers for corporate sustainability in Russia.

Despite, or precisely because of the apparent challenges, the emerging and "transitional" Russian business environment does offer ample opportunities for sustainability leadership. MNCs with a long-term vision about their participation in the Russian market have successfully transferred global best practices to the local context and in so doing have transformed and set benchmarks for the overall local sustainability landscape. Their social investments in Russia are examples of effective ways around the many external barriers to sustainability described above. Experience suggests that market leaders do not wait for guidance from authorities, but rather apply a proactive approach and so create and capture emerging market opportunities.

Notes

1. SKOLKOVO's Sustainable Business Lab, IEMS (2016). Sustainable Russia: A Guide for Multinational Corporations.

7

Unilever's Zero Non-Hazardous Waste Strategy

Achieving Sustainable Production Systems in Russia[1]

Andrey Shapenko

Unilever entered the Russian market in 1992 and it soon carried out its first major acquisition, the Severnoye Siyaniye cosmetics plant in St. Petersburg. By 2016, Unilever's Russian subsidiaries employed about 7,000 people, with Tula's food concentrate plant being the second largest production site in Russia. Commissioned in 1999, it uses the latest equipment and is one of the most advanced facilities specializing in the production of instant food not only in Russia, but also in Europe.

Unilever has prided itself on having led the Dow Jones Sustainability Index rankings for 15 years within the Food Products Sector (in 2016, a change in criteria led to it being ranked first in the Household and Personal Products category). In 2010, the company published the Unilever

The Life of Russian Business, pages 101–104

Sustainable Living Plan (USLP), the key goal of which was to double the company's business by 2020 whilst radically reducing its environmental impact. An indispensable part of the USLP was the reduction of the environmental impact of production waste. The issue of shipping waste to landfill was especially pressing in Russia; according to various estimates, only 3–4% of production waste there was recycled. This was unacceptable to company management, and in November 2013, the company set a goal of zero non-hazardous waste to landfill to be achieved by the end of 2014.

According to Unilever's global concept, the notion of "zero waste to landfill" implied that non-hazardous waste should neither be shipped to landfill or incinerated—rather, waste should either be completely eliminated at source or recycled at production plants.

Top management accepted this goal and rolled it out to international production divisions, including those in Russia, without any concessions for regional specifics. At Tula, the director of the Unilever production cluster, Konstantin Voytikov, was accustomed to achieving financial goals, but here he had to solve a problem that would likely lead to additional costs—at least at the beginning. Moreover, no other company in Russia had at the time achieved anything comparable to this—and Voytikov had only 10 months to find workable solutions.

By early 2014, Unilever plants in Russia produced tens of thousands of tons of waste, of which roughly 7,000 tons were shipped to landfills. About half of this waste—flotation foam, a specific type of waste formed after water treatment—came from the ice cream plant in Tula.

Due to the tight schedule, action had to be taken immediately. Voytikov assembled a working group made up of representatives from the key divisions. The team examined various options one by one, trying to find the most effective technological solution. It seemed that without contractors who would recycle waste, the company would have to build its own waste recycling facilities and incinerate most of the waste, which would be quite costly.

All solutions that the project team had proposed within the first month of the project implied significant capital and operational expenses that were not budgeted for by the company and were not welcomed by the head office in Moscow. The challenge was to find a solution that would be both operationally effective and cost efficient.

After a thorough analysis of plant operations, it became clear that through a process of sorting a significant amount of waste would be suitable for further use or processing. As Voytikov reflects: "We were surprised to find out that you can sell everything—all you have to do is put in a little bit of effort."

Firstly, a new procedure for measuring the scale of the waste problem was implemented. Previously, the company had calculated this based on volume, but now it began to weigh its waste. Secondly, a stricter process for sorting waste was implemented at the production line to minimize subsequent efforts. Thirdly, the range of types of wastes that could be recycled was significantly expanded. For example, initially, only clean film was recycled, but a supplier was later found who agreed to recycle dirty film as well. Even ice cream sticks and broken wooden pallets were no longer discarded, but stored in a special container.

By April 2014, a technological solution had been found for flotation foam sedimentation, which decreased its volume by 73% and doubled the output of solids. At the same time, the increase in annual costs for the disposal of flotation foam amounted to only slightly over EUR 1,000.

Together with these new processes of waste reduction, the procurement team began to search for suppliers of waste solutions. One of the most difficult tasks was finding contractors that would comply simultaneously with both the laws of the Russian Federation and Unilever's requirements. The company was confronted with a lack of highly skilled professionals in the market, and those that did offer services required detailed inspection. For example, Unilever demanded that contractors submit a video of the waste incineration process to make sure that it did happen. Only by September 2014, was it possible to find qualified contractors for most of the waste.

The methods selected were first found to be 6–8 times more expensive than simply shipping waste to landfill, yet a subsequent analysis proved that these additional costs did not lead to overall losses—on the contrary, the company began to make a profit by selling recycled waste.

Finally, Unilever Russia implemented a series of measures aimed at increasing employee awareness and getting them involved in waste reduction efforts, because it became clear that without their participation it would be impossible to complete such an unusual project in Russian conditions. Starting with sorting waste on the production line and in the office and through the use of promotional materials, the company introduced an annual "Clean-Up Saturday," which was attended by all the company's employees, including the cluster director and all top managers. They launched campaigns to collect waste paper and plastic which employees brought from home. All of these measures, as well as a commitment to the goals set by company management, made the initial lack of understanding and resistance on the part of employees disappear. They now often bring paper, cardboard, and plastic bottles to work to throw them in a special container set up in the office or in the production facility.

All of the measures undertaken enabled the plant to reach the goal of eliminating shipping waste to landfill by October 2014. Voytikov and his team were surprised by the fact that the implementation of zero waste procedures at the ice cream plant did not adversely affect operating expenses and in fact led to a two-fold increase in profit from selling recycled waste.

The Unilever Tula cluster became the company's second Russian production site after St. Petersburg to reach the goal. This became a historic turning point for the company in the country, and in early 2015 the project goal was officially declared completed. However, Voytikov and his team were not planning to stop, and have continued to improve the sorting, disposal, and monetization of waste.

Note

1. The is a shortened version of a teaching case study winner of the EFMD Case Writing Competition 2016 in the category "Sustainable Production Systems."

8

Enabling Russian Boards

Western Fancy?

Dmitri Melkumov

A generation has now passed since the Soviet Union came tumbling down. During this time, Russia has experienced a number of drastic transformations. The democratic, but economically unsuccessful tenure of President Boris Yeltsin saw the lack of the rule of the law, institutional voids created by the destruction of the former planned economy, and the absence of a solid system to replace it. This period is also synonymous with fraudulent privatization, unlawful and shady business dealings, expropriation of state monies and assets, and thriving corruption. President Vladimir Putin's reign which started in 2000 brought stability and funds to the economy. Some attribute the success to the significant rise in oil and gas prices. Others argue that restrictions on the economic and political freedoms of firms and individuals associated with an increasing role of the state did also play a factor.

The Life of Russian Business, pages 105–108

The relationship economy is one of the key characteristics of Russian business practices. Deeply rooted in Tsarist Russia, it continued to persist through the Soviet regime. Favors and "blat" networks[1] were used to gain access to otherwise unavailable or scarce resources. In the context of modern Russia, the relationship economy has evolved into a more structured, transparent, and formal network economy. The state participates in formal and informal control of private firms by means of direct or indirect majority or minority ownership in these firms, or by appointing presently or formerly politically engaged individuals to their boards and/or to their top management teams. The omnipresence of the state in the Russian economy, which according to some experts may reach up to 70%, is a key reference to evaluate business practices in Russia. It is regarded that to be successful and gain access to (state controlled) resources the firm has to, in some way, participate in the network economy and have solid connections to the "right" individuals.

At the same time, Russia has engaged internationally experiencing significant technological development, increased labor mobility, and cross-border financial flows. International managerial and organizational expertise is easily accessible. Many Western firms have established businesses in the Russian market ranging from sales networks to independently functioning production facilities with local Russian management. Moreover, recently, many Russian companies have started expanding internationally and their numbers continue to increase. These developments have brought Western values and practices into Russia. These include managerial styles, ownership structures, the role of transparency, and internationally accepted reporting principles. Importantly, we also see an increased reliance on formal structures and expertise as opposed to (or in addition to) the network economy. This alternative (Western) approach has infiltrated all organizational levels. For example, many employees seem to prefer democratic leadership styles as opposed to the inherently Soviet power-based approach. In short, we see the coexistence of two economic models: the relationship-focused network economy and a Western-inspired "formal" economy.

The coexistence of these two competing logics is reflected in the functioning of corporate governance in Russia. Strong owners undermine the power of independent directors making Russian boards passive observers squeezed between stockholders and corporate executives. While in the West, boards of directors constitute the apex of organizational decision-making, in Russia, boards have often been underutilized. Their role is further impeded by the lack of clear requirements and enforcement by the authorities in terms of implementing internationally accepted principles of corporate governance. For example, the code of corporate conduct[2] is not a legal requirement but only "recommended" for firms with over 1,000 employees.

One of the most active actors on Russian boards is the state, which in recent years has significantly increased its ownership stakes in several strategically important organizations. State controlled or affiliated organizations also increasingly participate in board decision-making thereby compensating for the presence of institutional voids through direct control of the business sphere.

Traditionally, research has found corporate governance irrelevant on boards of organizations with a high ownership concentration and/or owner-run organizations. This stems from their inability (or the perceived non-need) to perform their mandate to monitor management decisions. Of course, beyond monitoring there is much more that the engaged board can do for the organization. For example, the board might provide resources including access to political decision-makers, international expertise, funding, and business elites.

At the end of the day, regardless of whether a firm operates according to the network relationship model or according to the more formal Western approach, an active and enabled board offers considerable value to the organization.

In the network economy, the board can be an important channel for communication, knowledge sharing, and contact to the political and/or business elites, which often is crucial in Russia.

At firms leaning towards the Western, more transparent business model, the board can be of considerable value by creating legitimacy in the eyes of foreign partners and financial markets. Indeed, Russian organizations with independent directors on their boards are deemed more transparent and reliable, especially if those directors are foreign. The board may serve as a channel for the introduction and the development of both "Western" values and business practices such as hiring practices or talent retention. Very importantly, the board might help identify key managerial talent inside and outside of the country.

There are instances where Western style boards move a firm away from old-fashioned network economy governance. For example, Russian financial conglomerate Sistema has consciously and continually introduced and upheld a Western approach to corporate governance. Alongside the inevitable conflicts with various players associated with the firm's network economy past, companies that make this move do modernize and become more transparent.

Notes

1. Editor's note: Blat refers to the system of informal arrangements based on the exchange of personal favors, such as those rendered to obtain access to scarce goods and services—it is often associated with corruption.
2. Editor's note: The code is available at https://ecgi.global/code/russian-code-corporate-conduct and further background can be found at: Roberts, G. (2004). Convergent Capitalisms? The Internationalization of Financial Markets and the 2002 Russian Corporate Governance, *Europe-Asia Studies*, 56(8): 1235–1248.

9

Corporate Diversification and Value Creation

Should Russian Firms Diversify?

Irina Ivashkovskaya
Irina Skvortsova

Corporate diversification is the expansion of firm activities into different business areas, both across industries and product markets.[1] Diversification is a key strategic choice and a competitive issue faced by firms worldwide. In Russia this challenge is exacerbated by the inherited complexity and uncertainty of the business environment. At the same time, and despite a growing body of studies on corporate diversification practices in Russia and other emerging economies, there is still little agreement on how diversification affects a company's value creation.

The complexity of the diversification-performance relationship in Russian companies can be explored through three distinct frameworks.

The Life of Russian Business, pages 109–111

First, via the *institutional framework* which focuses on how institutions shape the purpose and impact of diversification strategies. Under conditions of insufficient development of markets in capital, goods, and labor, as is the case in Russia, diversification can provide firms with an advantage. That is, it gives firms a superior ability to raise capital, increase the efficiency and speed of resource allocation, diversify risks, exercise control over operations, and create an internal pool of well-trained managers. In essence, institutional gaps are compensated for via diversification.

Second, according to the *resource-based framework*, diversification can benefit firms that compete on the basis of generic resources rather than on the basis of industry-specific capabilities. Obtaining licenses, arranging financing, securing technology, and managerial know-how are generic resources when they do not depend on industry-specific capabilities.

Third, the *financial framework* focuses on the corporate risks associated with high levels of diversification, mainly due to the conflicts of interests between powerful parties in organizations. If a firm is managed by the owners or entrepreneurs or when the managers own large stakes, the agency conflicts between managers and owners are less present. At the same time, a high level of ownership concentration in the hands of few large shareholders can result in minority expropriation due to agency conflicts between majority and minority shareholders. Therefore, the financial framework suggests that diversification strategies at Russian firms with high levels of ownership concentration negatively affect performance.

Our research of 71 listed Russian firms studied the performance effects of corporate diversification and found that compared to other BRIC countries, Russian firms have the highest level of diversification. For example, the total entropy index (which measures diversification) reaches 0.69 in Russia compared to 0.47 in Brazil. Paradoxically, investors in Russia are the most pessimistic about management decisions to launch corporate diversification strategies. If this contradiction was not enough, financial markets also react negatively to the announcement of a decision to engage in diversification compared to, for example, investors and markets in China or South Africa.

Interestingly, when it comes to the performance of diversification strategies, our results show that an increase in the number of product lines in the business portfolio of Russian firms is associated with profits well above the risk-adjusted rate of return. That is, product diversification increases the fundamental profit generation ability of firms. Performance is further improved by diversifying into unrelated industries. What could the reasons be for this? There are lower investment project risks for firms boasting broad product portfolios. This might be the result of the ability to smooth cash flows from different product markets. Such added stability in an unstable market such as Russia helps to improve debt capacity and hence results in lower costs of financing.

Despite the above findings, and as suggested previously, we found that product diversification lowers the expectations of investors regarding future performance. Negative perceptions from investors and the financial markets could be based on the belief that many Russian management teams lack the expertise to operate simultaneously in different industries and new markets. Of course, profits and general performance show otherwise. This paradox has complex explanations. For instance, there are benefits when Russian firms diversify to overcome business environment imperfections. But cross-subsidization of various business lines, especially in the period after the economic crisis, is likely to result in inefficient resource allocation.

There is another interesting finding regarding the diversification strategies of Russian firms. Firm size is a negative associated with performance. Attempting an increase in competitiveness through the simple growth of the firm no longer seems feasible. In today's environment, the way forward is through improved management and innovation, rather than obtaining favorable terms through greater market power.

In conclusion, diversification strategies are both a challenge and an opportunity in terms of value creation in Russia. On the one hand, diversification is a source of competitive advantage and contributes directly to the creation of firm value. On the other hand, diversification is associated with increased risks for investors and thus also destroys value due to negative market reactions. When considering diversification, Russian managers face a dilemma, as they have to take into consideration more than just the synergies they expect to generate through diversification. It is equally important that they ask themselves about how likely these synergies are in a highly uncertain and volatile environment with skeptical financial stakeholders.

Note

1. See, for example:

   Rumelt, R. P. (1974). *Strategy, Structure, and Economic Performance.* Cambridge, MA: Harvard University Press.

   Pitts, R. A. and H. D. Hopkins. (1982). Firm Diversity, Conceptualization and Measurement. *Academy of Management Review,* 7:620–629.

   Palepu, K. (1985). Diversification Strategy, Profit Performance, and the Entropy Measure. *Strategic Management Journal,* 6:239–255.

10

Independence in Russia's Finance Industry?

The Birth of the Analytical Credit Rating Agency (ACRA)[1]

Tomas Casas i Klett
Vladimir Korovkin

Russia has been constrained by a choice made over two decades ago. The *Global Three* international rating agencies: Standard & Poor's (S&P), Moody's, and Fitch Group, had de facto been given a near exclusive position in Russia's financial market. This choice resulted in an unbalanced market for credit risk assessment. The market was split between international oligopolists in rent-seeking mode on one side and a small cohort of minor local players on the other. That meant that Russia's finance industry had a problem: significant unmet demand for independent sources of market information and credit ratings. In November 2015, the government decided to act and, in the words of an insider, "re-balance the playing field." Yet how did Russia get to this situation?

The Life of Russian Business, pages 113–118

The End of Cherry Picking

In Russia, as elsewhere, it was the government that created the original demand for ratings. Russian laws on ratings were nonexistent in the mid-1990s and the Global Three had entered Russia while other emerging market countries, such as China, did not allow American agencies to operate (at least until President Trump's "early harvest" deal in May of 2017,[2] which was soon overtaken by events in the Sino-U.S. relationship). The Russian blue chip companies such as Gazprom, Rosneft, Lukoil, Sberbank, or Vympelcom were certainly always duly rated. Yet others, such as pension funds, leasing companies, second tier corporates, and asset management firms also needed proper credit ratings based on the latest methodologies and solid jurisdiction-specific statistical research. Without high quality ratings, all of these financial sector areas found it difficult to contribute to Russia's financial infrastructure and economic development. In short, the Russian government was disappointed at the Global Three's "cherry picking" strategy.

Not that the strategy was irrational. The three firms served the 250 most lucrative Russian blue chip clients, as the biggest profits were in cross-border bond sales. Unless domestic markets were deep, such as in Brazil, China, and Mexico, it made little sense to go down-market; the margins were simply not comparable. In short, the triage strategy that ignored smaller Russian players because of "too much work for too little profit" made sense for the Global Three, but not for Russia.

The government's position was clear. After years of profits in Russia, the foreign players were not reinvesting enough; nor were they playing the expected institutional development role. Moreover, they were now becoming a constraining factor and a bottleneck of sorts. The beginning of the economic crisis coupled with a jump in inflation at the end of 2014 threatened to destabilize the country, bringing back memories of the difficult 1990s. The Central Bank of Russia (CBR) intervened and vigorously stabilized the situation in December of that year. Part of the anti-crisis measures included the provision of government funds to support Russian industry and banks. Some funding was deliberately channeled to smaller corporations. Even local firms outside the large cities became eligible for government funding, many of which had not been rated by the Global Three. This vacuum was met with an incentive plan for local rating agencies to provide services.

The local ratings agencies, which had some strong players such as Expert, had mostly followed a strategy of aggressive price competition against the Global Three. Their ratings were affordable even to mid-size Russian companies. When new legislation on ratings was introduced, the local agencies went on to boost their market presence. At the same time, there was a feeling in some quarters that their fast growth and low cost advantages were in part the result of simpler assessment methodologies.

At this point, many pundits thought that the market could only change by means of enlightened regulation. Between 2013 and 2014, Russia's central bank worked out, as a first step, a detailed concept draft for the industry. From September 2014 onwards, the CBR became the Russian finance industry "mega-regulator," responsible for "everything financial," including banking, insurance, investment companies, and even credit cooperatives. With its new extended mandate, the CBR would also have the authority to supervise rating agencies, which had previously been the subject of very mild regulation by the Ministry of Finance.

The second step was the implementation of regulation. A guiding principle of the new financial governance was licensing. That meant having a legal entity in the country. In Russia, the global rating agencies were present in the form of branches, not as locally incorporated subsidiaries. That is, "they operated in Russia, and paid taxes in London." The government's strategy was designed to avoid regulatory arbitrage. In the words of a person in the know, the message to the Global Three was:

> We welcome you, but please transform your operations into subsidiaries. We create demand for your products. We must apply the same regulations as we do to anybody else operating in the market.

The international ratings agencies rejected such proposals. As a result, they could continue to work for Russian clients from Moscow and rate top Russian entities (such as Gazprom) for international investors, but lost their regulatory recognition for domestic market purposes. 2015 saw the passage of the "Law on Rating Agencies" (reference FZ 222). The objective was unequivocal: Russian ratings agencies functioning with the highest international industry standards.

ACRA: "We Are Russia's Rating Agency"

The CBR went on to encourage the creation of a new Russian credit rating agency with standards and operating principles comparable to the Global Three. The Analytical Credit Rating Agency (ACRA) was thus born in November 2015. Ekaterina Trofimova, a former senior vice president and member of the management board of Russia's third largest bank and possessing over 11 years of experience at S&P, became ACRA's founding CEO. In an interview on CNBC she tackled head on the key issue for long-term success in the financial industry: independence. The role of the CBR would be limited to granting a license to operate, as well as encouraging any interested initial investors. As soon as the new ratings agency was founded it would have to face market forces on its own strengths.

> To succeed we need to have full independence. It might sound strange, but it is actually very easy to figure out when a given ratings decision has been done under interference.

Trofimova's comment applied as much to Russian as to Wall Street ratings. At ACRA, independence meant independence from politics, from its own shareholders, and from clients. It also referred to the implementation of corporate governance principles. However, independence would come at a price, as the ACRA team would discover.

Independence was the guarantee of an "exclusive position in the market" and was reflected in its basic governance principles. Of great significance was the diversified shareholder structure. There were 27 shareholders, balanced by sectors with each owner controlling 3.7% of the shares. There was much pride in this state of affairs, as Trofimova commented: "We have the most diversified credit rating agency shareholder structure in the world." To further underline the board's full independence from the government she noted: "There is no single former state employee or manager in our board."

The supervisory board itself consisted of Trofimova and five highly reputable and very experienced directors from Europe and the United States. The emphasis was on good governance. Karl Johansson, an American with deep business expertise in Russia and emerging markets, was invited to become the Chairman. Johansson accepted because he viewed the ACRA leadership and team as able to make both a difference and a contribution to the market. He articulated the needs and desires of Russian state and the financial market players, emphasizing the importance of transparency and accountability:

> Russia wants the same thing that we want in the US or Europe. That is, not a controlled market, not a closed market, not an inefficient market.

Not yet having a brand and a decades-old reputation meant that ACRA would have to be extremely accurate with its rating process. Ratings would have to be valid ex post facto to woo investors. The challenge was not minor: Under 2010 Dodd-Frank rules, ratings agencies in the United States were obliged to publicly evaluate their ratings performance. Would ACRA's ratings performance, enable it to build the most precious asset to be had in finance—credibility?

The Price of Credibility and Independence

ACRA had to develop a business model for a market whose size was not easy to determine. It estimated market revenues to be between US$ 50–100 million annually. The top 20 financial institutions would have 2 to 3 issues annually that needed to be rated. The pricing for rating such issues varied considerably. For example, it was reported that the price VTB bank paid for its ACRA rating was 3.6 million rubles (US$ 60,000). At the same time, a local competitor's price—Expert was cited—was in the range of 0.7–3.5 million rubles.[3]

By January 2017, ACRA had only nine published ratings, significantly less than expected at its launch. Why was this key milestone in the original business plan not being met? Results were off even against conservative targets.

Some industry observers deemed ACRA's approach as too "tough" for Russia. At the same time, a reputation was clearly being established. Integrity lay behind the praise lavished on ACRA in an early 2017 article in *Vedomosti*[4]—a rare occurrence in Russia's highly contentious business press. The emphasis was on ACRA's quality levels, which were seen as comparable to the Global Three. Rigor, even if at odds with the expectations of some Russian firms, was welcomed. For instance, Alfa Bank's ACRA rating was in line with earlier Global Three ratings. Some of those interviewed in the article stated that ACRA had actually requested more documentation than the Global Three. This was, of course, a double-edged sword. The article implicitly linked high quality and rigor to ACRA's few issued ratings at that time.

Was there a trade-off between growth and integrity? "If we had the support of the government we would have grown faster—independence has its price." ACRA executives emphasized that, ". . . reputation is all we have." As if to bring this point to life, it had also been reported that VTB, one of Russia's largest banks and a shareholder in ACRA, underwent the ratings process. The bank stated that it was unhappy about the rating process result and opted not to publish it. ACRA's commitment to independence—both from the government *and* from its clients—was deemed to be the indispensable prerequisite for long-term success given its newcomer status in the market.

ACRA's CEO saw "accelerating growth" around the corner. By early February 2017, new ratings were being issued every couple of days. By the end of the month, the number of newly issued ratings equaled the total number released in 2016.[5] By mid-July of 2017, ACRA had publicly rated 47 firms and 34 issues, with more ratings assigned but not publicly disclosed by the clients. The benefits of independence and credibility were starting to materialize.

Notes

1. This contribution is based on the case by the authors "Taking Risk Out of Risk Assessment: Analytical Credit Rating Agency—If Not Us Then Who?" published at the CaseCenter (ref. no 817-0108-1).
2. Donnan, S. (2017). Critics pan Trump's "early harvest" trade deal with China: President accused of being outplayed by Beijing as "gigantic" agreement draws derision, *Financial Times*, May 14, available at: https://www.ft.com/content/16a9b978-3766-11e7-bce4-9023f8c0fd2e
3. Adamchuk, O. (2017). Национальное рейтинговое агентство АКРА буксует [National Rating Agency Came to a Halt], *Vedomosti*, January 31.
4. Ibid.
5. ACRA press releases February 20–25, 2017, https://www.acra.gov.sg/news_events/

11

High Net Worth Individuals in Russia

Evolving Needs

Ruslan Yusufov
Marianna Slutskaya

In the quarter century since the restoration of private property rights in Russia, private wealth in the country has significantly increased. Although there are no precise data on the size of private wealth in Russia, various sources estimate its total to be between US$ 1 and US$ 2 trillion, that is, an amount comparable to the country's GDP. As the size of private wealth grows, the needs of Russia's wealth possessors become increasingly complex. Our aim here is to provide an overview of the current state of Russian private capital owners. The research conducted by the SKOLKOVO Wealth Transformation Centre, reveals emergent trends in the wealth management of Russian high net worth individuals (HNWIs).

The Life of Russian Business, pages 119–122

Portrait of a Russian Wealth Possessor

The average age of the surveyed HNWIs is 48, with about one-third (32%) being over 50. HNWIs have several children (from two to six) of varying ages. Often the children were conceived at different stages of the HNWI's life and find themselves at different points in their own life; some are already starting their careers, while others are still too young to discuss business and wealth.

The owners of business and private capital are different from the general Russian population (data from the European Social Survey, ESS)[1] as far as one fundamental parameter is concerned: They clearly express a "strongly individualistic orientation." That is, two distinct values prevail among them: self-affirmation (an orientation towards achievement and success, the main resources of which are power and wealth) and an openness to change (characteristics of which include a high importance of novelty, a readiness to experiment, a lack of fear regarding risk taking, a strong propensity for independence, hedonism, and a "taste for life").

While the majority of Russian HNWIs are aware of the complexity associated with business succession, they do not always acknowledge its importance and relevance. Quite often, temporary solutions are taken such as, "remaining the owner of the business going forward" or "running the business for as long as possible." Nevertheless, some do understand that their present choice is a short-term fix and that the succession issue will arise again in 5–10 years.

Families of HNWIs

For the majority of HNWIs, doing business relates very closely to individual values, norms, and motivation. Family values and parenting are extremely important for entrepreneurs; but a child's personal growth and their "appropriate" attitude towards money are not the only concerns. A relevant topic for Russian wealth possessors is a special upbringing and education. Evidently, education focuses on pragmatic questions of wealth management and business succession, even if the children will eventually choose a different career or self-realization path.

The relationship between the family and business domain varies greatly between Russian wealth possessors. Five strategies of managing the relationship between business and family were identified.

The first is "isolation," when the family is not involved in the discussion of any business issues. In its strictest variant they are even excluded from any discussions regarding the estate.

The second strategy is "cooperative autonomy." In this case, the HNWI takes on the role of an investor. Those family members exhibiting interest in business activities gain the opportunity to attract investments for their "projects" (usually as a one-off). They can then develop the project more or less autonomously, maintaining a partnership on issues regarding the family's wealth.

The third strategy is providing an "education via the business." Children are provided with experience and should try to make independent decisions, experiencing both achievements and failures, in order that they may understand whether they wish to work in the business.

The fourth strategy is the "clan history," which occurs when the business starts to form through the activities or mergers of different parts of the family and business connections. This represents a broad yet closed environment of mutual support among several family members or groups of business owners.

The fifth approach is the traditional "family business," where business activity is intertwined with family relationships and many family members have actives roles in the enterprise.

Wealth Management and Philanthropy

In global practice, one of the key instruments serving the interests of HNWIs and their families is the family office. In recent years, the term has grown in importance in the Russian market. However, the views on what constitutes a family office in the Russian context and what services they provide vary significantly. Family offices in Russia, like elsewhere, serve a number of functions including management, placement and structuring of capital assets, acquisition of real estate, succession planning, and the implementation of philanthropic projects. They are often also employed in resolving family conflicts.

Given the integration of Russia's HNWIs in global networks and their extensive experience communicating with Western financial institutions, domestic Russian providers need to increase the quality and scope of their services in order to compete with international providers. One area of differentiation where local private wealth management providers can excel is in the support of philanthropy in Russia.

Philanthropy can be regarded as form of wealth transfer, even if it's an unconventional one. It might seem surprising to some but all the wealth possessors surveyed in Russia participate in some kind of charitable activity. Most of them prefer direct participation in charity and philanthropic activities, without institutional mediation. In general, Russian entrepreneurs view philanthropic activities in the traditional way: as help to the needy, excluding those that are seen as part of so-called deviant groups (such as those with criminal records or the homeless). They are keen to support those who lack independent political or economic status (such as sick children or orphans). Philanthropic HNWIs are, however, very cautious about media exposure as discretion is seen as prudent.

In summary and as elsewhere, the needs of Russian HNWIs go beyond personal wealth management and are increasingly related to the family welfare, as well as to philanthropic ventures.

Notes

1. Further details available at http://www.europeansocialsurvey.org/data/themes.html?t=values?

12

Troika Dialog's Investment Banking Journey

Are Values an Advantage, or Not?

Irina Kulikova
Yuliya Ponomareva

At the end of 2012, Ruben Vardanyan, the leader and chief shareholder of Russia's flagship investment bank, Troika Dialog, completed the integration process with Sberbank, the massive state-owned leading financial institution in Russia. As the deal, with a price tag of US$ 1 billion in cash plus earn-outs[1] hit the finishing line, Vardanyan reminisced about the company's rise. Starting out in the planned Soviet economy, Troika had been managed to meet international best practice and had led the development of investment banking in Russia.

He recalled 1991, when, as a Moscow State University (MSU) fourth-year student, he joined Troika Dialog. At a time when the Soviet Union

The Life of Russian Business, pages 123–129

was falling apart he bet his future on a newly founded financial firm led by Peter Derby, an American Wall Street banker of Russian descent. Back then, proper financial institutions were largely non-existent in Russia. Commodity and raw material exchanges dominated the market. The banking sector was almost unregulated and the spreads[2] were huge, to the order of several 1,000 basis points,[3] pointing to a rather immature and volatile environment. In those circumstances, most companies strove to maximise their short-term income. Few businessmen thought about the future.

During its fledgling years, Troika dealt with asset acquisition deals for Western investors and engaged in financial consulting. The company also took part in the first auction of government short-term bonds (GSTB) and became the leading trader in vouchers dealing with the state property privatisation programme as well as with IPOs of state-owned companies. In addition, the firm offered asset management and private banking, merchant banking, private equity and venture capital services.

Troika's competitive advantage was based on values: Service-orientation, a long-term focus and respect towards both clients and stakeholders. On the other hand, these very strong ethical values came at a cost. The company turned down many opportunities, clients and transactions that were not in line with its principles. That made it more difficult to compete with other rising players in Russia's financial scene. For instance, Troika did not take part in shares-for-loans auctions,[4] neither did it acquire assets for its shareholders with clients' money.

Stress Test and Then the "Fat Years"

In August 1998, disaster hit when Russian federal government declared a default and devalued the rouble, which subsequently slumped by 400%. The national economy was disastrous in September of that year and markets froze in terror. The three things most feared happened simultaneously: devaluation, government default and a payment blockage.

Troika lost over US$ 6 million on transactions with GSTBs. With a capitalisation of US$ 24 million,[5] the company had monthly expenses of approximately US$1 million, which meant that Troika had enough money to survive about 18 months without income.[6] This 'safety cushion', rare for Russian companies in the 1990s, allowed Troika to maintain its professional standards. At the same time, the company made adjustments.

Troika chose a conservative approach, focusing first on cost reductions. Salaries were cut by 40%. This was the way to keep Troika's unique team. The only exception made was for traders; reducing their wages could have had an adverse effect on their motivation, which was key to maintaining the company's cash flow. To the management's surprise, traders made a commitment to have their salary cut like the rest of workers, or else they would leave the company.

Soon after the crisis, Troika regained momentum and managed to close several major transactions, including Telenor's acquisition of a blocking stake in VimpelCom. By 2000, the total turnover in the Russian investment banking industry amounted to US$ 400 million; Troika was earning US$ 60 million. Its expenses amounted to US$ 45 million.[7] The economic shock meant that those that had survived were now leaner.

Troika gradually diversified the range of its financial services. By 2002, it had a retail business in addition to its investment and wealth management services. Troika also participated in the pension reform and was soon a leader in pension savings management. The company expanded its geographical presence by opening offices in 21 cities, both across Russia and abroad in Almaty, Kiev, London, Nicosia, and New York. The company's share of the total trading turnover at RTS[8] MICEX,[9] over-the-counter ADR[10] and GDR[11] markets amounted to 11%.

In 2005, the Russian market switched into furious growth gear. Troika was keeping up with the pace. The company led Russia Deal League Table ratings in investment and banking transactions. It also saw through the two largest IPOs in Russian stock market history (AFK Sistema and Novatek). The company established the private equity fund, Russia New Growth Fund, in partnership with Temasek Holdings (the largest financial corporation of Singapore), as well as three venture funds in partnership with the regional governments of Krasnoyarsk and Moscow, and for the Republic of Tatarstan. Troika was the first company to start option trading in the domestic market. The company was growing by 30% to 40% annually and doubling its capital every two years.

By 2007, the retail side of the business had grown significantly and the company's share in the mutual funds market exceeded 30% with up to 70,000 investors. Troika had the highest returns for managing pension funds over three years (27% versus 7.9% at Vnesheconombank, the Russian government-owned development bank). By that time, Troika's total assets under management reached the then equivalent of US$ 10 billion.[12] At that successful juncture, the company received a buy-out offer from JPMorgan worth US$ 2.8 billion. Although attractive, the offer was rejected, as independence and the strategy of being a 'local champion' were prioritized over money.

More Than a Storm

The financial crisis of 2008 started on September 15th with the crash of Lehman Brothers. Banks all over the world stopped to trust even their most reliable partners and closed credit facilities one after the next. The business model that had recently yielded such generous profits to investment banks ceased to exist overnight. For Russia, it was the end of 'ten fat years'. The crisis of 2008 also demonstrated the high degree to which Russia was integrated in global financial systems and exposed to risk. Despite being of U.S. origin, the global crisis was crushing its markets and causing a liquidity crisis.

The situation was more challenging than in 1998. The entire global financial system was on the verge of collapse. It became clear that the Russian government would not offer support, while Western clients and investors were rapidly withdrawing their funds. Many investment firms faced liquidity troubles and were unable to fulfil their obligations to their partners. Vardanyan claimed that Troika lost "more due to Lehman Brothers than due to the Russian rouble devaluation."

Again, a salary reduction was applied to top management. Salaries below US$ 3,000 a month remained unchanged. Still, this time, 20% of staff was fired.

Troika was struggling. It was losing money in its private equity fund and had serious problems on the asset management side. Western banks, facing their own liquidity risks were closing down their credit lines to their Russian counterparts. Frightened clients were cashing out their investments.

The company would survive thanks to its strong reputation and long-lasting relationships with its clients and business partners. In its most challenging hour, Troika was saved by client and team loyalty.

In a cliff hanger, Troika had only two days to settle its payments. Miraculously, three international banks refrained from turning off their credit lines. The decisions were in some cases not made by the official risk committees but informally, by managers who personally knew Troika's management team. Moreover, and to everybody's surprise, some clients even increased the size of their investments instead of liquidating their holdings. That demonstrated deep trust, a direct result of Troika's values. In the past, values had come at the cost of short-term profits, but now they differentiated the firm from other investment houses that did not survive.

Not a Crisis but a New Reality

The crisis was relatively short, but its effects were long term for the whole financial system. Analysts predicted that recovery would take several years. It resulted in a substantial capital outflow that in turn significantly impaired the investment climate in Russia. Companies cut their borrowing activities, M&A slowed to a near standstill, as did IPOs. In Russia, the situation was aggravated by the increasing market power of the state-owned banks, namely VTB and Sberbank. Private investment houses found it difficult to compete with the almost unlimited financial power they were afforded. Surviving in the new shrinking market and within the parameters of state capitalism was a tall order.

Troika's management realized there was no way for the investment house to proceed without having its own bank, and that concentrating its efforts on the market of a single country implied certain limitations. It seemed necessary for Troika to diversify its risks in different regions around the world. As a result of these reflections, management concluded that a focus on a combination of Africa, China and Russia would be optimal and synergistic. In March 2009, Troika entered into a strategic alliance with South Africa's Standard Bank by selling a 33% stake for US$ 200 million. Under the deal, Troika also received Standard Bank's Russian business.

The partnership with Standard Bank was expected to further capitalize on growing Russia–Asia links. After all, the Industrial and Commercial Bank of China (ICBC) was a major shareholder in Standard Bank. With this in mind, Vardanyan hoped that the alliance would see the build-up of new business flows between Russia, Africa and China, along an increased presence of Russian corporations in Standard Bank's natural territory, Sub-Saharan Africa.

Troika had managed to recover. In 2010 it boasted profits of US$ 42.3 million against 2009 losses of US$ 49.6 million.[13] However, Vardanyan's ambitious plans were fated to fail due to the tightening of the global financial market regulatory environment, as well as a number of unfavorable developments. For instance, after the crisis, the main criterion clients used for choosing their financial institutions was no longer professionalism. Rather, it was a call on which institution was best equipped to survive any further shocks to the financial system. Vardanyan understood that in this new reality only large players would survive. One option was to focus on newly emerging niches such as boutique investment services. Another was to be bought out. Yet, given Troika's significant market value, few players were able to absorb the firm.

In March 2011, the purchase of Troika by Sberbank was announced. The deal was closed in January 2012. Sberbank CIB was then created as a new entity to take over Troika's business and work with Sberbank's key clients. Troika's team integrated well into the new organization and increased its buyer's investment banking powers. For shareholders, the transaction meant a substantial premium for the brand, reputation, employees and client base. It did not escape pundits, however, that Troika's valuation was significantly lower than the offer received form from JPMorgan only a few years earlier.

Looking back, Troika's long-term values served it very well. The bank survived two severe crises, assembled the very best team in Russia and lead industry growth in the good times. It was saved at its most critical hour by its loyal team and by international banks keeping open credit lines because they valued what Troika represented. Of course, there were times when it was not able to live up to its values, as when it had to lay off a fifth of its workers.

An important point for reflection is whether adherence to its values—independence and being the local champion—pre-empted Troika from accepting JP Morgan's impossible to refuse offer. In other words, did these commendable values destroy shareholder value? How predictable was the massive economic crisis and the resulting new reality that would see Troika eventually ending up losing its independence at a much lower value?

Notes

1. Mauldin, W. Russia's Sberbank to buy Troika Dialog, *Wall Street Journal,* March 2011.
2. A "spread" is the difference between the purchase price and the selling price of the same asset at the same time.
3. For example, inflation in Russia in 1992 was 2600%.
4. Shares-for-loans auctions in Russia were a privatisation mechanism. In 1995, major companies such as YUKOS, Norilsk Nickel, and Sibneft carried out such auctions. Under this mechanism, the government received loans from several commercial banks, who got shares in state-owned enterprises as collateral. The banks had been granted the funds for the credits by the Ministry of Finance. After a certain period of time, the government had to either repay the loan or lose their shares to the banks. This overall schema has been referred to as "siphoning off public money."
5. Shekshnya, V. 2004. Ruben Vardanyan at the helm of Troika Dialog, INSEAD Case.
6. Asker-zade, N., Safonov, B. (September, 2010). *Anti-crisis aid of the government was costly for Russian business* [«Антикризисная поддержка государства дорого обошлась российскому бизнесу»] Vedomosti, https://www.vedomosti

.ru/newspaper/articles/2010/09/30/krizis_pokazal_chto_kapitalizma_u_nas_net

7. Shekshnya, V. 2004. Ruben Vardanyan at the helm of Troika Dialog, INSEAD Case.
8. The Russian Trading System (RTS) was a stock market established in Moscow, in 1995, consolidating various regional trading floors into one exchange.
9. The Moscow Interbank Currency Exchange (MICEX), established in 1992, was one of the largest universal stock exchanges in the Russian Federation and East Europe.
10. American Depositary Receipt (ADR).
11. Global Depositary Receipt (GDR).
12. Troika Dialog History, retrieved from https://sberbank-cib.ru/eng/about/history/archive.wbp
13. Asker-zade, N. (May, 2011). *Troika Dialog could have missed its profits in 2010* ["Тройка диалог" могла остаться без прибыли в 2010 г] Vedomosti, https://www.vedomosti.ru/finance/articles/2011/03/09/trojka_vyehala_na_dvojke

III

Innovation and Entrepreneurship

SECTION III

Introduction

Human talent and genius are associated with Russia. The country has given the world many renowned mathematicians, writers, musicians, and painters. It put the 20th century into orbit with the launch of the first man-made satellite, the Sputnik. Its scientists and engineers have discovered or invented an array of breakthroughs: from stem cells or vitamins, to radio or famously the world's leading assault rifle. However, few Western executives, when asked whether Russia is innovative, will answer in the affirmative. This section is structured by the dialectic of individual inventive genius, on the one hand, and what are, apparently, signs of emerging innovation and venture spirit on the other.

The first two pieces by global innovation scholar, Max von Zedtwitz and colleagues, make an initial assessment of Russia's innovation and entrepreneurship system and then examine foreign multinationals and their local R&D efforts (Chapters III.1, III.2). This bird's eye view is followed with a general analysis of the innovative winning strategies of fifteen selected SMEs (Chapter III.3). Thereafter, four cases bring the characteristics of Russian innovation in organizations to life. Atlantis Pak shows innovation in engineering through, of all products, sausage casings (Chapter III.4); SPLAT innovates with niche oral hygiene products, so unique that they seduce demanding Chinese consumers (Chapter III.5); Neurosoft, with its medical devices and emergent global niche strategy, provides a case of masterfully implementing "accidental innovation" (Chapter III.6); finally,

The Life of Russian Business, pages 133–134

SPIRIT DSP is a software venture whose engines silently power many of the applications we use everyday, an exemplar of Russia's "silent innovation" (Chapter III.7).

The section continues with an examination of the venture capital (VC) industry (Chapter III.8). Start-ups aiming at high-growth and VC largesse need peers to scale, as it is well known that innovation seldom occurs at the single firm level, but within ecosystems. Here, the cybersecurity sector is benefitting from Russian mathematical talent and from certain dynamics that appear to give Russia a global advantage (Chapter III.9). Promobot (Chapter III.10), on the other hand, hit global headlines when its robots "escaped" from its factory in Perm, a future cluster for robotics? More broadly, we will see how the founder of the Internet Initiatives Development Fund (IIDF), an entrepreneur of entrepreneurs with state backing, is working to build a massive accelerator platform that overcomes the knowledge, funding, and legislation gaps that inhibit the emergence of highly scalable ventures in Russia (Chapter III.11).

Is there such a thing as a Russian innovation model? The pieces in this section don't attempt to develop a concept or even answer that question. Yet they do recognize a thread that articulates common characteristics, as well as the strengths and weaknesses, of Russian innovation and of the organizations and ventures that drive new technology. The role of institutions is also apparent, since barriers for economically viable innovation are to be overcome not only by a vibrant new class of firms, but also by the state. For the Western or Asian businessperson the practical question might well be one of strategy and management: How can one invest in Russian inventiveness and profit from Russia's innovation potential and its talent?

III 1

Technology-Based Entrepreneurship in Russia

How the Cold War-Era Innovation System Is Being Upgraded Into a Modern, More Open Innovation Ecosystem

Max von Zedtwitz
Ekaterina Vainberg

Another revolution is now taking place in Russia: an entrepreneurial revolution bringing innovation, new technologies, and new products onto the market. Russia is slowly improving its standing in surveys such as the Global Innovation Index or the World Economic Forum's "Global Competitiveness Ranking" placing in the top 30 or 40 most innovative countries. At the same time, with almost 30,000 patent applications in 2015, the country filed the most since 1992.[1] Scientific publication output has also grown—by nearly 50% since 2003. But more importantly, the creation and quality of

The Life of Russian Business, pages 135–139

startup companies working on innovative technologies and business models has accelerated, especially in key high-tech sectors.

Experts note that we are now witnessing the fourth major phase in Russia's innovation transformation. The first phase mostly dealt with the stabilization of science and technology in the post-Soviet 1990s. Soviet technology had fallen behind global benchmarks, but the country still had a solid scientific education and research infrastructure. The country went on to establish a new mission and self-understanding for its many scientists and engineers. Key research centers were either restructured or built from scratch.

During the second phase, around the turn of the millennium, Russia put in place some of the predecessors of today's innovation and technology centers. Yet times were not favorable for innovation, and both state firms and private companies focused on building competitiveness by alternative means, only tentatively investing in technology.

In the mid-2000s, Russia established key legislation (e.g., the new patent law) and enacted other institutional reforms with long-term development potential. There was a new focus on small- and medium-sized enterprises, technology parks, special economic zones, and the Russian Venture Corporation was created. One of the landmark initiatives of this third phase was the SKOLKOVO cluster, a small town on the outskirts of Moscow, the new "blacksmith of Russian innovation." The time frame from about 2005 to the recent past saw the rise of startups and the creation of a more complex ecosystem around them. The first incubators, accelerators, and university entrepreneurship programs were launched, complementing early venture funds and angel networks.

We have now entered the fourth phase, where all of these building blocks are starting to fall into place. New universities and business schools are graduating young people whose start-ups try to emulate the successes of Russian trailblazers such as Kaspersky (anti-virus), Yandex (search engine), and Mail.Ru Group (social networks). In addition, we see a new wave of entrepreneurs, supported by venture capitalists, technology transfer offices, incubators, and accelerators. This generation builds on the experience of the previous phase: the overall number of startups is lower than before, but the quality and sustainability of the ventures is better. IT and Internet-based startups took the early lead, but increasingly we now see startups in aerospace, cleantech, oil and gas, and in other industrial fields. This is quite important, as large corporations—in Russia as well as elsewhere—find it difficult to pursue entrepreneurial innovation from within, entirely on their own. While the fourth phase has only barely started, it is being additionally fueled by the onset of digital transformation. Last but not least, in terms of culture, it is now fashionable to become an entrepreneur.

Key Components in Russia's Innovation Ecosystem

The dominant sector of Russian startups is in IT; specifically, e-commerce, games, cybersecurity, service-platforms, and social networks have received 90% of accumulated venture investments. Following far behind are biotechnology and industrial startups. Increasingly, experienced professionals are now joining the startup scene, including engineers and former corporate employees aged 35–40 years and older. Moscow is the center of this trend and the 2015 Global Startup Ecosystem counted around 3,000 technology startups in the capital alone.

Some of Russia's most prominent startup names might be familiar to foreign pundits including VK (social networking service), Lamoda (online fashion retail), Ozon (e-commerce retail), Ivi (streaming media), 3D Bioprinting Solutions (biotech), Astro Digital (satellite imagery), Avito (classified advertisement website), LinguaLeo (online language learning service), and OneTwoTrip (travel booking website). Telegram, launched by Pavel and Nikolai Durov (the founders of VK) in 2013, is an instant-messaging service that allows users to send and exchange messages, photos, videos, and also stickers. By early 2018, it had close to 200 million monthly active users, and completed a US$ 1.7 billion ICO (Initial Cryptocurrency Offering) even as it cancelled its public sale component.

At the same time, established companies are transforming their R&D centers and becoming more market-oriented and internationally competitive. The number of corporate accelerators in Russia has greatly increased with pioneers such as Kaspersky Lab, Life.SREDA, and Alpha Bank, being joined by giants such as PepsiCo, Faberlic, Morton, Diksi, and several other banks. Some of the companies have also announced the creation of their own corporate venture units. The Kaspersky accelerator is a remarkable success story. Created in 2015 with the support Luxembourg-based venture fund, Mangrove Capital, it eventually became a fully-fledged incubator that developed about 200 entrepreneurs inside the company and about 1,000 startups outside of it.

The domestic VC industry is still nascent and, in some aspects, underdeveloped, with many prospective Russian startups still seeking offers from international investors. At the same time, VC firms and other startup service organizations are being created across many cities in Russia supported in part by the state, and increasingly also by private industry and wealthy individuals. Meanwhile, the VC deal flow is being supported by an increasing number of venture accelerators, entrepreneurship programs, and incubation networks. The innovation ecosystem necessary for high-tech entrepreneurship is slowly taking shape. In 2014, the Internet Initiatives Development Fund (IIDF) was established and is now supporting an enormous number of start-ups (see the complete IIDF story in the final contribution of this section).

It is worth noting some of the ever-growing list of initiatives. The Scale-Up program for growth-focused entrepreneurs is operated by the Center for Entrepreneurship and its partners in eight Russian cities. Launched in 2016, it claims to be the first of its kind, dedicated to accelerating and expanding existing businesses instead of supporting the ideas phase only. In less than 2 years over 250 entrepreneurs completed the program, resulting in an average business growth rate of 50%. The SKOLKOVO Technopark, launched in 2016, had more than 140 startups within a year, mostly in space technology, IT, bio-technology, nuclear energy, and energy efficiency. Increasingly, there are also more private initiatives in the funding sector. In 2016, the Gutseriev family, one of the richest in Russia, created the Larnabel venture capital firm with an initial US$ 100 million endowment for investment in AI technologies. Also of relevance in this context are the targets for technology growth by the National Technological Initiative, which has an ambitious mandate in nine key sectors: NeuroNet, Marinet, SpaceNet, FoodNet, FinNet, AuroNet, HealthNet, SafeNet, and EnergyNet.

Triggers and Facilitators

What are some of the catalysts of these new developments? For one, many of the new startups are not constrained by traditional business resources. Innovative new technology enables the individual Russian entrepreneur to capitalize on ideas faster and more powerfully than established companies tied down by old-style legacy systems.

The rise of social networks allows people to more intensively communicate across disciplines, organizations, and market-spaces to explore new opportunities. Many startups have team members located in several Russian cities as well as different countries but pursue joint business opportunities as well as—or even better—than companies limited in their geographical reach.

Russians, especially the younger generations, have also adopted a much greater tolerance to failure. Working with the lean-and-agile methodologies of product development, many startups reduce the risk of failure and increase their rate of experimentation. “Learning by doing” has become a new mantra for young entrepreneurs and innovators, increasing the success rate of their startups. We are seeing the rise of a new generation of people whose mindset accepts entrepreneurship as a legitimate means of career development, preferable to working in the civil service, at state corporations or at established companies.

Of course, there are still many obstacles, and as the innovation ecosystem develops, interdependencies between Russian institutions and entrepreneurial startups will increase. Lawmakers and regulators must closely observe the trends and promulgate new guidelines and laws intended to make investments more reliable. We claim that challenges notwithstanding, the overall trend is nonetheless clear. Russia is seeing the emergence of a new class of entrepreneurial competitors that will challenge established domestic firms and even foreign multinationals. At the heart of these developments, the indisputable fact is that new technologies are leveling the playing field for smart entrepreneurs and will lead to slow but significant wealth generation across the board.

While we are in the midst of the fourth phase of Russia's innovation renaissance, the fifth wave is already appearing on the horizon: the pervasive startup economy, with entrepreneurial initiatives in all sectors, investing in globally cutting-edge technologies, and launching these into international markets. Somewhere among the young and daring startup entrepreneurs of today are Russia's future captains of corporate and social innovation. Some of them will surely have a global impact.

Notes

1. World Intellectual Property Organization (WIPO), (2016). WIPO Patent Report: Statistics on Worldwide Patent Activity.

III 2

Foreign R&D Investment in Russia

How to Translate Into Innovation?

Max von Zedtwitz, Zeljko Tekic,
and Kelvin Willoughby

As the country with the world's 12th largest nominal GDP, and by some accounts the 6th largest in purchasing power parity-adjusted terms, Russia is naturally a destination worthy of consideration by the decision-makers of any multinational corporation (MNC). The rationale for such investment is not only market access, but also to strengthen the firm's global innovation activities.

Thus, Russia continues to attract international R&D investments, helped by virtue of a strong reputation in science and technology. Russian engineers in R&D centers in Moscow, St. Petersburg, and elsewhere are contributing to the development of new technologies and products sold worldwide.

The Life of Russian Business, pages 141–146

Our analysis of a global R&D location database with more than 10,000 R&D centers shows that Russia is host to more than one hundred foreign R&D centers, or approximately 1.5% of all transnational R&D establishments. This puts Russia in 17th position worldwide, ahead of other popular regions such as Taiwan, the Netherlands, or Switzerland. However, given the size of the economy and especially the size of the country itself, this number still seems rather small. Why is this the case?

Market Attractiveness, Technology, and Talent

Traditionally, and as already noted, a key reason to set up R&D in a foreign country is access to local customers. MNCs are profit-oriented organizations that aim to remain competitive by improving technologies and products—and the best way to increase local sales in a country is to customize offerings to local standards, customs, expectations, and preferences. This requires product localization, usually done best by a local R&D center.

These market forces are also at work for many of the R&D investing companies in Russia. But GDP growth in Russia is often flat and in recent years has even seen some negative growth years. The economics for the establishment of an R&D center to serve local markets requires the host country to show market growth otherwise the investment is unlikely to be recouped by the parent MNC. Strong local market growth can overcome many other challenges that keep MNCs away from countries that are too small, relatively underdeveloped, or culturally too different from the parent company's home country. Hence, slow market growth has not played in Russia's favor to attract more foreign R&D. Nevertheless, the absolute size of its market, driven by a population of more than 140 million, translates into a sizeable product localization business opportunity.

Russia's reputation for science and technology, along with an abundance of scientific and technological talent, matters. Firms that seek to invest in fundamental science and technology development also put local market considerations on the backburner. They will, instead, focus on acquiring input factors such as highly educated scientists and skilled engineers. The presence of advanced research institutes and universities is also of importance.

Russia is doing quite well in the educational domain, with several top-ranked universities in various global rankings. The location of these universities coincides with the two main economic and scientific centers in Russia: Moscow and St. Petersburg. This reality is in turn reflected in the location choices of many foreign R&D centers, as Figure III.2.1 shows. Foreign R&D

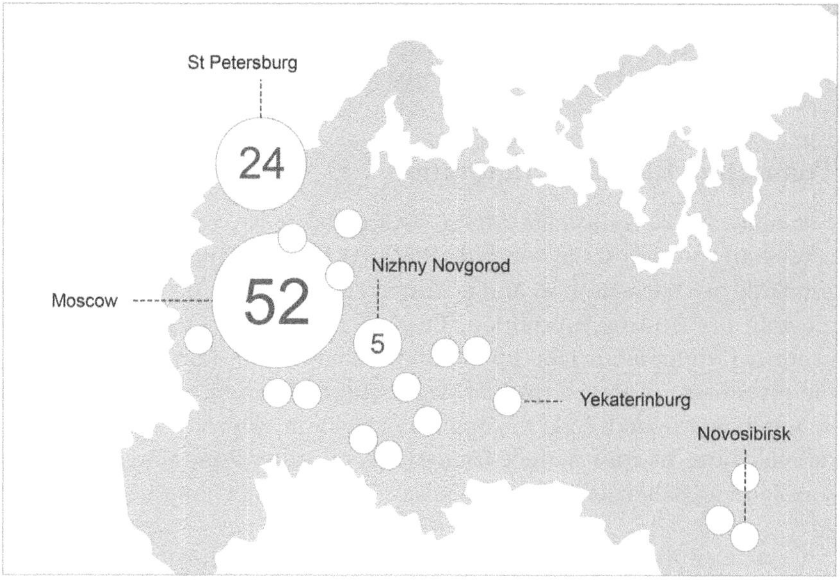

Figure III.2.1 Location and number of foreign R&D centers in Russia. *Source:* GLORAD Database.[1]

centers are also found in Nizhny Novgorod, Tomsk, Perm, Kazan, Samara, and Novosibirsk. In leading Russian cities, especially in Moscow, it is relatively easy to hire high-quality R&D staff.

Motorola was one of the first MNCs to establish an R&D center after the dissolution of the USSR in 1990. Since then, many others have followed from almost every conceivable industry; the list of companies includes Microsoft, IBM, Siemens, and AstraZeneca. China's giant telecom equipment producer, Huawei, set up an R&D center in 1997 in order to strengthen its position in Russia by localizing its products and services early on. From the very beginning, Huawei's Moscow R&D center was designed to be as local as possible, promoting active collaboration and joint training with major local institutions in the telecoms industry such as the Ministry of Informational Technologies and Communications, the Central Research Institute of Communications, and the St. Petersburg Research Institute of Communications.

Others gave their Russian R&D centers a decidedly fundamental research mandate, such as IBM, General Motors, and Samsung. In 2007, Hewlett Packard established a research center as part of its global HP-Labs network in St. Petersburg, to tap into the local technology workforce, focusing on various research areas in computer science and to further develop the foundations of digital technology. St. Petersburg was chosen because of its emergence as an IT hub, its long history in science and education, and also because it was Russia's second largest city—a natural magnet for talented scientists from elsewhere in the country.

Translating R&D Into Innovation

Generally speaking, foreign MNCs seek to be part of a local innovation ecosystem through their domestic R&D. At Russian companies, R&D has primarily two tasks: support and maintenance of existing product lines, and creating breakthrough products. Product maintenance and incremental product development take up the lion's share of an R&D budget, while the investment in long-term R&D lags behind. Therefore, there is a lot of technology-oriented R&D making the transition to product innovation a difficult one. Besides market factors, several other conditions make this transition a challenging one in Russia:

- Genuine entrepreneurship is mostly found in flexible startup companies founded by young engineering graduates, and not yet in the R&D departments of larger, more process-oriented and established companies, whose R&D staff are typically much older. Some of the senior management in these large R&D intensive companies undertook their training during the old Soviet-style planned economy. Yet their technical expertise makes them irreplaceable. Thus, foreign R&D centers have cautiously hired such senior managers while also preferring individuals with experience both in Russia and abroad.
- While basic research at Russian academic institutions can be quite advanced, there is still not enough collaboration with industrial, startup and even foreign R&D initiatives. Much of the university-based R&D is too academic. Even university spinoffs are often more interested in pursuing R&D for the sake of technology at the expense of taking an invention to market. This makes the effective integration of the strong fundamental R&D capacity of academic institutes challenging for both for foreign and Russian firms.
- Since many of the large Russian companies are still vertically integrated, much of the R&D is in-house, with significant competition between and within firms. Western concepts such as "open innovation" are therefore difficult to implement. This adversely affects foreign R&D, as MNCs seek collaborations with local technology partners, local component suppliers, and local market leaders.

What about government support for R&D? It has proven to be an important force in creating startups, Science & Technology (S&T) parks, and bolstering corporate R&D. Although still bureaucratic, the government itself has become more innovative, improving S&T project park administration across Russia.

The recent sanctions imposed by foreign governments on Russia have, in fact, led to a certain improvement in the overall R&D situation in Russia, slowing down the brain drain and even bringing back to Russia many highly qualified expatriate scientists.

A more fundamental positive trend revolves around Russia's improving innovation situation in comparative terms. This is evidenced by the growing emphasis on international patent applications relative to domestic patent applications. Figure III.2.2 illustrates the increasing international density of Russian-sourced patent applications worldwide, compared with the global norm. The variable plotted in Figure III.2.2 ("IPAD") is the percentage of a country's worldwide patent applications in a given year that is accounted for by international patent applications, normalized relative to the global mean for all countries. A country exhibiting "average" performance in international patenting in a given year would register an IPAD score of 1.0.[2]

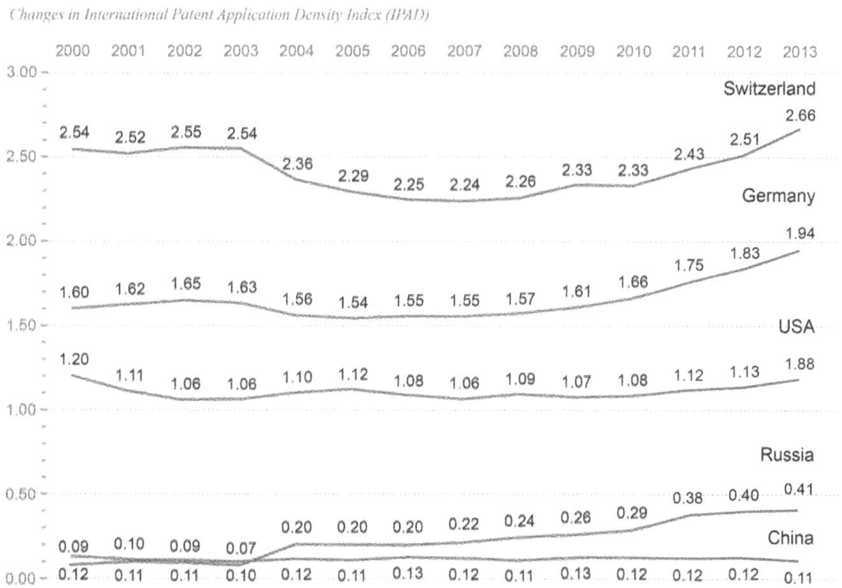

Figure 3.2.2 International density of total patent applications, Russia and selected countries. *Source:* [calculations and chart]: Willoughby (2017).[3] [raw data]: World Intellectual Property Organization.[4]

Russia, which began the new century with a very low IPAD score (lower than China), has now a much stronger international orientation than China, and actually strengthened its international patenting orientation faster than, for instance, the United States, during the studied period.

All in all, Russia's innovation capabilities seem to be strengthening. At the same time, foreign R&D in Russia is very much driven by the quality of the country's science, technology, and talent, as well as by government policy. And yet, while an important number of MNCs invent technology in Russia, this technology is marketed primarily overseas. As economic conditions and market growth further improve, these foreign MNC R&D centers will step up and be more than just local nodes of global MNC networks. This will ultimately lead to something we welcome: a spillover of young, well-trained talent capable of injecting global entrepreneurial innovation into Russia's domestic innovation ecosystem.

Notes

1. GLORAD Center for Global R&D and Innovation. No date. 'R&D Locations' database. Available through http://www.glorad.org.
2. For a detailed explanation of the International Patent Application Density Index, see Kelvin W. Willoughby, *Endogenous Innovation, Outward-Bound International Patenting and National Economic Development* (Working Paper, SKOLKOVO Institute of Science and Technology, 2017), available from the author at kelvin@skoltech.ru.
3. Willoughby, K. W. (2017). Endogenous Innovation, Outward-bound International Patenting and National Economic Development: China and the World, Keynote Lecture, China Intellectual Property Conference, Nanjing University of Science and Technology, College of Intellectual Property, Nanjing, China, 15–16 December.
4. World Intellectual Property Organization, WIPO IP Statistics Data Center, WIPO Statistic Database, http://ipstats.wipo.int/ipstatv2/index.htm(accessed 1 April 2015).

III 3

The Winning Strategies of Russian SMEs

Beyond Resilience in an Unpredictable Landscape

Ekaterina Molchanova

The state of small- and medium-sized enterprises (SMEs) in Russia is generally overlooked. Indeed, the country—so strongly associated with natural resources—is not traditionally viewed as a welcome environment for dynamic private business ventures. Yet Russia's private sector has been growing over the span of more than two decades, and it continues to grow at an increasing pace. While industries related to natural resources constitute almost 95% of Russian exports, these account for only about 15% of Russia's GDP. Remarkably, the remaining 85% is generated by other sectors of the economy—and this is where Russia's new, dynamic and entrepreneurial businesses are found.

Research presented in the "Unknown Russia: Powered by Entrepreneurs" report[1] showcases 15 leading Russian SMEs from industry sectors other than natural resources. These so called "Selected 15" are remarkable

The Life of Russian Business, pages 147–153

for several reasons. With the majority of them launching in the turbulent 1990s, these companies have managed to survive economic downturns and post outstanding results, despite the continuously evolving and often unpredictable landscape of Russian business in this period. These companies outperform, or at least challenge, international players not only in Russia, but also often in the global marketplace. Their success is attributable to their ability to address and navigate the idiosyncratic Russian context.

Key Russian Challenges

The Selected 15 managed to survive and thrive in the turbulent Russian business context. The reasons behind their success have paradoxically and to a significant extent been determined by what would be considered in the West as extremely adverse local market conditions.

Poor Market Institutions

The political and economic crises of the early 1990s left Russia with relatively undeveloped market institutions, high levels of unemployment, a poorly functioning legal system, low purchasing power, and a weak national currency. Basic market institutions such as banks, capital markets, intellectual property legislation, and private property rights enforcement simply were not available for Russian business pioneers in the early 1990s.

Deficient Business Infrastructure

The Russian economy was sharply restrained by deficiencies in the local infrastructure—impaired transportation and logistical systems, both of which are crucial given Russia's vast territory. A deficit of commercial real estate was also a business deterrent. These factors led to uneven development among industry sectors, which, in turn, significantly hampered the implementation of otherwise proven business models.

Absence of Entrepreneurial Culture

Besides the infrastructural and business environment gaps, Russian culture also acted as an impediment to the development of a vibrant business sector. For a long time, entrepreneurial activity of any kind was perceived negatively. The only business model familiar to the broader population—tracking down scarce goods and then selling them to those who needed them—operated for many years as a shadow component of the Soviet economy.

Lack of Trust

The Russian business community is characterized by an insider-dominated culture emphasizing a need for a high level of control over decision-making. Internal approaches to strategic development (such as vertical integration) are generally preferred over the exploration of potential partnership opportunities outside the company. From a customer perspective, the general lack of trust between the purchaser and the seller has precluded firms from employing advanced transaction mechanisms. As a result, Russia, even to this day, remains to a great extent a cash-based economy.

These serious obstacles dissuaded many foreign competitors from the Russian market, leaving more space and time for local businesses to develop. Russian entrepreneurs started to emerge, and were forced by market conditions to learn rapidly from their own experiences. In addition, the Russian mentality and the Soviet legacy have shaped Russian ventures to become more inward looking. Unlike their Chinese counterparts, who have aggressively entered global value chains, Russian mid-sized companies have largely disregarded international expansion.

Winning Strategies

The adverse market conditions, regulatory gaps, infrastructural deficiencies, and lack of established business practices and trust make the success of Russian medium-sized firms even more remarkable. Drawing on an analysis of the Selected 15, four generic strategies for success have been identified (See Figure III.3.1). Below we analyze these creative responses and strategies that harnessed the challenges of Russia's market to their benefit. Despite the diversity of the strategies, there is one common feature across all of them: rapid deployment and a preference for market penetration strategies targeting the long tail of the market.

Best Adaptation

The Select 15 exclusively focused initially on the Russian market and used innovative operational strategies to successfully adapt global best practices, despite shortcomings in the local infrastructure and the general immaturity of the market. Creative operational strategies were key. The most

Figure III.3.1 Russian SMEs winning strategies matrix.

common solution was "in-sourcing"—building an in-house competence as a substitute for outsourced services.

By applying a best adaptation model, Russia's largest retail chain, Magnit, outperformed local peers and global players competing within Russia. This was made possible thanks to in-house logistics and in-house programmers. The company maintains a homegrown, tailor-made enterprise resource planning (ERP) solution that is responsible for ensuring sufficient quantities of fresh goods on store shelves. In combination with a strategic decision to first focus on small cities while competitors were targeting the more obvious opportunities in large cities, Magnit managed to secure the trust of customers and gain market share, while remaining almost invisible to competitors. As a result, it was too late for competitors to react once Magnit had already achieved a critical mass.

Local Offerings

These companies concentrate on the local market and outperform their global and local competitors by offering distinctive value propositions tailored to Russian consumers. Their success has been determined not only by their creativity, but also by a deep understanding of the current needs and future expectations of Russian customers.

Qiwi, a leading provider of next generation payment services, is an example of how the inefficiency of the local market can be converted into a promising business opportunity. In a predominantly cash-based Russian economy with rapidly growing cellular phone penetration, many people struggled to keep their phone accounts funded—payment points were rare and usually very busy. Qiwi installed tens of thousands of cash payment terminals in public places where people could immediately top up their phone accounts with cash. The success of this entrepreneurial solution was obviously ephemeral, but it helped Qiwi to win the trust of customers, to build its brand, and to gain a reputable global partner—the international payment system, VISA.

Global Niche

The Select 15 are dedicated to world-class single product excellence and outperform competitors by developing a strong and constantly improving core product, and then offering multiple variations and versatile applications to their customers globally. No matter whether a company deploys a cost-leadership or a highly focused product strategy, the key success factor is attracting highly qualified people with strong academic backgrounds.

Alawar, now a leading global player in the publishing and distribution of casual games, started as a game developer in Novosibirsk, the home to some of the best engineering schools in Russia. Ascon, originating from the military-industrial complex in Kolomna, challenges global leaders in computer engineering and design. Prognoz, founded by a team of economists and scientists from Perm State University, successfully challenged Oracle in the creation of business intelligence applications. Transas, founded in the late 1980s by sailors who enjoyed programming as a hobby, is now the leading global company in navigation systems.

Global Citizens

In addition to product or service excellence, market acumen, and best-in-class operational performance, for some firms, internationalization eventually becomes a priority with the setting up of multiple locations and hiring talent worldwide. This is not what one would expect from a Russian company, and so examples of aggressive internationalization are rare. Perhaps one of the best examples is Luxoft, which provides offshore software development. The company outperforms low-cost Indian competitors by focusing on developing sophisticated solutions for Western blue chip companies. Most importantly, the company has service and delivery offices not only in cost-effective locations such as Russia or Vietnam, but also in locations with immediate proximity to the customer—such as the United States and European Union. This is a model the company calls "near-shore" software development.

Looking Forward

Despite the country's well-documented challenges, positive economic forces are at work in Russia. While generally off the radar, particularly to the international audience, these private companies represent a new generation of Russian business leaders that have entrepreneurial culture and behavior as part of their very core.

Still, the companies' winning strategies, which once were their strengths, may make them vulnerable in the future. Given the relatively undeveloped market conditions that existed in the late 1990s, these companies have done well by focusing mainly on product, brand, and on distribution in their innovation repertoire. Yet such inside-out thinking, which puts the product at the center of the business model, might not work well in the face of today's challenges of growing competition, and increasingly demanding consumers.

Today's challenges call for more sophisticated innovations and necessitate outside-in thinking that relies on creative business configurations and enhanced customer experience. To respond to the changing business landscape, these companies need to preserve their entrepreneurial competence through deploying creative, flexible, and consumer-centric business models. Only then will Russian SMEs survive and thrive in the face of global competition coming from Western, Chinese, and other emerging market multinationals.

Note

1. This contribution has been derived and updated from the report "The Selected 15: The Winning Strategies of Russian Entrepreneurial Champions" by E. Molchanova and SKOLKOVO IEMS research team was presented in the "Unknown Russia: Powered by Entrepreneurs" report produced by the World Economic Forum's Global Agenda Council on Russia, 2015.

III 4

Atlantis-Pak

Russia's Bespoke Atelier for Meat Packaging[1]

Ekaterina Molchanova, Oleg Remyga,
Maria Cristina Di Vito, and Ksenia Sokolova

Atlantis-Pak was launched in the southern Russian city of Rostov-on-Don in 1993 by six partners who, with their diverse skills, teamed up during the difficult years after the collapse of the Soviet Union. The founders had previously been involved in a variety of sectors including cable production, tobacco and packaging before settling on casings, which are enclosures of meat filled products, such as sausages.

The decision to focus on casings for the meat production sector was the result of a trip by one of the founders to St. Petersburg. He visited a natural casings (i.e., intestines) plant and learned that demand in Russia significantly exceeded supply. As the team was new to the industry, they arranged to meet with scientists at the National Russian Meat Research Institute to gain a better understanding of the kinds of casing products that were

The Life of Russian Business, pages 155–158

already on the market. Eventually, the entrepreneurs placed their bet on plastic (artificial) casings that were not widely used at the time but in their view had the largest growth potential. The group bought its first production line from a German plant that was scheduled to close. The equipment was superior to Russian offerings and this gave the company an immediate local competitive advantage. Even at this incipient stage, the firm had ambitious goals, as CEO, Igor Perepletchikov notes: "From the very beginning, the company was centered on two guiding principles. First, we wanted to create value through innovative products and cutting-edge manufacturing. Second, we aimed to expand internationally."

Although innovation has played an important role in the company's success, its first attempts at product development were chaotic at best. While in Europe plastic casings had already been on the market for some time, in Russia, the technology was new. Sergey Borodayev, the former chemist who had previously been involved in cable production, was entrusted with leading new product development. Through trial and error, a first batch was produced and shipped to the Armavir meat processing plant for testing. Upon delivery of the order, the team received a call from the outraged client stating that the casings had exploded during application. Later, it was discovered that the product's edges had been worn out because of poor transport conditions. Atlantis-Pak was quick to learn from this and many other mistakes, which in retrospect laid the foundation for its innovative practices.

Innovation in the casings industry is a combination of advanced chemistry—new products are created from the same basic polyamides—and manufacturing technology. Polyamide casings possess valuable properties such as high mechanical durability and stability in high temperatures and humidity, but they also have a number of disadvantages, as they can only be used for sausages with larger calibers, have an unnatural appearance and do not allow sausages to be smoked. The in-house laboratory worked on new solutions and the first big success came in 1997, with the world's first plastic casing for frankfurters and wieners. Within just a year, the innovative casing gained a 22% share of the massive frankfurter and wiener product category in Russia. There were other breakthroughs in innovation, the most notable of which was the introduction of permeable casings[2] for dry and semi-dry sausages. The company has now registered numerous patents and received a number of national and international awards including the DuPont Silver Award in the Packaging Innovation category.[3] The company markets a quality product and does not compete on price.

Yet, product innovation is only half the battle in this industry. Atlantis-Pak's main competitive advantage lies in its customization and service offering. That is, in its ability to quickly accommodate the needs and preferences of different consumers across the globe. The remarkable speed and adjustability at Atlantis-Pak is made possible by its original manufacturing lines. Unlike its competitors, who buy ready-to-use integrated production lines, Atlantis-Pak has developed its own production lines from imported parts, sometimes doubling the output of a line compared to the industry standard. This manufacturing innovation enables responsive services and is led by an in-house team of skilled engineers. The company had been fortunate to find top engineering talent in Rostov-on-Don, as the city was previously home to a large defense plant. Perepletchikov drove home the firm's emphasis on customization: "We are the largest atelier of 'bespoke' (meat and cheese packaging) products. Standards of production are very different from country to country; size, color, and temperature requirements differ. We are unique in that we fulfill all orders as we receive them."

Customer-centric internationalization is also important to the company's success. As early as 1994, Atlantis-Pak began serving CIS countries such as Ukraine and Belarus. Initial efforts to expand internationally were unsophisticated. In the early years, top management traveled by train with a suitcase full of samples. In Eastern Europe, nine countries would be visited in a single trip, pitching the casings to meat processing companies.

By the late 1990s, the firm had hired a young team of English and German speaking sales professionals to reach the attractive German market and the rest of Europe. Germany was pivotal to the establishment of Atlantis-Pak's reputation in Europe as the country boasts a strong "sausage culture" and a sophisticated industry. Atlantis-Pak's fast service response and flexibility were much appreciated by its European partners. By the year 2000, their products had successfully entered various European markets.

By 2010, the casings market in Russia began to stagnate and in 2011 the company was acquired by Russia's Agrocom Group,[4] which gave Atlantis-Pak further impetus for internationalization as well as diversification into the new product category of barrier shrink films, which block oxygen permeation, thereby extending shelf life.

On the international front, in 2013, Atlantis-Pak obtained BRC (British Retail Consortium) Global Standard certification. Although it took nearly two years of paperwork, it granted access not only to the United Kingdom market but also to many other countries worldwide. In 2014, in order to also reach the large Islamic markets, such as Indonesia and the Middle East, Atlantis-Pak obtained International Halal certification. The company had already been certified locally to serve Russia's Muslim population, estimated at close to 20 million people, thus facilitating the process.

Atlantis-Pak's international pursuits on the back of its innovative product range have been fruitful. Today, the firm sells to over 80 countries and the share of exports in the company's turnover is close to 60%. The economic downturn in Russia also seems to have played to the company's advantage. With a weak ruble, the company works at full capacity to satisfy growing international demand. As the CEO emphasizes: "We, Russians, think of Russian products in lower terms than they actually deserve. Outside of Russia, people think that if we can fly into space then we can manufacture a good product too."

Notes

1. This contribution has been derived from the report "Russian and Chinese Mid-Sized Business: Internationalization Strategies" report (by SKOLKOVO IEMS and with kind support by EY, 2017)
2. Petrova, Y. (2012). Колбасный глянец [Sausage glamour]. Magazine "Kommersant. Secret of Firm" №9. Available at: https://www.kommersant.ru/doc/2000667
3. DuPont Packaging & Printing Media Center. (2013). 25th DuPont Packaging Awards Winners. Available at: http://www.dupont.com/industries/packaging-and-printing/media/press-releases/25th-2013-dupont-packaging-awards-winners.html
4. Agrocom Group is one of the largest private companies in Russia with assets in a variety of sectors.

III 5

SPLAT's Leap of Faith

Niche Strategies of a Russian Medium-Sized Company[1]

Benoit Leleux, Tomas Casas i Klett,
Ekaterina Molchanova, and Yuliya Ponomareva

Making bold decisions was not new to Yevgeni Demin. Yet in 2004, he was, at best, an entrepreneur in the ranks of the "living-dead."[2] His company had hit rock bottom, leaving him with unpaid bills and no salary. Worst of all, the crash of Demin's once profitable firm was the result of his own venturing decision to pivot from distributor to brand business.

Only 2 years earlier, in 2002, the firm had enjoyed annual sales of 60 million rubles (approximately US$ 2 million), reasonable profitability with 5–7% margins and stable annual growth. It was a promising distribution business of health and beauty products. Yet, it was not what Demin had dreamed about. He had envisioned building a high-growth business based on his very own innovative and branded product. That very vision was, after

The Life of Russian Business, pages 159–163

all, what in 1996 had taken the young tourism management graduate from Sochi, a city far away in Russia's south, to the nation's capital.

In Moscow, Demin started his business career as an employee of a small firm affiliated with Moscow State University (MSU) that produced parapharmaceuticals. Soon, he bought the brand and established his own company. For a short while, the company continued to produce and sell dietary supplements but soon switched to a more lucrative distribution business model. The move provided the founders a comfortable living but this was not Demin's driving motivation. He was still determined to launch and market his own branded product in the same category of health and beauty products with which he had become familiar. After careful consideration, he decided to bet the house on his own SPLAT-branded toothpaste and make it "the best toothpaste in the world."

By 2003, revenues at the firm started to decline and profit margins went into negative territory. Like water and oil, it seemed that the distribution business could not coexist with his new proprietary brand. For Demin, it was time to let one of them go. The distribution business was gradually wound down and was terminated in 2005. In the absence of profits, the company had to rely on its cash reserves to finance the new venture's development. That safety cushion was essential since access to formal financial sources was out of the question due to high interest rates in the range of 20–25%.[3] Just like other Russian entrepreneurs at that time, Demin had nobody but himself to finance his dreams. Energized by the new vision and the enormous pressure to turn a financial corner, the team went to "work harder than ever."

The Battle for Survival

The company's very first product, SPLAT Professional, was a medicated toothpaste which had therapeutic effects and targeted specific problems. Such a value proposition was completely new to the product category and represented a rather daring move. The Russian market, though on its way to recovery after the economic crisis of 1998, was still dormant. The oral care category was rather underdeveloped. While young people in big cities understood the value of brushing teeth as a preventive measure, consumers in the rest of the country had low awareness of oral hygiene and health. Western oral care giants were dominating the mass market with standard products in the mid-price category, while Russian producers were offering cheaper alternatives.

With its innovative formula, the SPLAT toothpaste was positioned in the emerging niche of professional products. The timing appeared perfect, as the segment was clearly unserved. SPLAT chose to cater to middle-aged educated families concerned with the health of their teeth and looking for professional solutions. Soon after the launch of the first product, Demin and his team continued to widen the line of professional toothpaste solutions each targeting a specific problem, such as enamel damage, gum diseases, and sensitive teeth.

Having an exceptional product meant little unless it had a presence on the shelves. This was a challenge for several reasons. Modern retailing was not developed in Russia at the time. Most trade took place outside of the organized sector—in kiosks or small convenience stores. Big chains required large down payments, which a small start-up like SPLAT could not afford.

The company targeted pharmacies at first. The sales team, and Demin himself, would visit and introduce the product. Usually, before their visit, they sent some friends to ask about this wonder product called SPLAT. Surprised pharmacists wrote down the name of the toothpaste and a few days later, when the sales team would turn up at the doorstep, they would recognize the name. Sometimes, the sales team would explain to a pharmacy unwilling to stock the product that its rival up the road had already placed an order. Every new sale was a result of painstaking work. After almost 1 year of camping out on the doorsteps, SPLAT products started appearing in pharmacies.

Now, as SPLAT found traction with pharmacies, Demin saw the need to strengthen communication with consumers. He believed in the importance of emotional connections and decided to make personal contact with people who had bought his toothpaste. He wrote a "letter to the client," randomly inserting the missives in the packaging of the toothpaste tube. To his surprise, consumers responded with suggestions, complaints, or compliments, but most importantly they provided his team an impetus to grow and improve. Over the years, Demin has continued with his "tradition" of sending monthly letters, and spending about 1.5 hours every day reading and answering responses from consumers.[4]

Niche for Growth

By 2006, SPLAT's battle for survival had been won. When the 2002 annual sales figure target of 60 million rubles was amply surpassed, it was clear to all that the hard-fought transition from distribution to the independent brand business had been accomplished. SPLAT was now poised for double-digit growth rates. Yet, still limited in resources and small in size, the company had to be inventive, being both daring and cautious at the same time. Demin's strategy was to move gradually, build up competencies and aim for the long-term. This was a non-trivial decision at the time when most other businessmen were focusing on projects that offered short-term gains to minimize risks in the uncertain Russian environment.

In the course of the next decade, SPLAT grew from a small venture into a solid mid-size company with annual turnover exceeding US$ 100 million. Its share in oral care was on the rise, hitting 8% in 2014. In the toothpaste category, SPLAT was the number two brand, with 12% of the market, tied with international giant, Colgate-Palmolive.

Nevertheless, by 2015 it seemed that SPLAT had exhausted the growth potential within its niche. Pushing for higher market share in Russian oral care meant direct competition with large players—something that Demin was not keen on doing. The overall market performance of the oral care category also began to deteriorate. The decline was attributable to a combination of gradual saturation and the expansion of modern retailing, which made oral care products more accessible and affordable.

The decline of the market intensified competition. German professional oral care company Lacalut, continued to be SPLAT's main competitor in its segment. However, as the industry's battle for market share escalated, many other players began to creep into niches that they had previously ignored, with professional and medicated oral care being at the top of the list. The continuing premiumization of the market supported the trend. Colgate-Palmolive launched the whitening toothpaste, Colgate Total Pro Whitening. Domestic player, Concern Kalina, acquired by Unilever in 2011, introduced a two-in-one toothpaste and gel with herbal balms under the Forest Balm brand. With more consumers looking for novel offerings in oral care, market analysts anticipated an increasing number of innovative product variations in the years to come.

SPLAT's response to the intensified competition was to aggressively explore niche opportunities in new product categories and geographies, a strategy for which the company had laid the foundations long before the market downturn. Always on the lookout, SPLAT had spotted niche opportunities in adjacent product categories. At first, these pursuits were of an experimental nature, but soon they crystallized into a long-term strategy. Besides oral care, four other categories were on the company's radar: baby care, body care, home care, and hair care. For each of them the company introduced a new brand.

Expansion across product categories was done in parallel to international expansion. SPLAT's pursuits outside of Russia started in 2007 with the active expansion into CIS markets. This was evidently a natural choice for a

Russian company. Geographical proximity, similar mentality, language, and common trading agreements allowed Russian companies to expand into the post-Soviet republics with relative ease. SPLAT started with neighboring Ukraine and Belarus, subsequently moving further south towards Kazakhstan, Georgia, and Armenia. Eventually, SPLAT ventured into Europe and Asia. Demin saw himself as an ambassador for Russia: "It is important for me that the image of Russia be associated with cool products, from IT to food to personal care."[5]

Yevgeni Demin believes that the challenges of creating new products and winning over new segments can be met with existing capabilities. "After all, SPLAT has always been about staying ahead of the game." In his mind there is no doubt that SPLAT's calling is to carve out new profitable niches based on brash unique offerings. Mistakes are not welcome anymore—after all, this time he has much more to lose.

Notes

1. This contribution is a derivative work based on the case by Casas i Klett, Leleux, Molchanova, and Ponomareva "SPLAT's Venture Dilemma (A&B)" published at the CaseCenter (ref. no 316-0238-1).
2. The living-dead are theoretically described in: Casas i Klett, T. and Hilb, M. (2016). Founders in the Living-Dead Trap: A Theoretical Exploration at Entrepreneurship's Dark Core. *Entrepreneurship Research Journal*, 6(4), 401–423.
3. Devyatanayeva, N. V. (2013) Проблемы кредитования малого и среднего бизнеса в России [Credit Problems of Small and Medium-Sized Business in Russia], *Molodoi Ucheny*, 6: 317–320.
4. Agaeva, M. (2008). Зуб даёт: директор SPLAT Евгений Дёмин учит продавать без рекламы [*Bet the Farm: SPLAT CEO Yevgeni Demin Gives Lessons on How to Sell Without Advertising*]. Retrieved from http://www.sostav.ru/articles/2008/03/28/ko1/
5. Shainyan K. (2015). Евгений Дёмин, SPLAT: "Полка магазина—это не доступ к трубе" [*Yevgeni Demin, SPLAT: "The Store Shelf is Not Access to the Pipeline"*]. [online]. Available from: https://republic.ru/posts/54542

III 6

Neurosoft

From Accidental Innovation to In-House Strategy[1]

Ekaterina Molchanova, Oleg Remyga,
Maria Cristina Di Vito, and Ksenia Sokolova

Neurosoft was established in 1992 by a team of professors and researchers at the Ivanovo State Power Engineering University and the Ivanovo State Medical Academy. The group was brought together by chance. Doctors from the local hospital approached the engineers asking for help: Their electroencephalograph (EEG) machine, used to record electrical activity in the brain, had broken down. At that time, an EEG device was a stand-alone bulky piece of equipment. The printing component had malfunctioned and its replacement was expensive.

The engineers decided to develop a device that would digitalize the signal and transmit it directly to a computer. This, in turn, allowed the use of standard printers. Unknowingly, the team created a computerized EEG,

The Life of Russian Business, pages 165–167

an innovation at the time. The news quickly spread in the industry and the team then set up the company.

At the beginning, Neurosoft did not have its own production facility and relied on contract manufacturing in its home city of Ivanovo. The firm focused on the development of both software and hardware. The business grew, and in 1996, the company moved from its cramped office into a larger space and established a production facility. Neurosoft has become a rare player in the Russian medical equipment market, dominated by international firms, where Russian companies operated mostly in lower value added technology segments. Neurosoft's DNA made it different—being a research spinoff it prioritized innovation from the very beginning. Although breakthrough innovations are rare in the field of electrodiagnostics, it aggressively realized a large number of incremental innovations that ultimately led to success. But for a firm aiming to be an innovator, success in Russia's market was not sufficient.

At the beginning of the new millennium, Neurosoft's management considered international expansion. Interestingly, the company's initial pursuits coincided with important developments in the international market for medical equipment. Before the turn of the century, medical equipment producers mostly served their domestic markets. But as a result of a wave of mergers and acquisitions activity, newly consolidated companies were streamlining their distribution channels. Most distributors had run out of products and were looking for new vendors.

It was one such distributor in France, Pierre Scholl, who contacted Neurosoft in 2002. The team immediately responded to the request by sending its devices. Scholl's initial assessment was not positive: "These devices are not bad but nobody will buy them," due to their poor interface. However, he still agreed to give them a try and eventually became the official representative of Neurosoft in Europe, guiding the company's application for relevant ISO and later CE certifications, which meant that Neurosoft's products were assessed to meet high safety, health, and environmental protection requirements. The CE approval from EU authorities was highlighted during the MEDICA 2004 exhibition in Dusseldorf, Germany. The company used the event to officially launch its global expansion plan and sign its first international contracts.

The team's decision to enter international markets was key in developing the company's long-term competitiveness. Due to stiff competition in foreign markets and higher quality requirements, many products and new features were first developed specifically for the needs of foreign clients. Only later were they introduced into the Russian market.[2] Obtaining local certifications for both the products and of the entire manufacturing process and quality control procedure was a laborious effort, but one that paid off in the long-term. That became especially true for Neurosoft's first US FDA certification in 2011.

Operating in over 70 different countries and with exports now accounting for more than 50% of sales, Neurosoft is very careful to uphold its reputation. It has had to work harder than its international competitors to earn its global reputation and clients' trust. The lack of depth of the Russian supplier network and its comparatively small market size has conditioned this strategy.

The development of software and programming constitute the core competencies of the company, but Neurosoft has also had to bring in-house a whole range of auxiliary operations to ensure quality and cost control. It is difficult to find reliable suppliers and outsourcing options in Russia. This has meant, for example, mastering vacuum forming technology used in the mass production of plastic goods, or introducing its own silicon rubber molding technology. One challenge has been that, because of its size, Neurosoft has low buying power, making it costly to import necessary components from abroad. As a result, it even makes basic USB cables in-house because existing options do not meet the required specifications or are too expensive.

The firm is flexible and continues to adapt to remain competitive. At the moment, Neurosoft is exploring the opportunity to outsource some of its production to Western Europe. That would be financially beneficial—avoiding import duties—and it would also increase the brand perception as being not "Made in Russia." At same time, Nickolay Smirnov, chief commercial officer of Neurosoft, articulates the benefits of in-house production as a strategic advantage: "Standard practice is to outsource all non-core activities. At Neurosoft, we produce everything. We just can't trust anything to be outsourced."

Notes

1. This contribution has been derived from the report "Russian and Chinese Mid-Sized Business: Internationalization Strategies" by SKOLKOVO IEMS and with the kind support by EY, 2017.
2. Skvortsov, A. (2013). Ивановскую медтехнику покупают даже в Бразилии и Франции [Medical Equipment from Ivanovo Is Bought Even in Brazil and France]. Ivanovo newspaper dated on July 28, 2013. Available at: http://ivgazeta.ru/read/11796

7

SPIRIT DSP Software

Engine Inside

Ekaterina Molchanova, Oleg Remyga,
Maria Cristina Di Vito, and Ksenia Sokolova

In 1990, Andrey Sviridenko developed his first software product while still a computing mathematics and cybernetics student at Moscow State University. He and his classmate had developed an Artificial Intelligence (AI) software product. While on a student exchange in Germany in 1991, Sviridenko was able to sell 10 licenses of the software product for about US$ 10,000 to a small German software reseller. This was an exceptional amount of money in light of the Russian economic situation at the time. He invested the proceeds into launching SPIRIT DSP company, buying computers and hiring a team of 10 young programmers each on a salary of US$ 30 per month.

In 1994, another classmate went to live in Japan, and Sviridenko suggested that he set-up a local Tokyo office for SPIRIT DSP. This first "office" was really just a desk with a computer in the Russian–Japanese Business

The Life of Russian Business, pages 169–171

Council building. It soon became apparent that the Japanese were not very interested in the AI software. Instead, in 1995, NEC Corporation (the largest global chip producer at the time) suggested that SPIRIT develop communication and navigation software products for NEC DSP chips. SPIRIT accepted the offer, which was worth about US$ 500,000.

In the middle of the project, the project management engineer entrusted with the development of the communication software announced that he was moving to live in Germany to work for Siemens, taking along key programmers with him. With the NEC contract delivery deadline approaching fast, Sviridenko looked for other high-quality programmers that could help him with development, eventually asking his father for help. Vladimir Sviridenko was a university professor and a communications and digital signal processor (DSP) technology guru. He decided to quit his job at Rockwell Semiconductor R&D Center in Moscow and join the young team as project manager. In the end, the NEC project was successfully executed and the founder's father remains with the company as chief technology officer to this day.

SPIRIT DSP is a niche player. Its success in the global market rests on its ability to make high performance embedded communication software engines for media processing. Although the firm has explored different software product categories throughout its existence, ranging from telecommunication systems to AI to navigation, it has always focused on very specific solutions with cutting-edge software. The company's main business vertical market is telecommunications. Until 2011, SPIRIT's software business was almost 100% exports to the United States, Europe, and Asia.

Today, the firm is a global leader in mobile Voice and Video over IP (VVoIP) engines and its software products are used by more people than Skype; in fact, Skype licensed SPIRIT video technologies. The company's innovative voice and video software platforms allow telecom carriers, equipment manufacturers and software developers to deliver superior quality and integrated VVoIP services. SPIRIT DSP's software products have been licensed to or integrated in popular product brands including Apple, Adobe, Avaya, AT&T, BT, Broadsoft, China Mobile, Huawei, HP, HTC, Korea Telecom, LG, Microsoft, Mavenir, Mitel, Oracle, Texas Instruments, Polycom, Reliance, Toshiba, Skype, Samsung, Viber, and ZTE amongst other global 200 technology leaders. The combined SPIRIT DSP embedded software products user base exceeds 1 billion people in over 100 countries.

Over time, SPIRIT DSP has adapted. As competition intensified and Microsoft and Google began to develop VVoIP engines in-house (they acquired SPIRIT competitor companies), it shifted its attention towards emerging technology giants in Asia. It has also evolved its product range; in

1995 it launched GPS-GLONASS (outdoor) navigation systems and in 2010 it switched to integrated navigation software systems (indoor+outdoor). Unlike outdoor navigation, which mainly relies on satellites, indoor navigation is much more complex, as GPS-GLONASS signals do not reach inside a building. Therefore, indoor navigation uses radio waves, magnetic fields, and built-in step counters. SPIRIT DSP's developments in this area have won several global technology contests, including one run by Microsoft in 2015. In early 2016, SPIRIT DSP sold its subsidiary, SPIRIT Navigation, to a global public mobile technology company headquartered in California (the buyer's name is covered by an NDA).

The firm has come a long way, and its CEO reminisces how they winged it in the early days:

> In the beginning, we didn't have anything. When the NEC people wanted to meet our team in Moscow, we asked our friends if we could move into their office for a day and pretend that it was ours. During the visit, the Japanese managers talked with the team and said "Okay, we believe in you."

In 2007, eBay made an offer to acquire SPIRIT DSP along with Skype, but the company declined as it planned to grow organically into new geographical and product markets. In 2011, VideoMost, HD videoconferencing software for workgroup collaboration was launched. Unlike other solutions that require expensive video conferencing hardware, VideoMost is pure software and does not need any dedicated hardware or infrastructure, while delivering top video quality on PC, web, and mobiles. Unlike SPIRIT software engines, which are integrated into somebody else's products, VideoMost is a stand-alone enterprise product ready for distribution by service provider partners in a cloud (SAAS) delivery model. VideoMost serves the Russian enterprise market as well. Sviridenko admits that selling innovative software in Russia has been a challenge as clients give preference to large international software companies that provide integrated solutions. Yet, he believes that the combination of high performance and competitive pricing give VideoMost a strong edge.

Sviridenko faces unsurprising challenges: "In Russia, bureaucracy can nullify even the most obvious advantages of home-grown high-tech products." On the other hand, the new Russian government policies on import substitution are changing the dynamics of the local IT market. In the past, government procurement tenders were primarily awarded to U.S. software giants. Today, the push for local technology companies to substitute the software of global monopolies is an opportunity. Sviridenko hopes to make the most of this initiative.

8

Venture Capital in Russia

Re-Emergence, Hype, and Looking Abroad

Yuri Mitin
Vitaly Polekhin

The Russian venture capital (VC) market is still relatively young, having only come into existence about a decade ago. After an early peak in 2012, the activity in the VC market began to decline. Yet, despite the current economic slowdown in Russia, the market is still alive and given the overall circumstances, remains relatively robust. While the crisis has manifested itself in declining transaction volumes (i.e., fewer venture deals), many existing Russian investors have stayed committed to the venture business model. They have adapted by becoming more selective in their choices for less risky late-stage investment projects. To further minimize risks, investors target "safer" software projects over hardware.

How does Russia fare on a global scale? Russia's formal VC market as a percentage of global VC investments stands at less than 0.2%, meaning

The Life of Russian Business, pages 173–175

that annually about US$ 250 million are invested. By other measures, the Russian VC market represents about 0.03% of the country's GDP. In this sense, the VC market's size is not unlike that of other nations, as only in the United States and Israel does VC funding clearly exceed the OECD average of 0.05% of national GDP.

There are important differences between Russian and foreign VC investors. The first of these is the source of capital. Foreign VC funds are generally funded by corporations, sovereign wealth funds, university endowments, insurance companies, pension plans, Ultra High Net Worth Individuals (UHNWIs), and High Net Worth Individuals (HNWIs). Russian VCs have a much narrower investor base and are funded primarily by corporations, UHNWIs, HNWIs, and by the state.

Differences also exist in terms of sector emphasis. Global VCs have diverse investment targets ranging from IT to life sciences, from food to renewable energies. In Russia, IT is the most active sector by far, constituting about 90% of total venture transactions and invested amounts. Key sub-sectors of IT include e-commerce, cloud computing, fintech, and social networking. Fintech is one of the most promising areas with several hubs thriving in Moscow. In this vein, 2017 saw the emergence of a new hype, initial coin offerings (ICOs). Everybody now wants to raise the next $US 10 million in tokens. Vitalik Buterin, the Russian-Canadian 24-year old co-founder of Ethereum[1] has achieved guru status in Russia and is inspiring a new generation of founders. In 2017, the total amount of investments in blockchain startups with Russian roots exceeded US$ 200 million,[2] comparable to the total VC market in the country.

Another interesting trend is the corporate ventures led by the likes of Sberbank, Alfabank, Rostelecom, PepsiCo, MTS, or Ikea—large Russian and international corporations that are trying to work with startups and opening both accelerators and incubators. Government affiliated entities are also jumping in with new funds like Vnesheconombank, the Bank for Development's VEB.2.0.[3] The fund boasts over than US$ 1 billion in assets under management and plans to invest on Series A, B, and C venture rounds. At the opposite end of the spectrum, Russian business angels are making a comeback but this time they are working with angel clubs, preferring to syndicate. They are also using crowdfunding platforms such as NABA (National Business Angels Association), Venture Club, or StartTrack.

Finally, Russian startups are trying to go global. Some have set their eyes on the United States and aim to raise money in Silicon Valley. Examples include Cinemood.com ("Your favorite YouTube Videos and Channels on a Big Screen and On the Go"), VisaBot ("an AI-powered solution for streamlining the U.S. visa process"), or Mubert ("Increase your productivity with seamless AI music"). In parallel, Russian VC funds and business angels are also setting their sights beyond the domestic market, investing in global startups. The United States, Canada, and Israel are their main destinations, along with Singapore and Switzerland.

Notes

1. Ethereum denotes a "decentralized platform for applications that run exactly as programed without any chance of fraud, censorship, or third-party interference."
2. Belov, V., and Kolesnichenko, S. (2017). Инвестиции в цифрах. Как ICO меняют венчурный рынок [Investments in Numbers: How ICOs Change the Venture Investments Market]. Available at: http://www.forbes.ru/finansy-i-investicii/351141-investicii-v-cifrah-kak-ico-i-kriptovalyuty-menyayut-venchurnyy-rynok
3. http://www.veb.ru/en/index.php

9

Russia at the Heart of Cybercrime Prevention

How a Cybersecurity Startup Became a Global Leader

Ruslan Yusufov

It all began with a book written by FBI insiders Chris Prosise and Kevin Mandia, *Incident Response: Investigating Computer Crime.* Ilya Sachkov, a 17-year old freshman in the Information Security Department at the Bauman Moscow State Technical University, read the book "in one gulp" and decided to set up a detective services start-up, Group-IB. That was back in 2003 when the state, represented by the Ministry of Internal Affairs and the Federal Security Service (FSB, formerly KGB), had a monopoly on investigating cybercrime in Russia. "We had no friends in high places and no connections. But we were greatly inspired and burning with desire to work," Sachkov recalls. His brother lent him US$ 5,000 and said "Go for it!"

The Life of Russian Business, pages 177–179

Quite a lot has been achieved over the last decade and a half. Sachkov's team has successfully conducted over 150 high-profile investigations, with guilty verdicts being passed in over 30 countries. He has built-up an international high-tech company. *Business Insider UK*, a business news aggregator and analysis website, has listed Group-IB among the top 7 key global cybersecurity companies along with FireEye, Palo Alto Networks, and Kaspersky Lab. How has this been possible?

Group-IB started out by focusing on computer forensics and cybercrime investigations for such crimes as website and email hacking, DDoS attacks, and money theft from online banking systems. However, Sachkov soon came to realize that conducting investigations was not enough for creating a scalable international business. Its breakthrough was a combination of technology and business model innovation when it switched from services to products.

As early as 2011, ahead of later efforts by other private firms and the government, the company created CERT-GIB—a 24/7 response center for cybersecurity incidents. The company also developed both software and hardware solutions designed to identify malicious activities in corporate networks, as well as sophisticated malware and remote control detection systems. Threat Intelligence, an early warning system for proactive cyber defense became the company's flagship product. But while top analysts such as Gartner and Forrester rank Group-IB among the best providers in the world, there is another twist.

The most advanced technologies will not work unless you know who your enemy is, how he acts, and what tools he uses. Knowledge lies at the heart of security systems in the modern digital world. During its nearly 15 years of investigating cybercrime, Group-IB has now built up a vast database. From the very start, Sachkov and his team collected information about hackers—the people, rather than Trojans and their signatures. The company's database now contains over 100,000 profiles of criminals and hacker groups. The company's specialists monitor underground hacker forums tracking criminal activity and new malware.

For many years, no one else apart from Group-IB was able to get insider information from the darkest corners of the cyber world. Let's not forget that huge changes have taken place over the years. The era of geek hackers is over. Cybercrime has become organized, technology-based, and transnational. Major companies that invest astronomical amounts of money in cybersecurity are still affected by major incidents and face ongoing and evolving challenges. Their enemies are formidable organizations.

Money is the key motivating factor for cyber criminals. Nearly 98% of all global cybercrime involves money theft. Getting hold of cash with minimal risk is the prime aim for cyber criminals, which is why they now choose banks, financial institutions, and their affluent customers as their main targets.

Hackers have chosen Russia as a testing ground. Since the beginning of the new century, all the new cybercrime schemes and tools have been tested in Russia—it is only after they have proved to be successful that they move on to international targets.

Major threat intelligence companies today are mostly American and British. They probably have a perfect understanding of the general landscape of cyber threats, but are not always up to speed on the local specifics. This is due to linguistic, mental, or psychological differences between different parts of the world. According to Europol (the European Union's police service and an official partner of Group-IB), 85% of all cybercrime investigations are related to Russian-speaking gangs (both from Russia and other post-Soviet countries). "Russian hackers" has become a brand name of sorts and today, many gangs around the world pose as coming from their midst; for instance, the North Korean Lazarus group, or even hackers with links to Western security agencies.

Group-IB is able to foresee trends. Its HI-TECH CRIME TRENDS 2016 report was the first to warn of the risks of new types of attacks against critical infrastructure facilities. Unfortunately, the forecast turned out to be correct. That year, the Black Energy group attacked Ukraine's power grid and financial systems. They had obtained new tools that allowed remote terminal units (RTUs), responsible for the physical opening/closing of power grids, to be controlled from far away. Recently, European Union and United Kingdom companies have also become the targets of such attacks.

The laws of economics apply to the cyber world: The most innovative solutions are created in free and highly competitive markets. Russia is where a majority of the vulnerabilities, viruses, and delivery methods are prototyped and used by criminal gangs, which compete viciously with each other in attacking their targets—preferably financial institutions. These criminals develop digital weapons that can also be used by both security services and terrorists. At the same time and given the economic rewards of successful cybercrime, states are in a difficult position; acting independently they lack sufficient resources to guarantee cybersecurity.

Private companies, including those deeply embedded in Russian networks such as such as Group-IB, are therefore key players in the combat against global cybercrime, and making the world a safer place in the digital age.

10

How to Sell Roses?

Russian Robots on the March

Dmitri Sinitsin

An unorthodox Russian company has been making the news in the West for the last couple of years. Its products are neither extracted from Russia's rich soil, nor used to kill or wreak cyber havoc. Few would expect Russia to feature prominently in robotics but Promobot often steals the show with its charm and adventurousness.

Established in 2014, Promobot has quickly become Russia's largest manufacturer of humanoid entertainment and service robots. A high-tech startup from the provinces that refuses to move to Moscow (which usually sucks in talent from all over the country), Promobot quickly got the attention of journalists. After attracting the interest of President Vladimir Putin, Prime Minister Dmitry Medvedev, and Moscow mayor, Sergey Sobyanin at various shows, it even became a media darling. By August 2017, the company had deployed over 240 robots priced between EUR 8,000–16,000 in

The Life of Russian Business, pages 181–184

numerous locations across Russia, China, the Czech Republic, Kazakhstan, and Ireland. The bots go into service as promoters, store and service center assistants, museum guides, concierges, and indoor delivery boys. At the moment, the management is considering branching out into robot applications for other businesses.

Promobot is owned by the five founders and the Internet Initiative Development Fund (IIDF), which invested 150 million rubles (about US$ 2 million) in late 2016. The team behind Promobot initially got together with the idea that the residents of Perm, a city in the heart of Russia close to the Ural Mountains, would love someone else to shoulder their snow shoveling burdens. The city gets 150 snowy days per year on average. Their first robotic snow plow didn't sell all that well, but led the team to an incubation program in Russia and eventually brought them in touch with their second angel investor and future CEO, Alexey Yuzhakov.

Hailing from the same town and university as the team, Yuzhakov had already earned his stripes in the digital space as the successful CEO of a large regional specialized IT integrator. Decisive and extremely focused, he immediately pivoted the product and implemented it as a promotional device to benefit his own 2,300 square meter "smart flower greenhouse." He was looking for a way to boost the retail sales of roses. The promotion campaign ramped up sales by 240%, and Yuzhakov decided he had struck gold. His relentless networking helped the team quickly sell the first twenty Promobot V.1's to malls around Russia for a total of 9 million rubles.

V.1 looked like a water dispenser with a screen in its belly and two blue eyes in a table tennis bat-shaped head. Discontinued by January 2015, it was succeeded by the much more attractive V.2, which quickly became the most frequent robotic entertainer at various exhibitions and conferences in Russia.

While V.2 was an upgrade of V.1, Promobot V.3 was conceived as a parallel product with vastly expanded functionality. Launched in October 2016 and equipped with a powerful cognitive engine, it found its way to such customers as the Russian Pension Fund, Sberbank, Azbuka Vkusa (an upmarket grocery chain), Henkel, and the Russian Modern History Museum, performing a repertoire of roles including receptionist, concierge, store assistant, bank teller, and museum guide.

V.3 is promoted as an assistant robot that can replace human staff in a variety of functions. This positioning works since the "wow" effect of an entertainment bot soon wears off. Service robots are a burgeoning industry valued globally at over US$ 10 billion per annum and predicted to grow at a compound annual growth rate (CAGR) of 16.5% for the next 5 years.

The fastest growing segment of the industry is household cleaning bots exemplified by Massachusetts headquartered iRobot's Roomba autonomous robotic vacuum cleaners (over 12 million units sold worldwide) and its numerous imitators. Promobots, however, belong in a niche with professional service robots, such as those used for surgery or firefighting that account for two thirds of the total service robot sales.

While the global robotics market is expanding rapidly, competition is fierce. According to the International Federation of Robotics (IFR), in 2016 there were 625 service robot manufacturers globally. At the same time, the Russian robot market is still in its infancy—in terms of industrial robot density, Russia ranks second from the bottom according to IFR data,[1] and service robot penetration is similarly low. In total, less than 1% of all robots worldwide are being operated in Russia, and domestic manufacturers mostly focus on defense and space applications. However, the growth potential is significant as Russian demographic and economic trends will make robots ever more attractive, while approximately a thousand robotics engineers graduate every year from Russian universities, according to the SKOLKOVO Robotics Center.

Promobot's fast-growing R&D team designed V.3 as an advanced platform that incorporates leading technologies. Simultaneous detection of several people helps the robot communicate better; payment terminals and check printers make the robot a mobile point-of-sale; a cognitive engine based on a neural network allows the system to master new knowledge quickly; and wireless collection of data supports faster and deeper analysis of customer interactions. Promobot is happy to engage with their clients in joint development efforts, customizing robots for individual applications—for instance, teams are now exploring different business cases with a large Russian bank.

The company also has a knack for PR stunts. Every 3 months or so, their robots escape test grounds, save children from falling racks and run marathons. YouTube videos featuring the "robot escape" have amassed millions of views, and the media loves the R2D2-like personality implemented in new Promobots.

Today, Promobot is among the market leaders and its relatively low costs have helped it succeed in the domestic market and attract a growing cadre of overseas clients. However, Promobot's CEO is keenly aware of a likely industry consolidation in the near future, as well as the sheer market power of service industry giants such as Softbank and Google, and industrial robotics leaders such as KUKA or FANUC. Any of these companies might easily enter its niche if they see the potential for a good return. To continue to be successful, the firm needs to scale up and extensively leverage global standards.

This leads to another challenge—capacity. The company has a manufacturing facility in its home city of Perm which caps production at 200 units per year. To take on Softbank's Pepper (positioned as an "emotional robot" intended "to make people happy" and mostly used as a receptionist), or Pal Robotic's REEM-H2 (which targets the same market of promotion robotics), Yuzhakov believes that Promobot will need to start producing at least 5 times that number.

Note

1. IFR (2016). World Robotics 2016 Edition. https://ifr.org/ifr-press-releases/news/world-robotics-report-2016

11

The Internet Initiatives Development Fund (IIDF)

Kirill Varlamov's Public–Private Partnership to Accelerate Entrepreneurship

Tomas Casas i Klett
Jiatao (J. T.) Li

"Only a few years ago nobody invested in pre-seed projects; early stage ventures got nothing," noted Kirill Varlamov, the founding CEO of the Internet Initiatives Development Fund (IIDF), at the beginning of our lunch interview. Ambitious start-ups in Russia faced a variety of insurmountable obstacles, but the lack of proper institutions seemed to be at the core of this unhappy situation. According to Varlamov:

> The Russian legal system lacked key instruments for entrepreneurship, such as shareholder agreements and different share classes. Young start-ups were forced to structure the deals in jurisdictions abroad. This was both expensive and time consuming.

The Life of Russian Business, pages 185–189

Much has changed since the founding of IIDF in 2013. IIDF is a venture capital (VC) fund plus start-up accelerator launched by Russia's Agency for Strategic Initiatives at the behest of the country's president. Varlamov's mandate at the helm of this public-private partnership goes beyond identifying early-stage technology and Internet venture teams in Russia. What was his initial key task? Obviously, "to provide cheap money."

To do so, Varlamov and his team had to contribute to the industry's development, by introducing a number of legal initiatives. They took a total of 14 rules from British law and "reconstructed them" to fit Russian practice. For instance, *option agreements*, a legally binding conditional obligation to buy or sell shares upon the occurrence of a specific event, were introduced. So were *representations and warranties*, contractual and statutory requirements to provide a counterparty with reliable and truthful information and compensate losses derived from supplying false information. *Indemnity*, the obligation to compensate counterparties in case of direct and indirect negative consequences of one's actions, even if not known at the moment of transaction signing, was also not part of the Russian legal code. The Russian legal variants are not copied word by word, but conceptually are very advanced. As a result of IIDF's efforts, by 2017, "Russia's legal framework for start-ups is on a par with the best of the world."

Good laws, however, are not sufficient. These need to be enforced and Varlamov recounts his own reaction when the first court judgements testing the newly introduced legislation came out, "we were surprised, positively." Specifically:

> We have always been worried about the courts. We thought they could not understand the new legislation. But you know what, they did very well. Correct judgments on complex matters like stock options were passed.

IIDF is getting support from the top. On the wall behind Varlamov's desk hangs a picture of him next to the Russian president, similar to one at the fund's homepage.[1] This is a double-edged sword of sorts, as such support from the top means significant pressure to perform. That means that at the end of the day, IIDF will be judged on the results at the four acceleration program levels that it offers.

The first top-level program is now in its fourth year. It consists of intakes of 35 companies that are accelerated over a period of 3 months. By the end of 2017, the 13th intake had gone through the process. Besides acceleration, start-ups also receive an investment in rubles worth US$ 35,000 ("This amount gets you very far in Russia; in Silicon Valley this is the equivalent of US$ 150,000"). How much equity does IIDF get for its investment?

"Always 7%, as early stage firms are impossible to value." This is the same 7% pre-money valuation Y Combinator[2] takes, albeit in exchange for about US$ 120,000. At IIDF, as is the case at other accelerators, only firms that complete the acceleration program receive the funding. How different is Russia's main acceleration program from programs elsewhere?

> We did worldwide research in places like Israel, the United States, and Germany and we realized we cannot copy exactly what they are doing. The maturity of their startups is quite different than in Russia. That is, there is much less knowledge here in marketing and sales, while we are usually very strong in programming. We also have to emphasize that the focus of a start-up is *business*. Our program has two parts. First a tracker, a hard coach, who pushes the founder team through the process, asks unpleasant questions, determines areas of improvement and recommends what to learn. Then we offer expertise via master classes. Every single company we meet claims, "We are seed." No matter, we tell them, "You have to run through our program. Afterwards you are seed."

Unlike the first level acceleration that occurs at the Moscow premises, a second level acceleration program takes place across Russia's 10 biggest cities. Over two months, IIDF supplies education, experts and tracking. It invests no money in the ventures and does not take any shares. About 500 companies go through this level each year and Varlamov believes "the program is still not big enough."

The third level offering is online acceleration and limited only to tech entrepreneurs. The main purpose of this level is to answer one question: "What do I do with my idea?" This level is based around a survey of 450 items, which are filtered for each type of project (on average it takes 105 answers to complete the form). Then there is a library of 45 videos, each 5 to 10 minutes in length, that cover specific topics related to the survey questions. What started with 2,500 firms in 2015 has scaled to 7,000 projects in 2017. One of the reasons of its attractiveness is the "industry acceleration" angle. IIDF has invested in industry profiles such as medical, telecoms, finance, retail, and even railroads. Experts and leaders in the different markets are invited to develop the content and offer master classes. "We fill in the knowledge gaps. We propose a very standard way to structure ideas. Investors can then decide whether to invest, or they can have a Skype call with the founder teams."

The fourth level is acceleration at universities. Here, the flipped classroom pedagogy is employed; lectures are online and in the classroom the professor works on the student's questions. This initiative's extent is massive on the delivery side; about 300 professors from 144 universities are involved. The program's emphasis, as the name, *Technological Entrepreneurs,* reveals, is on "how to find the right idea for my startup." In 2016—its first year—5,000 students enrolled; in 2017 the number doubled to 10,000. This service is free.

What about the VC angle of IIDF?

> Of the 7,500 companies per year that go through our first three program levels, we invest annually in 75 to 80. This adds up to 350 companies already funded, for a total of US$ 70 million. Besides the graduating firms funded by ourselves after acceleration, we see about 30% of start-ups making it to the next round on their own. About 25% shut down, which is what we ask them to do if they don't succeed. Another 45% are zombies, meaning they make some money, but do not grow fast enough to be interesting for venture investors.

An accelerator is a long-term bet and IIDF is still young; to ascertain its financial success will take another two to three years. But confidence is not an issue with Varlamov. Could IIDF launch global unicorns expanding into America or China? "Yes, we are ready."

Along with the acceleration program and beyond its performance metrics, Varlamov's mission is to build an ecosystem. Its 5,000 square meters facilities in the center of Moscow have a genuine creative space look and feel. Three old refurbished buildings were connected and retrofitted with the latest equipment while the walls are still the original red brick. The atmosphere and buzz is no different from that of any accelerator in the West. The ecosystem focuses on founders, but also aims to become the biggest investment platform in Russia. Its existing 50 investment partners are a start.

As critical to the ecosystem as entrepreneurs and investors are the large established firms seeking innovation by teaming up with new ventures. This intrapreneurial angle of IIDF is coming to life and at the end of 2017 there were about 70 different pilots where corporations paid for the use of start-up services or products. This side of the ecosystem is also valuable in terms of education. It is a known fact that established firms in Russia do not know how to deal with entrepreneurs. "No big companies want to buy start-ups. Hence we have to teach them—both sides—to be comfortable with each other."

After lunch we returned to Varlamov's office and he pointed to the building next door; the landlord is converting his 3,000 square meters of space into a start-up incubator. When I asked him if he welcomes the move, Varlamov responded in a matter of fact way: "Are you asking me if they are competition? Not at all, this is also part of our ecosystem. Their investment confirms that we are igniting something in Russia."[3]

Notes

1. www.iidf.ru
2. Y Combinator has been called "the world's most powerful start-up incubator" by the U.S. business magazine, *Fast Company*. (https://www.fastcompany.com/section/the-y-combinator-chronicles)
3. This contribution was researched and prepared in 2017 and early 2018. A comprehensive and more recent account of IIDF situation and development dilemmas is available in a teaching case study. The details are: Tomas Casas and Jiatao (J.T.) Li, "Accelerating Russia: The Internet Initiatives Development Fund (IIDF)," The Hong Kong University of Science and Technology (HKUST) and Moscow School of Management SKOLKOVO (SKOLKOVO) case no. HS1 (HKUST and SKOLKOVO, October 2018), via HKUST Thompson Center for Business Case Studies, http://www.cbcs.ust.hk, accessed 31 October 2018.

IV

Internationalization, Outbound, and Inbound

SECTION IV

Introduction

Russia is the proverbial bridge connecting East and West. It is the only state that has borders with both the EU and China and even has a maritime border with the United States. It is at the heart of Eurasia with strong links to both the Muslim and Jewish worlds. And yet, Russia does not figure prominently in global trade and investment accounts. Beyond the modest macro figures, however, Russian firms are starting to look outwardly and learn how to expand internationally. As latecomers to the game, their internationalization approaches can be both bold and original. Equally interesting is how foreigners approach Russia. The country and the CIS have become emergent destinations with various degrees of attractiveness for many companies—and not just Western multinationals.

The subject is framed by the *Wall Street Journal* version of the classic article by Fey and Shekshnia: "How to Do Business in Russia" (Chapter IV.1). The section then turns to the East, with a paradoxical view: "Why We Need to Look to the West to Turn to the East" (Chapter IV.2). To illustrate the challenges of the pivot to China, we follow with two riveting cases from the frontlines written by Egor Pereverzev, a China hand from the Belgorod region, that showcase how opportunities are actually pursued (Chapters IV.3 and IV.4). The next turn is West, to the Baltics, where Timurs Umans, an academic based in Sweden, questions whether Latvia's love–hate relationship with Russia could bridge the gap between Russia and the West (Chapter IV.5). In terms of who can perform the actual bridging, what is

The Life of Russian Business, pages 193–194

the role of expatriate Russians? The perspective presented in "The Enchanted Generation" is why Russian managers are not in high demand abroad (Chapter IV.6).

Three cases of outbound Russian firms follow. Their travails, ingenuity, and, yes, success, depict at times unconventional but also effective approaches to internationalization (Chapters IV.7, IV.8, and IV.9). The two final pieces in this section change the vantage point with inbound perspectives. The entry of foreign manufacturing technologies into Russia is reviewed by referencing Soviet industrialization. There is a continuity of sorts today with joint ventures and other cooperation arrangements made by some of the world's leading multinationals (Chapter IV.10). Individuals, too, have come to Russia seeking to realize their entrepreneurial dreams, which might not always turn out to be all that sweet. One Swiss entrepreneur, Walter Denz, closes the circle with the section's final article as he shares the remarkable story of his own venture launched in the legendary 1990s. In "Russia Is About Business" he provides essential practical advice (Chapter IV.11).

From East to West and from inbound to outbound, these pieces aim to expand the business repertoire of foreign investors and traders wishing to do business in Russia, or with Russians. Surprising and even shocking in some respects, the thoughts and ideas are entertaining throughout. For the international management scholar, wishing to understand the particularities of emerging market firms reaching out to global markets, this section is likely to be a treat.

IV 1

How to Do Business in Russia[1]

Carl F. Fey
Stanislav Shekshnia

Russia has much to attract foreign investors—a fast rate of growth in gross domestic product, a large population and a substantial expansion in purchasing power. But its unique and sometimes murky business environment has left Russia with a reputation as being a difficult place to set up shop.

How can international companies overcome the difficulties and reap the rewards of doing business in Russia?

Based on interviews with executives from 36 foreign companies operating in Russia, as well as our own business experience there, here are eight commandments aimed at helping Western companies prosper.

The Life of Russian Business, pages 195–197

Commandment 1: Practice Authoritative, Not Authoritarian, Leadership

Russians value strong, highly involved leaders who gain authority and trust through competence. Effective leaders in Russia communicate a compelling vision, deliver superior results, and share responsibility and success with followers. A hands-off management style, on the other hand, is often mistaken for weakness.

Commandment 2: Build a Strong Organizational Culture With Visible Foreign Elements

Russians are drawn to work cultures where employees are respected, made to feel part of a team and encouraged to achieve their full potential because these weren't traditional elements of Russian national work practices. Western companies should preserve and play up these qualities, even as their top management becomes more Russian. A strong organizational culture also helps guide employees' actions.

Commandment 3: Work to Create an Empowered Organization, Step-By-Step

Convincing Russian employees to make decisions and show initiative is difficult because they weren't encouraged to do so in the past. Creating an empowered organization should be a gradual process that begins with a promise not to punish employees for making honest mistakes.

Commandment 4: Respect Local Rules, But Play Your Own Game

Don't try to copy the business models of Russian partners or competitors because it is tough to beat them at their own game. The foreign companies that most often flourish in Russia are those that apply, with some local adaptations, the business models that have led to success elsewhere.

Commandment 5: Stand Firm on Major Goals and Be Flexible on Details

In Russia's changeable environment, some say planning is impossible. We say it is a necessity. Setting and sticking with long-term goals, while being flexible about the way those goals are pursued helps guide employees through the sea of uncertainty.

Commandment 6: Learn to Live and Manage in a Crisis

Russia is very predictable—something unexpected is sure to happen every day. Companies must be prepared not only to put out fires but to spot the opportunities that grow out of them. Firms can work to reduce surprises by implementing early-warning systems—such as additional checkpoints on long-range projects to spot delays at early stages.

Commandment 7: Recognize That Corruption Is Omnipresent in Russia and Must Be Managed

Managing corruption is a necessity in Russia. To deal with it, companies can try several options. They can outsource to other companies activities that are prone to corruption. They can preempt corruption by proposing a deal that doesn't violate the company's ethical standards. One firm we know of offered complimentary products to officials in return for daily reports on the products' performance, testing from which the company benefited. Companies also can wait to enter the business at a later stage, or they can pass on deals in which corruption can't be avoided. Russians will test a company's corruption strategy, so standing firm is key.

Commandment 8: Cultivate Relationships With Government Agencies at All Levels

Getting to know people is important in Russia, where politicians and government agencies continue to have arbitrary power over business. Often attention, and not bribery, is what is most important. A company's top executives should make regular visits to government officials, invite bureaucrats to visit and get involved in local welfare or training programs.

Note

1. This article is republished with permission from Fey, C. F. and Shekshnia, S. 2007. The key commandments of doing business in Russia. *The Wall Street Journal.* October 19, 2007: R4.

IV 2

Russia's Pivot Towards Asia

Why We Need to Look to the West to Turn to the East

Andrey Shapenko

After Vladimir Putin's visit to the APEC Summit in China in late 2016, Russia's mass media started to discuss "the pivot to the East" with renewed enthusiasm. This is ironic, as Russia has previously underestimated China's potential. We are now at the other extreme, our earlier bias replaced by an overestimation of the opportunities. If Russian firms do venture to the East they ought not to overlook the challenges that their Western counterparts have experienced in China over the last 20 years.

There is no question that Russia will have to build a closer relationship with China. The pivot to the East is not a short-term approach to avoid inconvenient Western partners; it is the restoration to its proper significance of the Asia-Pacific region in Russia's foreign economic ties. But today, China has become a very complex market even for experienced global players. It is evolving from an enormous assembly site into a fully-fledged

The Life of Russian Business, pages 199–202

global competitor with advantages beyond just cheap labor. That has meant "repatriation" of production facilities for global firms like Caterpillar, GE, or Ford. Other global players, including Revlon, MediaMarkt, Yahoo, and Tesco, have had to leave China for good due to growing local competition or falling profitability. What challenges does Russia need to tackle to be able to play its Eastern card with full effect?

First, there is the matter of vast geography and the lack of infrastructure. Despite seemingly in close vicinity, the two countries' key regions (in terms of demographics and economic activity) are very far from each other. About 80% of Russia's population and 70% of its GDP are concentrated in the Western/European part of the country. At the same time, 70% of the Chinese population and up to 80% of China's GDP are accounted for by the 15 South-Eastern provinces of the country. The distance between Moscow and Shenzhen is equal to the distance between Moscow and New York. This, coupled with the low density of population in the territories in-between, makes China a rather distant business partner. There will always be opportunities for close economic collaboration and growth, and especially for cross-border trade, between the neighboring Russian Far East and China's Heilongjiang province, but these are marginal in terms of the greater economic picture.

The second obstacle is a significant difference in culture and business practices. China has historically seen Russia as a Christian culture with its values being closer to those of European or even Arab countries, rather than those of Asia. One example of such cross-cultural differences that lead to a heated international discussion was President Putin's act at the APEC summit: He wrapped a shawl around the shoulders of China's first lady who was getting cold—something Western culture would interpret as a gallant gesture was seen in the East as a violation of private space.

A third obstacle is joint ventures. For Western firms, like Volkswagen, these have proven to be an effective method of gaining entry to the Chinese market. But, joint ventures have never been a characteristic strength of Russian business and virtually no national company has succeeded in international expansion through such partnerships in recent decades. Even joint ventures in the Russian market often become business cases on how to study corporate conflict, with the Russian-British TNK-BP oil venture being a stark example.[1]

A fourth challenge is the issue of negotiation with Chinese partners, who are used to conducting them from a position of strength and always seek specific economic benefits. The position of Russia here is hardly enviable, as China does not seem to desperately need anything Russia can offer, other than possibly raw materials, space, defense, and nuclear technology. Two thirds of Russian exports to China are natural resources and wood, while Russia imports Chinese high added-value products, such as equipment and vehicles, as well as many commodities. China is Russia's second most important trading partner after the European Union, while Russia as we saw in Chapter I.3, seldom makes the top ten list of the most important trading partners of China. Russia needs China much more than China needs Russia, and her Chinese trading partners cannot help but take advantage of that fact. One example is the Russian gas supply negotiations that continued for more than a decade before Russia had to make significant concessions.

A fifth challenge is shortage of China expertise. If Russia aims at increasing its trade volumes with China several-fold, it must, as soon as possible, train many more specialists capable of interpreting China's culture codes, conducting negotiations, penetrating the twists and turns of intra-party strife and navigating the regulatory environment, all while setting up successful businesses.

A sixth challenge is that after President Xi Jinping came to power, China launched an uncompromising struggle with corruption which affected many top politicians and businessmen. Being fearful of prosecution, local entrepreneurs are now far more cautious and thoroughly vet their partners, especially for major projects. This can impact cooperation with Russia, given the existing—and less than rosy—image of Russia and major government corporations. Should Russian business become more westernized in order to positively change its image when venturing East?

The answer, I believe, is yes. Generally speaking, and in the spirit of Chinese stratagems, before turning to the East, Russia must work more closely with the West. First, most of the large infrastructure projects Russia is currently planning cannot succeed without Western technologies. Even flagship projects like the "Power of Siberia" gas pipeline are unlikely to be completed without Western equipment. This opens up many opportunities for trilateral economic partnerships, the benefits of which should put any political issues on the back burner.

We should welcome existing and former top managers of global Western companies to become our guides in the Chinese market. Sometimes, the Chinese are the first ones to look for such experts in order to expand their businesses or to bring new projects and technologies to the country. The international experience accumulated by China over the last 20 years is mostly based on Western engagement models.

The pivot of the Russian economy towards China is a comprehensive and long-term objective which cannot be implemented without massive effort and learning. In this regard, it is necessary for Russia to more effectively leverage European and American experiences in China.

Note

1. TNK-BP was a joint venture between British BP and AAR, a consortium of three Russian oil firms. At its peak, TNK-BP was a Global Top 10 private oil company and number 3 in Russia. While very profitable, the venture was plagued by corporate scandals stemming from disagreements between British and the Russian partners. The venture was acquired by Russian state-controlled oil company Rosneft in 2013.

IV 3

Fighting for Every Cent and Fen

Russian Firm Builds Lean Sourcing Network in China[1]

Egor Pereverzev

Russian companies builidng supply chains and sourcing networks in China face enormous challenges. Compared to their U.S. and European counterparts, Russian firms had a very late start. By the late 1990s, only a few Russian firms had the competencies necessary to produce and purchase in China, and there was scant understanding of the Chinese market, value chains, industry structures and the cost of capital. This has been changing rapidly over the last decade.

In 2002, two young businessmen from Moscow, Alexander Goldman and Sergey Nestorov, owners of EK Electric, met with Chinese entrepreneur Wang Li. At the time Wang was the export director of Zint—China and the world's largest producer of circuit breakers and low-voltage switchgear. The meeting took place in Wenzhou, a city in Zhejiang, a province famous for the acumen of its business people, and was organized by a Russian

The Life of Russian Business, pages 203–206

consultancy, Tex Logistics, that had recently established a company there. Business was so good that Director Wang left his job at Zint to organize his own manufacturing enterprise, SEA Electric. In the next few years, his business model became clear: SEA Electric was purchasing thousands of stock keeping units (SKUs) from the local suppliers. It would then add packaging and stickers and sell the equipment to Tex Logistics at a reasonable margin. They would then in turn sell products to EK making money on the 17% VAT rebate, logistics, and also charging 3% for quality control and new product search. In a few years, this cooperation created three large companies: EK Electric, Tex Logistics, and SEA Electric.

A decade later in 2012, the Russian market was very different from when the business model was conceived. All the signs of saturation were present, with suppliers competing hard for a small group of key customers. That is, suppliers were no longer gaining market share; rather they would take it from each other in exchange for a costly cut in their own profit margins. Chinese suppliers further aggravated the situation by flooding the market with low quality products. Unlike the established brands, who were keen to ensure that their products satisfied international safety norms, small firms were importing switches that did not possess any protective functions. Such products would often cost less than half the price of a piece of normal equipment, looked the same, but did often not protect from electric shocks or overload. Last but not least, the world's leading brand, Schneider Electric, had acquired Deliksi—the second largest Chinese producer of circuit breakers—and soon followed suit by buying the Russian brand DeKraut. Using this new strategy and cutting costs both upstream and downstream, Schneider's DeKraut products were sold in Russia at very low prices, aggressively expanding their market share in the low-end segment. The era of fat profit margins was over.

At the Chinese end of the supply chain the situation was even worse. In 2007, Chinese Premier Wen Jiabao had famously stated: "The Chinese economy as it currently stands is unstable, unbalanced, uncoordinated, and ultimately unsustainable." The policies that followed led to an increase in taxation and salaries within the industrial clusters of China's coastal cities. Migrant workers, who were the bulk of the blue-collar workforce in the East, started relocating nearer to their native homes where they could work on government infrastructure projects while staying closer to their families. The situation was further aggravated by demographics: Over the previous 30 years the average population age had gone from that of a developing country (around 27 years of age) to that of a developed country (over 37 years of age). The Chinese workforce had become increasingly scarce and expensive.

Cutting Out the Middleman

From 2010, the EK owners had been working hard to cut costs within the supply chain. The company's turnover exceeded US$ 10 million, but in Russia, EK now faced difficulties competing. The multiple cost-reduction projects with SEA Electric and Tex Logistics had little impact on overall cost savings. Meanwhile, prices in the Russian market kept decreasing, posing a growing and considerable threat. The owners realized that a conflict of interest existed across the partners in the value chain, which effectively inhibited further cost cuts. The status quo gave SEA and Tex sizable margins at the expense of EK's interests. It was time for EK to take the supply chain under its control.

Within a few months, EK was working hard to hire world-class product and quality engineers, beefing up its China product management team and creating a China-based export department. The China headquarters were in Shanghai, structured as a 100% foreign-owned export company.

By the end of 2013, EK had taken control of over 80% of its business in China. The hardest part was to negotiate new direct cooperation with suppliers, as many of them had been very comfortable cooperating with the Chinese-owned SEA and were not willing to delve in international trade.

The high risks of international credit transactions had traditionally acted as an impediment to trade between China and developing countries. To release this pent up potential, the Chinese government established the China Credit Insurance Corporation (Sinosure). Using insurance from Sinosure, Chinese producers could obtain loans from Chinese banks and use them to provide favorable credit terms to their clients in developing and under-developed countries. EK had all of its key suppliers join the Sinosure scheme, allowing EK to reduce the cost of capital by switching from Russian interest rates to significantly lower rates in China. This move unlocked considerable value, even though running one's own operations in China wasn't cheap.

With the newly gained market understanding, EK abandoned its previous single strategic supplier approach, even though this sourcing mode had been widely supported by consultants and was even endorsed by the business literature. The new priority was to define and contract two qualified suppliers for each product category. Most Chinese suppliers, which were clustered in Zhejiang province, had huge catalogues of products yet very few were quality manufacturers in a given product category. Most bought from each other and relabeled their wares. By 2014, EK had managed to find at least two key suppliers for each critical product category, and now could choose between SEA and an alternative. As a strategic counter-move, SEA invested into their own brand and operations in Russia, establishing an office in Moscow and hiring every EK staff member they could get their hands on. The two companies became competitors even though their business relationship continued.

In late 2016, favorable low price dynamics in the global raw materials markets changed against all expectations. Unsatisfied with low yields on real estate, Chinese speculators flooded the commodities markets rapidly increasing volatility. Within 2 months, prices for electric copper in China increased from RMB 37,000 to RMB 45,000 per ton. Iron, zinc, and other metals followed suit. Suppliers across the country started raising prices. SEA, squeezed by the high costs of its own Russian operations, raised prices by a ridiculous 8%, cutting deep into EK's profit margins. EK responded by transferring their orders to the second supplier.

It quickly became apparent that the second supplier did not have enough capacity to cope with the order volume required. EK found itself in a tough position: either forgo profit on half the orders; or reduce order volumes. The latter choice still meant producing as much as they could at their second supplier's factory. EK also had the option of trying to find an alternative third supplier, but that would take time. No matter what the negotiation outcomes would be, it was clear to the Russian company that taking over the supply chain to win every cent or *fen* in China came with its particular set of challenges and costs.

Note

1. This case is based on factual events while the company and protagonist names have been anonymized.

IV 4

One Tight Belt, One Hard Road

A Chinese Private Firm's Belt and Road Initiative (BRI) Investment[1]

Egor Pereverzev

He Lisan,[2] managing director of the Chinese family-owned New Horizon International Holdings, was sleepless on his flight from Beijing to Moscow. In his mind he kept returning to the critical situation he would face upon reaching his destination. How did it all end up like this? Only 18 months ago an engineering consultancy in Shanghai had proposed taking over the responsibility for his investment project in a post-Soviet country for a management fee the equivalent to 5% of its overall cost, a cool US$ 17 million. In no ambiguous terms they let He Lisan know that his firm had neither the critical technical skills nor the experience to run the multi-million dollar turn-key project. At that time He Lisan had laughed the proposal off, but now his rejection of the offer seemed absurd.

The Life of Russian Business, pages 207–212

It had all started in early 1990s, when He Lisan's father, He Jinyu, a former government official and a dedicated Communist Party member, laid the foundations for his family's prosperity by building a power station in a city in Northeastern China. This power station and a lucrative supply contract with China Railways that followed a few years later became the sources of steady revenues and soon the family had money to invest.

He Jinyu invested in a free-trade zone in the nearby Russian Far Eastern city of Nakhodka. The Russian Far Eastern region was heavily underdeveloped and in his opinion presented a great number of opportunities for international business: China, Russia, Japan, and South Korea were all located nearby. He Jinyu invested in building commercial real estate and a hotel. He then sent his younger son He Lisan to learn Russian and to help to develop the overseas business for the family.

He Lisan had a great time in Russia. A gifted and fast thinker he quickly learned very good Russian and immersed himself into emerging Russian capitalism. A combination of funds to invest, connections, and speed helped him make quick money virtually out of thin air. Yet by 2005, the scope of his trading business did not feel "big enough" and he decided to return to China. He was very good at dealing with people, he loved making profits, and he was agile at making deals. On the other hand, processes and paperwork did not fascinate him, so the family hired their first professional top manager, Xu Jianmin, to run the international trading arm of New Horizon International in Beijing.

The trading company expanded a very profitable cooperation with Chinese Railways and was selling railway stock made in China to Middle Eastern markets. To ensure smooth operations, New Horizon International employed former high-ranking officials at China's Ministry of Foreign Affairs and Ministry of Commerce (MOFCOM). A team of young Russian-speaking managers was hired and they started visiting the embassies of former Soviet Republics, now part of the Commonwealth of Independent States (CIS) countries. In the first year over 1,000 contacts were made, 200 meetings held and innumerable expensive dinners were enjoyed. The strategy worked: A former Soviet republic in Central Asia was having a hard time meeting deadlines for fit-out work at the Presidential Palace. It was a chance for He Lisan to show what he was capable of. It took 6 days for He Lisan to establish an office in Western China from where he coordinated the logistics of construction materials, furniture, and over 100 Chinese construction workers who were quickly sent to the construction site. Within 60 days the palace was ready and decorated to the joy of the country's president. A new business era for New Horizon International had begun. A decade later, this project would be considered part of China's Belt and Road Initiative (BRI).

The successful renovation project led to a stream of small- and medium-sized projects in the Central Asian republic. They were coordinated from a tiny unofficial office in the country's capital. The office was managed by a Muslim-Chinese manager, which opened many doors in the capital as locals enjoyed cooperating with a fellow Muslim rather than a non-religious Han Chinese. The stream of new projects lasted until top government officials involved in this cooperation were removed.

By that time, however, He Lisan's team had been working hard to open the markets of larger CIS countries, of which Russia represented the most interesting opportunity. In the early 1990s, Russia was buying virtually everything from Chinese factories. Russian companies paid with cash and used shadowy channels to minimize customs' duties. All players had excellent profit margins. By the end of the 2000s, the Russian market showed signs of saturation.

In 2005–2007, oil prices were high and Russia was bursting with business ideas. It seemed as if new business models could be tested. At the same time, China was building mechanisms allowing Chinese companies to seek international project financing from Chinese banks. Part of the model was the purchase of insurance from Sinosure, the state-owned export credit insurance company. Sinosure preferred to provide insurance to projects backed by state guarantees given by foreign governments. In case of insolvency of the local partner, the country's government would repay the Chinese bank, either with money or with an equivalent amount of natural resources. This was one of the biggest obstacles in doing business with Russia because the Russian government did not provide such guarantees. Rumors in Chinese investment circles suggested that by not providing state guarantees, Russia had effectively rejected loans of over US$ 50 billion by 2007.

In the mid-2000s, however, the government of the neighboring post-Soviet state created a plan for the modernization of its wood-processing industry. The newly appointed young minister of construction visited Europe and China to look for potential partners with experience in woodworking industrial projects. In Beijing, the ambassador introduced him to He Lisan. They liked each other and started considering possible ways of cooperation. After 3 years of meetings and bidding, a supply contract worth US$ 11 million in industrial equipment was signed. According to the contract, New Horizon International was to provide high-density fibreboard (HDF)[3] manufacturing equipment to one of the most modern wood-processing plants in the country. In this project, New Horizon International largely acted as a middleman, helping a professional firm from the North of China to carry out communications with the client. However, the project would soon run into difficulties; caused mostly by the laissez-faire attitude and Soviet-style bureaucracy on the one side; and by the lack of adequate engineering competencies on the other.

Amazingly, before this first project was finished, New Horizon International was invited by the government to bid on a new project of a very different magnitude. The state wanted to build a complex cardboard-producing industrial cluster in the north of the country. New Horizon International presented a project financed by the China Construction Bank and insured by Sinosure, with guarantees provided by the government. Having experienced the difficulties with the first project, He Lisan knew that that this was what the Chinese called "a hot potato." That is, a proposition that was both hard to reject and hard to keep in one's hands. However, the overall project volume of US$ 350 million was just too attractive for him to let this chance pass.

New Horizon International did not win the bid first time. He Lisan was devastated, but the friendly official explained to him in private that a little push could still help settle the project in his favor. He Lisan followed the advice and won the tender of his life.

However, very soon he was asked to sign two supplementary agreements, through which New Horizon International would take more responsibility for the project deadlines and delivery. He Lisan signed both agreements and explained to his father that after the project had commenced, he would solve any problems that might arise. Within a few months, New Horizon International received the first payment of US$ 50 million. It was then that He Lisan realized that Sinosure demanded an enormous US$ 27 million insurance fee to be paid upfront in full before releasing the financing. This was nowhere close to the amount New Horizon International had previously discussed with the insurer, but it was now too late to pull out of the project.

After New Horizon International paid the insurance fee, it was on the verge of disaster. Suddenly what was left of the substantial US$ 50 million down payment appeared nowhere near sufficient to purchase equipment, construction materials and deploy 1,000 workers to the country to start construction. And that was just the tip of iceberg. During the first months of work, the Chinese side could not understand why their partners cared so much about procedures, and so little about the goal: finishing the construction of the plant and starting production. It took months before they realized that they had misunderstood their partners from the very beginning. The former Soviet republic side wanted the Chinese general contractor to hire local subcontractors for almost every single job. They did so by asking the Chinese to provide local licenses for the sub-projects. Moreover, they also used other methods to increase their profits from the project including: forcing the Chinese to perform additional work, such as a railway road extension or the building of a bomb shelter; ad hoc, and rather onerous local taxation; and the levying of a slew of fines from countless governmental agencies. According to New Horizon International's estimates, 25% of the overall project value was thus wasted. New Horizon International was going through the circles of hell associated with Soviet-style bureaucracy.

As a response, New Horizon International started cutting costs including cancelling cooperation with the highly regarded engineering consultancy in Shanghai. They did so in secret, unbeknown to the client. This move and others effectively left them empty-handed in terms of technology and engineering capabilities. Still, there was not enough money to start the full-scale construction work. Six months passed by and the construction site remained abandoned farmland with wild grasses growing up to two meters high.

At that point, He Jinyu, the chairman of New Horizon International interfered in his son's work: He replaced the Chinese managing director on the site and appointed his younger son He Peiyang to join his brother and manage the project on site. On arrival at the construction site He Peiyang was shocked when he realized that there were no professional companies providing construction materials and equipment to the project. As managerial duties had not been clearly defined between the two brothers, the situation became increasingly ambiguous in terms of the subordinates' roles and reporting lines.

In any event, He Peiyang did hire Alexandra Ivanova, an experienced local manager who quickly gathered a strong local team of professionals. Alexandra quickly discovered that the bookkeeping done by the local accountants was woefully inadequate. This led to changing the team of accountants and bringing the firm through the painful process of restoring the ledgers and financial reporting. However, building on the construction site had started to progress and hopes grew that the project could still be made a success.

One year into the project, three things happened almost simultaneously. First, the friendly minister was replaced by an experienced government apparatchik, very risk-adverse, who only seemed to care about keeping his post by all means possible. The ministry became unhelpful or downright hostile. All attempts to establish proper relations with the new minister failed. Second, the government initiated a lawsuit against New Horizon International for the previous equipment supply project. They also made it very clear that they would soon consider legal action aimed at taking the second project away from New Horizon International and transferring it to a more competent Chinese firm who could meet deadlines. Finally, as if the existing problems were not enough, Xu Jianmin, the CEO of the Beijing trading arm of New Horizon International, jumped ship taking all his team and the trading business with him. Apparently, he disliked the fact that most of the firm's resources had been redirected towards the new project and used his decades-long connections with clients to grab the business from his former boss. The family patriarch, He Jinyu, would never forget the day he found an empty office when he arrived in Beijing.

Bankruptcy started to loom for the family and its business. Pulling out of the project at this stage was not an option any longer. The power plant they owned was after all the collateral on one of the project loans. On the other hand, continuing the project in a hostile foreign environment without the necessary skills could make the looming disaster even more devastating.

Thinking of all the troubles he faced, He Lisan felt panic in his stomach. He desperately wanted to smoke a cigarette. Yet cruising above the vast Eurasian expanse there were still two more hours before his plane would land in Moscow's Sheremetyevo airport for his connecting flight.

Notes

1. For a more detailed discussion on BRI initiative, also known as the New Silk Road, see contribution Chapter 1.2 "Russia, Perfect Partner? China's Bold Belt and Road Initiative (BRI)" by O. Remyga.
2. This contribution is based on a real story. The names of the participants and geographical locations have been anonymized for confidentiality reasons.
3. High-density fibreboard (HDF), is a type of fibreboard, which is an engineered wood product.

IV 5

Russian Speaking Latvians

A Bridge to the West or Trojan Horse from the East?

Timurs Umans

It was not easy to be a Russian-speaking citizen of Latvia in the 1990s. Sometimes, when on the bus or in the shops one could hear comments such as "Russians go home" or "Occupiers get out of our country." To those Russians who had come to Latvia on job assignments from the rest of the Soviet Union and had built roots in the country, this felt unfair. Many grew up in the country while some had actually been born in Latvia and called that country home.

Many Russian speakers ended up leaving what was actually the land of their birth, unable or unwilling to deal with increasing nationalism and hostile attitudes. Some, however, have stayed. These Russian speakers have chosen one of two types of strategies: "sitting in the trenches" and holding on to Russian culture while resisting everything Latvian; or, as is the case with the majority, trying to adapt to the order of their newly independent

The Life of Russian Business, pages 213–215

nation. This adaptation has included learning and using the Latvian language as well as gaining Latvian citizenship by passing a relatively easy examination. Today, there are a number of indicators of a well-integrated Russian minority in Latvia; with government ministers, members of parliament, and other high-ranked officials whose native language is Russian. There is also a high number of successful businessmen that are of Russian origin. There is a high degree of intra-cultural marriages with no less than the president of Latvia, Raimonds Vējonis, being the notable product of one such union. The list could go on. The nationalistic 1990s are long gone and for the most part a pragmatic business relationship prevails in Latvia. Occasionally, both Russian and Latvian media engage in bouts of demonizing the other side, but business is business.

Russian Latvians represent approximately 40% of the Latvian population compared to only 28% in neighboring Estonia. They comprise both a large consumer group and a key voter group in election after election. The pro-Russian party is one of the largest in the Latvian parliament. So, while at times the Russian media paints a rather sad picture of the Russian Latvians, in reality the group enjoys significant influence. So much so, in fact, that some raise suspicions over whether it may be a fifth column that one day will rise up against Latvia to open the gates for their "relatives" on the Eastern border.

Yet, having a comfortable life inside the European Union with steadily increasing living standards and promises of further subsidics for business goes a long way to ease such tensions. Latvian Russian speakers today are something of a hybrid type; while still positioned within the Russian sphere of cultural influence the overall mentality has become sweepingly European. They are increasingly fluent in both Latvian and English, and one cannot distinguish anymore whether the person you are speaking to is an ethnic Latvian or Latvian Russian (a distinction that in the 1990s was very apparent). Latvian Russians are becoming much more aware of the European nature of their Russian culture and are more than ever ready to do business with mother Russia while positioning themselves in their European/Latvian national context.

In a way, Russian-speaking Latvians are chameleons willing and able to serve two kings. On the one hand, they are aware of the value of their multilingual and multicultural ability (an ability that some Latvian speakers have lost, as learning Russian in the 1990s was not a priority of the education system); their skills are used as a bridge between Russian and the West. On the other hand, the sense of freedom, democracy, and liberalism that the European Union has infused in them might not make the Russian-speakers the Trojan horse of the East that some Latvians once feared. They do not feel the need for a strong Russian-Latvian leader and are happy with liberal parliamentary democracy (even though they will privately admit that both systems have their respective advantages and disadvantages).

Quite a few Russian businesses have spotted the opportunity of having European offices in nearby Riga, where almost everyone speaks Russian (even though the historical idea of Riga being a Russian port is now deeply buried in the past). Others remain skeptical, which is, I believe, a lost opportunity. Latvia is, after all, a small but vibrant European market with a strong Russian heritage. Leveraging Latvia and its sizeable Russian-speaking population as business partners is certainly a proposition worth considering.

IV 6

The Enchanted Generation

Why Russia's Top Managers Are Not Wanted Abroad

Andrey Shapenko

According to a recent survey conducted by Agentstvo Kontakt, in the next 2 years one in six Russian top managers plan to transfer to another country, while 42% of the total plan to emigrate at some stage in their careers.[1] Almost half of all potential emigrants aim for an executive position while one third are thinking about starting their own business. This prompts me to ask two questions. First, will global companies need all of these top Russian managers? Second, will people who have made quick careers during the oil industry boom and convinced themselves of their own super-competence be able to launch a successful business in very competitive and often low-growth overseas markets?

The Life of Russian Business, pages 217–220

Victims of the Crisis

A typical present-day Russian top manager is a man aged between 40 to 50 years old who started his career in the early- or mid-1990s. A manager who successfully rode the wave of recovery growth from 1999 and reached the upper echelons of the corporate hierarchy, bought several apartments, some located outside Russia. He has traveled the world not only as tourist, as he has participated in international projects and has received a business education in Europe or in the United States. His children study at a prestigious college abroad, and he feels fairly well integrated in the global world.

At the same time, Russian top executives as a class have suffered the most from the recent geopolitical and economic crises; the current situation directly affects their interests, lifestyle, and purchasing power. It is not surprising that with falling growth rates, curtailed projects, physical and mental fatigue, and a natural decline in drive, many representatives of this "children of the seventies" generation are seriously thinking of leaving for another country for good. There, they plan to either continue the type of work they have been doing in Russia, or to enter a qualitatively new stage of development and finally launch their own business.

The problem is that when people move to a different cultural and business environment, it is extremely difficult for them to maintain the same level of effectiveness, responsibility, remuneration, and living standard they enjoyed in their home country. The professional competence of managers is assessed by skills in three areas, namely: functional, industry, and soft skills. While functional skills are easily transferred from one culture to another and industry skills can be acquired, soft skills are usually a stumbling block for Russian managers striving to succeed abroad. We are reluctant to admit that apart from tacit knowledge of the Russian market and the Russian language, our managers do not have any fundamental advantages over their foreign counterparts. This is the case with most Russian graduates of foreign MBA programs that suddenly find themselves in a hyper-competitive market and have to actively "sell" themselves. There are thousands of other candidates who are no less qualified, so it is necessary to go far beyond one's competences and comfort zone in order to stand out. In addition, each and every country has "glass ceilings"—invisible barriers to career advancement that "aliens" do not always overcome. This is probably the reason why the majority of successful managers moving abroad in recent years, do, as a rule, still work with Russian or post-Soviet markets.

"Hungry" Competitors

Work experience in Russia does not make an executive's CV more attractive. To make a career in a global corporation, Russian managers need to forget what country they have come from. They will compete for recognition with people from more dynamic environments who are willing to work for less money, are "hungrier," more passionate at what they do, and are better at English. At present, we see more and more corporate CEOs who originate from emerging markets: the legendary Brazilian, Carlos Ghosn at Renault Nissan; the Indian, Ajay Banga at MasterCard; or the Ivorian, Tidjane Thiam at Credit Suisse. However, we have not seen a single Russian, or a representative of an Arab country for that matter, holding a similar office. The few Russians who have reached relatively high positions (CEO minus two) made their way up, as a rule, by obtaining a local education, gaining experience in various markets, as well as going through the painful process of cultural assimilation and the breakdown of mental stereotypes.

At the top echelons of large organizations in the West there are practically no examples of Russian top managers, with a few exceptions like Lev Khasis, who has held senior positions at Walmart. Research stubbornly indicates that most CEOs are nurtured from the inside—the appointment of an outsider is usually the result of a crisis, when boards of directors have no choice but to take drastic action. In this regard, the possibilities for Russian top managers abroad are extremely limited, since it is unlikely that many of them are ready to work their way up from the bottom and for less money. Again, the remuneration of managers in oil-boom Russia has for many years significantly exceeded that of their foreign peers.

Unnecessary Skills

It is no less difficult for a Russian to start a business abroad. There are many examples where Russians have successfully developed globally competitive businesses. However, most of these entrepreneurs have built their companies on the basis of expertise gained and perfected inside the country (ABBYY, Acronis, Kaspersky, Luxoft) and have taken successful businesses out of Russia in order to achieve growth through globalization. While many successful Russians are trying to do business "out there," very few of them succeed. Even the aggressive Evgeny Chichvarkin, founder of Russia's largest Russian mobile phone retailer, Yevroset, admits that he is "too Russian." This is the great obstacle—to fully assimilate and belong in a British or any other foreign business society.

As for Russian top managers wishing to emigrate, my advice is to take a few steps back. First, this is very difficult to do at 40 or 50 years of age. Second, Russian managers may have inflated conceptions of their own abilities. Enchanted by the economic advances of the 2000s, these leaders tend to ascribe these successes to their own individual competence and management skills in the dynamic Russian environment. Of course, for many this was really the case and the attribution is a fair one. However, personal success was essentially very often just a projection of favorable foreign economic conditions such as high oil prices.

Cosmopolitanism and globalist approaches need to be actively pursued and absorbed, but many lack the desire, time, or energy for this. Children of Russian top managers who have moved abroad will definitely assimilate into the new host culture, but not necessarily the top managers themselves. So, how will these high-end emigrants sustain themselves? Twenty-nine percent of the respondents in the survey mentioned earlier in this contribution said that they would either live on savings or from the rent on the real estate they plan to leave behind in Russia. We needn't worry about the wealthy. But those managers who plan to start a new life abroad without substantial savings might face a very, very difficult time.

Note

1. Volkova, O. (2016). Более 40% топ-менеджеров сообщили о планах уехать из России [Over 40% of Top Managers Have Plans to Leave Russia], https://www.rbc.ru/economics/06/06/2016/575597df9a7947f5eceacb1e

IV 7

Lighting Technologies and the India Connection

Illuminating Emerging Market Internationalization[1]

Ekaterina Molchanova, Oleg Remyga,
Maria Cristina Di Vito, and Ksenia Sokolova

Lighting Technologies (LT), established in 1997, began as a business importing and selling lighting fixtures. Its founders, Dmitry Nalogin and Sergey Mishkin, two students at Moscow State University of Commerce, quickly realized that it would be more profitable to produce their own lighting fixtures in Russia and so they decided to build a production plant.

The partners quickly realized that they lacked the expertise required to build such a plant and so they enlisted the help of an experienced Indian firm based in the United Arab Emirates with whom they had previously worked. They chose a location in Ryazan that was previously a repair facility for Kamaz trucks and completed the factory in 1998. Their Indian partners,

The Life of Russian Business, pages 221–223

Satish Ninkileri and Gopakumar Pazhedath, were each given a stake in the company as part of the deal.

At first, the Russian market showed great growth potential as consumers were increasingly requesting European style furnishings.[2] However, the company's first year proved to be tumultuous as the launch of its production facilities coincided with the onset of the economic crisis of 1998. Luckily, they had delivered their first order and received payment for it before the economic turmoil began, thus surviving the downturn.

Today, LT prides itself on the manufacture and design of quality, energy-efficient, and price competitive lighting solutions. Originally, the company's initial value proposition had been very much synched to the booming Russian construction market, with shopping malls, business centers, and industrial parks rapidly springing up. But this highly competitive environment attracted many market players, both international and local. Foreign companies offered high-end fixtures, while Russian manufacturers lacked comparable quality and targeted the lower end. This market gap provided a great opportunity and LT decided to focus on the mid-market segment. The company now admits that this meant copying European designs and making them cheaper by localizing production and sourcing.

Over time, LT grew to become the industry leader by being recognized as bringing the latest lighting trends to Russia. At the same time, the firm built a strong R&D department that allowed it to explore new opportunities. For instance, the company was involved in the development of Human Centric Lighting, which requires the effects of light on humans to be considered in lighting design with the aim of increasing the health and efficiency of workers in indoor settings.[3] In line with this innovation driven mindset, LT has been supporting a startup in the area of wireless technologies—Deus LLC, the first Russian company and one of the first in the world to produce wireless drivers for LED fixtures. LT also works with leading European and Russian designers to stay at the forefront of product and market trends. An example of this is the joint project with the Russian designer, Artemy Lebedev, with whom LT developed an innovative zebra crossing that integrates lights and enhances visibility for pedestrians and drivers.

Being focused on quality, LT has also obtained various international quality certifications and has even developed its own standard, SUN (Sustainable Usability Norms), which exceeds Russian norms. To control quality and costs, LT has increasingly chosen to produce components in-house as reliable suppliers are difficult to find. The company has its own plastic injection molding facility and die casting aluminum workshop, in addition to producing its own drivers and optic lenses, among other components.

In-house production also allows greater flexibility and is an important step in offering tailor-made solutions for clients, especially as LT expands its B2B large project business.

Until 2008, LT remained largely focused on the growing Russian market. However, in that year it acquired a Spanish plant, TRQ, specialized in emergency lighting. The purchase was mainly intended to strengthen LT's position in Russia, where it ended up gaining a 30% market share in the emergency lighting segment. However, LT's European expansion has been challenging. As it could not find Western European distributors willing to work with it, the company approached end-users for large projects directly.

The big turning point in LT's international strategy came as a result of stagnation in the Russian market. In 2014, LT opened its first India office with the help of its Indian partners. In 2015, the company completed a large production plant with R&D and design facilities near Bengaluru. The new plant serves the local market where significant growth is expected thanks to a boom in the construction sector. LT should benefit from relatively weak local competition and is expected to thrive with its range of products, flexibility, and speed of delivery—the formula that worked so well in Russia during the 2000s.

Initially, LT's strategy for internationalization was focused on Europe and while top management still believes it possesses a competitive product offering, the European market strategy needs better definition. Still, the company has plans to increase its overall share of sales to 60% from international operations. The aim is to become a top 20 global player and rank among the top 5 in India. The immediate plans are now to leverage its position in South Asia to enter the Middle East. As it does, LT will continue to explore new applications for its products, particularly in the growing medical and outdoor sectors.

Notes

1. Adapted from "Russian and Chinese Mid-Sized Business: Internationalization Strategies" report by SKOLKOVO Institute for Emerging Market Studies and with kind support by EY, 2017.
2. Ruban, O. (2012). Money From the Light (in Russian). Expert No. 15 (798). Available at http://expert.ru/expert/2012/15/dengi-iz-sveta/ [Accessed: 30 May 2016].
3. Krasnova, V. (2015). Light as the Expression of Feelings (in Russian). Special Report. Made in Russia Energy-efficient lighting and lighting solutions. Produced by MGK "Lighting Technologies," Moscow. Dmitry Nalogin, President of the company. Expert No. 13 (939). Available at http://expert.ru/expert/2015/13/svet-kak-proyavlenie-chuvstv/ [Accessed: May 30, 2016].

IV 8

Cooling Off the World With Evapolar

The Travails of a Radical Russian Born-Global Start-Up

Yuliya Ponomareva

In 2014, Evgeni Dubovoi, a new graduate from St. Petersburg University with a degree in applied mathematics was about to start his professional career as a software engineer. Development projects were exciting and paid fairly well, yet Dubovoi's true dream had always been to start his own venture.

Dubovoi's father, a nuclear scientist, had discovered and developed a unique derivative of basalt that can be used to protect systems from radiation. Fibers of this material are 1,000 times thinner than fibers of paper, and can absorb liquid up to 700% of their own weight. He was dreaming about using this technology in civil projects and soon after the fall of the Soviet system, obtained a patent. He named the material Evabreeze. While the technology has been proven to work, its commercialization has not been successful. The patent went largely unused for more than a decade.

The Life of Russian Business, pages 225–228

By 2015, his son was working on a business plan to bring Evabreeze technology to market.

Consumer air-cooling systems presented an attractive opportunity to commercialize the material. The systems work on the principle of evaporative cooling. The air is pumped and circulated over an excelsior pad. As the fan blows hot air through the wet surface, the liquid water is transformed into water vapor. This process reduces the temperature and increases humidity, producing a cooling effect. In comparison to conventional air conditioners, such air coolers are easy to install, less expensive, and more energy efficient. The disadvantage is less cooling power, when applied to large spaces.

Both air coolers and air conditioners are bulky and offer set temperatures for an entire space, while heat tolerance varies from individual to individual. Demand towards customizing indoor climates has already been noticed by auto and airplane makers. Yet many shared spaces, such as offices or gyms, have set temperatures that invariably create discomfort for some individuals. Dubovoi saw an opportunity in this incipient trend for climate customization. By decreasing the size of the unit, while maintaining the efficiency, he could make a cooling device that would create a personal climate.

Evabreeze material had several advantages over conventional cellulose filters, which are widely used in air coolers. Placed in the filter, it significantly increases the efficiency of water absorption, allowing a reduction in the size of the unit. Basalt fibers are also nonorganic which means that employing them in air cooler filters would avoid the spread of bacteria. All of these features were then neatly packaged in a small portable unit, which Dubovoi named Evapolar, a foundational product for the personal air-cooling market niche.

The next question Dubovoi faced was where to sell his Evapolar units. The Russian market for air treatment products had been dormant. Relatively cold climates in most regions of the country mean that there is low demand for air conditioning systems. Conversely, global demand is on the rise, led by the growing purchasing power of the burgeoning middle classes in China and South-East Asia. How could Dubovoi reach out to these customers?

St. Petersburg and even Russia in general was not the best location for such a global start-up. Reaching distant markets is difficult for Russian businesses not only because of customs regulations and the highly complex legal system—the biggest challenge is always to find the initial investment. Obtaining a loan is nearly impossible. For instance, during the 2015 economic slowdown, interest rates jumped to 17%. The market for equity financing is also almost nonexistent, with most of the interest coming from a few investors who prefer software projects that require no investment in fixed assets or production. Hardware projects are more difficult to evaluate, heavy on investment and a lot riskier as they involve many stakeholders. In exchange for these perceived high risks, some investors he approached asked for too large a portion of equity, which meant losing control—something that Dubovoi wanted to avoid. He decided to look for alternative funding strategies.

Crowdfunding seemed like a possible answer. But Russian platforms offered only modest resources, as crowdfunding is perceived as being more relevant to raising funds for charities and is dominated by cultural and social projects. Only a handful of projects are able to raise over 1 million Rubles (that is US$ 16,500).[1]

The U.S.-based platforms are a lot more attractive in terms of financing, but are also a lot more competitive. The leading one, Kickstarter, is only open to U.S.-based projects. However, IndieGoGo, the second largest platform, has a truly international scope, both in terms of the campaigns and the audience. The platform offers flexible-funding models, charging 4% of the total funds raised for fully funded campaigns and 9% if the initial funding goal is not met.

Dubovoi built a team from his university friends and they began work on the first prototype. While Dubovoi primarily focused on business development, Vladimir Levitin led the technological side of the project and became a co-founder of the company. In just 4 months, the team had its first prototype and continued to improve the technology.

The key challenge was how to market Evapolar on IndieGoGo and the first decision was whether to present Evapolar as a Russian product. After all, the country has not been associated with successful entrepreneurs, but Dubovoi decided to be honest with his customers from the very beginning. Evapolar's campaign began in September 2015. Once started, the team had 30 days to lock in early adopters as the success of the campaign is largely determined by the first month. Dubovoi and his team were working hard to reach out to potential customers through mailing lists, social, and local media. The goal was to reach the US$ 500,000 funding threshold necessary to start the production process.

Just 30 days after the start of the campaign the project had received US$ 250,000 in financing. In the following four months more than US$ 1.2 million were raised.

The thrill of the successful campaign was soon offset by the rigidity of Russian institutions. For example, very unexpectedly, his bank refused to wire the money Evapolar had raised as no product shipments to the purchasers had yet been made. If fact none of the banks they approached were willing to cash out the transfer. There were 7,500 orders waiting to be produced but the money needed to produce the units could not been transferred to Dubovoi. It took 4 months for him to convince the banks to provide him with access to his funds.

Once the funding was received, the team's efforts focused on delivering the product on time. While the core technology—basalt filters—was produced in Russia, the product casing and electronics were to be manufactured in China. Dubovoi and Levitin managed to build the supply chain in China in just 4 months. The hardest thing was to assure the quality of the product.

The community of backers was truly international, with orders from more than 30 countries. This led to a new problem: customs issues. Dubovoi had to push the promised delivery times back, spending precious resources on communicating production updates, and managing his customers' expectations.

When the product reached the first customers, various media outlets became interested in Evapolar. The first big breakthrough came through coverage by the trendsetting TechCrunch blog.[2] More positive reviews followed and it became clear that a good reputation for the new device was being built and the market was receptive to it. The traction with the early adopters pointed towards healthy demand, and new orders began to stream in. In his first year he sold 30,000 units in 45 countries. By early 2018, Evapolor was driving the industry narrative with an intelligent, Amazon Alexa integrated, air conditioner that creates a personalized microclimate.

Notes

1. Nosyrev, I. (2017). Россияне не идут на сборы: Почему отечественный краудфандинг не стал бизнес-инструментом [Russians Do Not Respond to the Calls: Why National Crowdfunding has not Become a Business Instrument]. Available at: https://www.rbc.ru/own_business/15/06/2017/594006559a794715c9d5819c
2. Biggs, J. (2015). Evapolar is a Mini Climate Control System for Your Desk, Techcrunch Blog. Available at https://techcrunch.com/2015/10/12/evapolar-is-a-mini-climate-control-system-for-your-desk/?guccounter=1

IV 9

Argus-Spectrum Securing the Future

Product Development in Russia, Production Plants Aboard[1]

Ekaterina Molchanova, Oleg Remyga,
Maria Cristina Di Vito, and Ksenia Sokolova

Argus-Spectrum was launched by five radio physicists from St. Petersburg's State Polytechnic University in 1993. The founder group included the current owner, Sergey Levchuk, who later consolidated and acquired all shares.

During Soviet times, the physicists served the state military institution developing high-frequency radio detection, location, and missile guidance systems. After the end of the Soviet era, the state-controlled manufacturing sector faced recession and uncertainty and was unable to fulfill the increasing demand for security systems. As a response to this situation, the Russian Ministry of the Interior (MVD) supported the creation of several private companies specialized in the design and production of security systems. It was the patronage of the MVD that ultimately determined the future

The Life of Russian Business, pages 229–232

of Levchuk's fledgling venture. In cooperation with the MVD, Argus-Spectrum was able to familiarize itself with technologies from the world's top security companies and to purchase the best equipment for its production needs. Initially, the MVD even assisted the company in obtaining financing and helped with other resources such as the rental of a bunker at a military plant for equipment testing.

Argus-Spectrum has today very much evolved into a family business with several members of the Levchuk family working for the company. Although, Sergey Levchuk is still the CEO, he has given his son, Mikhail Levchuk, increased responsibility over the years. The younger Levchuk is also a radio physicist and a 2002 graduate from St. Petersburg Polytechnic University, having previously completed his graduate studies at Uppsala University in Sweden. Mikhail Levchuk has worked at Argus-Spectrum in different capacities since 1995 and has been the Deputy CEO since 2011. He is also a business leader and activist involved in the improvement of legislation for the small- and medium-sized business sector.

In the 1990s, international firms dominated the Russian security equipment industry. Soon, however, their Russian counterparts began to outperform them as it became clear that local companies were better able to adapt products to the national context. In chaotic post-Soviet Russia, thievery and security incidents were frequently carried out by highly educated people, which required more sophisticated security products than were being offered by foreign competitors.[2]

In the early 2000s, as the economic situation in Russia improved, Argus-Spectrum decided to diversify its business by manufacturing fire alarm systems in addition to security systems. This coincided with a crucial point in the company's history, when it began delivering ready-to-operate systems and not just components. In addition, during this period, the rapid development of mobile telecommunications and fast internet connectivity drove Argus-Spectrum's breakthrough in wireless security technologies that gave them a significant competitive advantage over European and American companies still working with traditional wire systems. Argus-Spectrum was one of the first companies to start using wireless or hybrid platforms for alarm notification transfer. These systems proved to be more reliable and allowed firefighters to follow the dynamics of a fire and evacuate people accordingly. Using wireless technologies also allowed the company to achieve larger profit margins on finished goods.

In 2002, Argus-Spectrum opened a production facility in Italy in an effort to reduce European distribution costs and import duties. Through this operation, the firm soon realized that although the technical features of their products were excellent, the size, usability, and visual appearance of the devices clearly lagged behind those of foreign counterparts. They subsequently created an R&D facility to design components that were less cumbersome and had greater visual appeal. Today, the Italian facility still focuses on design while the R&D center in Russia focuses on the technical features. This combined approach led to the development of unique, reliable, and aesthetically pleasing products that were attractive to both the Russian and European markets, resulting in sales growth.

Argus-Spectrum's success was the result of innovation. For instance, it became the first EU-certified wireless fire alarm system, which triggered its expansion into Europe and enabled entry into other highly regulated markets. Today, Argus-Spectrum actively works with large multi-service companies that offer integrated services such as Honeywell and Tyco. These companies buy devices from Argus-Spectrum as white-label products and sell them under their own brands.

The internationalization of the company is clearly another reason for its success. Currently, the Italian facility employs 100 local staff including industrial engineers. Although it took 7 years for the plant to turn a profit, the Italian facility helped Argus diversify both its sales portfolio and client mix. In 2015, the company's long-standing partner, British Sterling Safety Systems Ltd, acquired a substantial shareholding in Argus-Spectrum. The two companies are now looking to tap into the synergies that the new relationship provides. According to Glen Jones, managing director of Sterling Safety Systems Ltd:

> This new relationship allows us to combine the specialist product design and manufacturing established by Argus with the marketing and field support expertise inherent in the Sterling business. This cooperation will enable us to offer all of our customers new and improved products and services whilst continuing to expand into fresh markets.[3]

Russia remains a key market for Argus-Spectrum and is growing fast. Consumers are starting to demand fire alarm systems in addition to security systems. Being a local firm also means less exposure to currency fluctuations, creating competitive advantage vis-à-vis foreign players. In addition, there are many new niches in the Russian market that have not yet been fully developed. For instance, Argus-Spectrum is now developing a new wearable electronics product category for use in occupational safety and health management systems.

At the same time, Argus-Spectrum is evaluating plans to enter the Latin American market, which might include localizing a plant. Product development will remain in Russia. The combination of centralized R&D and localized production and sales is the firm's preferred form of expansion. Lower logistics costs and import tariffs are a key consideration in this strategic approach. In addition, being physically close to target markets is helpful to understand the peculiarities and needs of the local market. Success has also pointed the way forward in internationalization. The United Kingdom experience has motivated Mikhail Levchuk to target new parts of the world: Commonwealth nations in Asia and the Middle East are high on his list.

Notes

1. Adapted from "Russian and Chinese Mid-Sized Business: Internationalization Strategies" report by SKOLKOVO Institute for Emerging Market Studies and with kind support by EY, 2017.
2. Imamutdinov, I. (2014). Try to steal! Science and Technology/Safety Systems. Soviet technological advance, savvy "burglar" and entrepreneurial talent have turned a start-up from St. Petersburg into a world technological leader (in Russian). Expert No. 38 (915). Available at http://expert.ru/expert/2014/38/poprobuj-ukradii/ [Accessed: 03 June 2016].
3. Argus Spectrum corporate website. http://www.argussecurity.it/news/article/n114-sterling-and-argus-stronger-together.

IV 10

Manufacturing in Russia

Still an International Affair

Pavel Bilenko

In 1929, the leaders of the USSR ordered the construction of tractor and crawler-type machine manufacturing plants in Stalingrad, Kharkiv, and Chelyabinsk. The construction of the tractor plant in Stalingrad was contracted out to the Caterpillar Tractor Company, the Kharkiv plant was built in partnership with International Harvester, while the Chelyabinsk tractor plant followed a technology transfer model. These were international cooperation projects of the utmost importance. The construction of all three plants was individually monitored by members of the USSR government, including the Politburo.

Lennart Samuelson describes in his book, *Tankograd: The Formation of a Soviet Company Town: Chelyabinsk, 1900s–1950s*, the details of this affair. In 1930, Kazimir Lovin, the future Chelyabinsk plant director, was sent to the United States and the United Kingdom together with a group of 40

The Life of Russian Business, pages 233–237

specialists to study Caterpillar, Allis-Chalmers, and other manufacturers. Candidates for the trip had all been selected by the local Communist Party, and underwent a short English course. They were joined by workers from the future Ford plant in Nizhny Novgorod, whose task was to absorb the latest advances in automotive manufacturing. A license production model was chosen. On that basis, a floor in one of Detroit's skyscrapers was rented out to host the design bureau of the Chelyabinsk Traktorplant. Russian and American specialists worked side by side to design a completely new plant.

By 1931, the technicians and workers had completed their training and returned to Chelyabinsk, where the assembly and installation of buildings commenced, on the basis of designs made in Detroit. The first tractor produced in Chelyabinsk was in many ways a copy of a Caterpillar tractor (model 1925–1931, 60 horsepower). The Russians gave it the name Stalinets-60. In World War II, many found military employment, towing guns and other heavy equipment.

Eight decades later, a joint venture (JV) was established in Chelyabinsk—TOP JSC.[1] The business model was different, but in essence, the experience of our grandfathers was being repeated. From 2014 to 2016 and in collaboration with the Italian partner, Termomeccanica (owner of a 25% stake in the JV), a cutting-edge manufacturing facility was built. The site was that of a dilapidated Soviet plant, which had just turned 80 years old. The European partner transferred technology, which is seen in Russia as a key component of international partnerships. The latest manufacturing technologies were implemented, such as hydrodynamic analysis and a unique test center processing several hundred control signals to monitor the functioning of pumps, electric motors, frequency converters, and heat exchangers. The JV also worked with leading global suppliers including Siemens, Voith, and Ebara. For Termomeccanica, the project was a success as the JV's trunk pumps for oil and water achieved significant market share in Russia and the CIS.

Some of the world's leading firms have been cooperating with Russia's largest industrial manufacturers. In 2017, Russia's oil and gas industry giant PJSC Rosneft signed joint manufacturing and cooperation agreements with General Electric[2] for the development of Russia's industrial internet. The JV includes building two factories (control systems and electrical systems for ships) and the development of digital technologies in such capital-intensive fields as refining and petrochemicals.

There is a second, more systematic approach to international partnerships in manufacturing that is based on the long-term support of a Russian institution. The Kaluga region represents a best practice case in this regard. The city used to be a trading post in the 19th century thanks to its location on the road that connected Kiev to Moscow, which is just 170 km away. This dormant area of 1 million inhabitants, of which about 330,000 live in Kaluga city, elected a new governor in 2000. With his appointment confirmed by the president in 2005 and still in office today, Anatoly Artamonov exemplifies the impact that enlightened officials can have on modern Russia. His goal was to turn Kaluga into a hub for large-scale manufacturing. His first step was to surround himself by a young and capable team of regional managers.

How did the governor realize his goal of developing Kaluga? The local government built an administration that was welcoming, fast and flexible, one that went to work with foreign investors. Over 150 firms have by now established facilities there including heavyweights such as Volkswagen, Volvo, PSMA (a Peugeot Citroën and Mitsubishi JV), and Continental. There are even two Chinese enterprises; FUYAO Glass invested US$ 200 million in a glass plant;[3] and YAPP, a producer of gas tanks, also opened a facility. The educated, relatively cheap workforce is a point of attraction. The quality of life in the Kaluga region is in some regards higher than Moscow thanks to lakes and forested areas that allow for outdoor dacha lifestyle possibilities. In addition, costs are lower than in Moscow with apartment prices just 40% of those in the capital.

Kaluga's transformation is also one of few successful examples of converting and repurposing the huge Soviet factories and industrial complexes for the 21st century—many have been abandoned or are barely ticking on "what is left." One solution is to convert them into industrial parks. Kaluga has twelve such industrial parks. In Chelyabinsk, the Stankomash factory, which during Soviet times produced frames for agricultural machines and machine components, is now a cluster of more than 10 companies focused on machine building. As Russia adopts modern manufacturing and the logic of clusters, how does its performance fare with global best practices? Volkswagen's Kaluga plant, for instance, managed to clone the group's conveyor system, and with modern automatization systems productivity levels are comparable to Germany. Yet there are fundamental challenges for Russia's future in manufacturing.

On the one hand the global economy has the American firms with their ultra-efficiency and smart manufacturing technologies—fully automatized factories such as Tesla's and Flex are exemplars. On the other there are the Chinese factories, with massive economies of scales, and still competitive labor costs. Russia's manufacturing could be squeezed on two flanks and crowded out by the American and Chinese models. Or, it could adopt both—the latest automatization technologies combined with the economy of scale possible in the Russia/CIS markets with its low land and energy costs.

In order to be competitive, automatization and manufacturing scale appear to be the only formula. Yet here, politics enters the scene and politicians want a happy electorate. For many government officials and state companies the main KPI for factories is the number of people they employ. Can this ever change? Yes, because competitive pressure gets higher every month. Jack Ma, the founder of China's Alibaba e-commerce giant has in a way already done it: "Do you know how long it took for a Russian girl to receive her products from China after she placed her order? Two years ago, it was four months. Last year it was done within one week. We crashed Russia's whole logistics system."[4]

Assuming politicians give the green light for the closing of inefficient sites, what will happen to Russian workers once their factory jobs are gone? Like employees in production elsewhere, they will need to be retrained. Blue-collar workers will need to become designers and programmers of robots. Pundits around the world ask if this is possible, but in our country we can definitely make it work. Russians of all social classes are talented and creative and take the initiative, having shown before that they are capable of reinventing themselves. In the 1990s I witnessed the transition from manual labor to computer numerical control (CNC) machine tools, in metal cutting. The workers that stayed on learned the new skills by themselves, without either the state or the firm providing any schooling. The mindset switch was immense—now we must do it again.

When heading a large manufacturing operation, I allowed every worker in my factory to come to my office at designated office hours to talk about any problem. The underlying philosophy was: "Upgrade yourselves and be ready to be part of the management team. You are the main source of your personal and of the company's development." In Russia, if a message of self-responsibility is genuine and associated with incentives, both positive (higher salaries) and negative (the alternative is joblessness), it usually works.

There is a final and harder challenge ahead of us. We will surely master cutting-edge manufacturing technologies and fast prototyping. But new technologies and good management are not enough. Moscow is said to be Russia's logistical bottleneck and it is the hub through which most goods and talents are moved across the country. In my opinion, the main bottleneck for economic development in Russia is the very low development of managers' soft skills.

To manage people in Russia, we have traditionally relied on vertical authoritarian power. Military style managers who demand respect (and who are not shy about making full use of Russia's rich vocabulary of swear words) are effective in traditional manufacturing contexts and in construction projects. When building a factory, the hard top-down management style does work. However, when it comes to the design of new machines, R&D or innovation projects, military management fails. One cannot elicit original thinking with hard power. Our focus must be the development of soft skills, such as teamwork, cultural intelligence, leadership and—yes—enthusiasm.

Notes

1. See article "Prime Minister Dmitry Medvedev Inaugurates Transneft Plant for Production of Main Line Pumps and Commencement of an Electric Motor Plant Construction in Chelyabinsk." Available at https://en.transneft.ru/newsPress/view/id/10552?re=en
2. See the January 2017 the press release on increasing cooperation, at https://chelorg.com/2017/01/30/rosneft-and-ge-expand-cooperation-in-shipbuilding-and-technologies/.
3. See article "Workers Busy at Russian Factory of China's Fuyao Glass in Kaluga." Available at http://www.xinhuanet.com/english/2017-08/18/c_136536730.htm.
4. Rose, C. (2015). Entrepreneurial Masterclass: Alibaba Founder, Jack Ma Interviewed by Charlier Rose. Available at: https://www.fin24.com/BizNews/Entrepreneurial-Masterclass-Alibaba-founder-Jack-Ma-interviewed-by-Charlie-Rose-20150210

IV 11

Russia Is About Business

Views from a Resilient Swiss Entrepreneur

Walter Denz

"Failing is not an option!" This, essentially, was the business plan when I and my business partner, Sven Lidén, both of us being young graduates from the University of St. Gallen in Switzerland with just a few years professional experience, decided to move to Russia in early 1992. The plan was to set up a language school teaching Russian to foreigners with the help of modern pedagogical techniques. It did not matter that neither of us spoke a word of Russian back then. We ended up picking up the language fairly quickly. While my business partner and friend moved back to Switzerland for personal reasons, I stayed in the country.

Starting a company in Russia in the 1990s was in no way comparable to what entrepreneurs face today. The start-up adventure was exciting but dangerous at times. It took Liden and Denz 5 years to break even and the company continued to face numerous non-financial risks well after that

The Life of Russian Business, pages 239–241

point. The absence of clear rules, complex and often contradictory regulations, plus criminal structures that seemed to be in control of pretty much everything, kept us distracted from strategic planning and achieving long term goals. This situation did not go down well with would-be investors.

In retrospect, we survived these difficult years largely because of three reasons: failing was not an option; our earnings were mostly in hard currency while overheads were low; and we managed to communicate in Russian despite being foreigners and, very importantly, we managed to understand the Russian mentality.

The third point remains essential even today. Speaking the language raises one's profile in one's Russian speaking network, whether in business, with officials or privately. Never mind that many Russians today speak decent English. Not knowing the language means being cut out of the communication flow and there will then always be a filter, which can lead one to wrong, sometimes disastrous decisions.

Since the 1990s, much has happened in Russia. Legislation on taxation has become increasingly business-friendly. Fairly low taxes for SMEs mean that many of them have now left the shadow economy behind and are slowly but steadily becoming tax compliant. Yet, many business sectors are still suffering from overregulation, from unnecessary licensing requirements, from antiquated public safety standards and other directives which have always been a cause of bribery and small- to medium-scale corruption.

Having run an SME in Russia for over two decades, my advice is simple. Striking "deals" with officials never pays off. It is expensive, will backfire, and—surprise—it is illegal too. Follow the rules, hire good lawyers, and challenge officials. Take them to court? Yes! But don't take shortcuts. You always lose. Especially as a foreigner, your visa can easily be revoked.

Being compliant raises your profile and at the end of the day, officials will respect you, as will others. Your business partners, your staff, and your customers will all appreciate your no-nonsense approach to doing business in Russia.

Corruption remains a huge problem in Russia. However, in our sector and given our size (about 80 staff) it is fairly easy to stay out of trouble. This has not always been the case. It took us years to convince our staff members that paying their social security contributions (amounting to approximately 30% of their salary) would actually be beneficial for them (e.g., making it easier to get mortgages and receiving higher payouts during maternity leave). The benefits for us as an employer are clear: outsourced accountancy, automated payroll system, no cash lying around, and no possibility of blackmail.

The dynamics of the private sector have also evolved over the past decade. The last time a customer threatened to annihilate our business and burn down our building because he was not happy with our services was a few years ago. Things have calmed down a lot. Russia is a much safer place now than it was 2 decades ago. Even manners have dramatically changed—for the better. This is even visible on the roads where Russian drivers now stop for pedestrians. Well, most of them do!

The 1990s brought a lot of adventurers (like myself) to Russia. Many of us had no track record in running a business anywhere else and had a scant knowledge of the local language or mentality. Blaming "the mob" or the difficult environment for failure was all too easy. Yet, from my personal experience, it is clear that many of those who failed and left Russia, would also have failed elsewhere.

It is clear that the country has democratic deficits that need to be addressed. Living in Russia today runs in many ways counter to Western values, but I strongly advise foreign investors or other expats against getting involved into Russian politics, even on social media. But then, would you seriously challenge the political system in China? As an expat living in Russia for over 25 years, I have never taken part in the debate on whether a "Western" type of democracy would be a better fit for Russia. I simply don't know. What I do know is that this is something for Russians to decide.

Despite all the shortcomings and uncertainty, I am confident that the business climate in Russia will now not change for the worse. If the past is any guide, we have had more than our fair share of shocks since the early 1990s and each time the economy recovered faster than was generally anticipated. Will this be the case the next time around too? Two forces in combination are central in answering this question. First, a highly educated and motivated workforce is determined to live better than their parents. Second, firms and entrepreneurs today are enabled by low taxes. In short, I believe that modern Russia means business.

V

Leadership

SECTION V

Introduction

Foreign professors teaching executives or EMBAs in Russia are generally very impressed by their students' business savvy, entrepreneurial talent, and quite a few also show mastery of hard skills such as finance or operations management. Asked about the biggest weakness of Russian executives, many will invariably respond with "soft-skills." Properly addressing cross-cultural management, teamwork, and leadership in the Russian organization will provide high returns.

This section is introduced by leading academic, John DeKrey, who sees authoritarian leadership in Russia through the lens of the transformation witnessed in China over the past two decades (Chapter V.1). This comparative view is followed by two critical pieces on Russian leadership; one hones in on "seven delusions" of Russian businesses leaders (Chapter V.2), while the other considers how culture and hierarchies interfere with doing business (Chapter V.3). The not altogether unknown links between Russian leadership and culture become essential in Outila's article where Russian leadership styles are articulated from insights supplied by proverbs (Chapter V.4). How then should foreigners lead in Russia and regard culture? German lawyer, Karl Eckstein, whose vantage point in Russia traces back to 1982, is unambiguous: "Culture First" (Chapter V.5). The cultural journey continues with a metaphorical view on leadership employing a close up examination of leadership dynamics at, of all places, Russian saunas (Chapter V.6). Two Israeli contributors with strong Russian connections

The Life of Russian Business, pages 245–246

then discuss specific aspects of leadership: Negotiations "Russian style" (Chapter V.7), and sales leadership (Chapter V.8). Konstantin Korotov, from EMST business school in Berlin, examines the challenges of leadership development (Chapter V.9). We conclude with a look into the future and the prospects for the next generation of leaders in a piece by the former deputy mayor of Moscow for economic issues and, today, the president of SKOLKOVO, Andrei Sharonov (Chapter V.10).

The fact that the leadership section closes this book is intended as a message. Russia is losing no time in transforming itself. We saw critical reflection and fast and furious movement when we examined formal institutions such as credit rating agencies and the health system, and informal ones such as entrepreneurship culture or succession planning.

Foreigners have always known that in times of emergency, when Russia mobilizes it becomes unbeatable, whilst in normal times the opposite seems true. Russia will continue its high-stakes journey to re-configure its institutions. The biggest transformation ahead, however, will be one of leadership—in times of ordinary business.

V 1

Authoritarian Business Leadership

Losing Sway in China and Russia

Steven J. DeKrey

One of my goals in relocating to Asia from the United States in the mid 1990s was to understand Asian leadership and its impact. During the period from 1950 to 1990, the Asian Tigers of Hong Kong, Singapore, South Korea, and Taiwan astonished the world with their fast economic growth. Businesses in those countries were becoming role models for other developing nations. There was a need to understand the secrets of the Tigers and also to observe how China was going to handle its own growth that had now begun in earnest. From my vantage point at the Hong Kong University of Science and Technology (HKUST) I would be able to garner privileged insights.

The best sources of my learning were the MBA and EMBA students at HKUST enrolled at our Hong Kong campus. The self-awareness instruments we used with them provided insight into their leadership styles as

The Life of Russian Business, pages 247–249

they completed their graduate programs. As a former psychologist, I interpreted the results and compared them over the years reaching some interesting data-driven conclusions.

The psychometric instrument PDP (Professional Dynamic Process) measures five basic leadership styles that coincide fairly well with the five big factors of personality that are: openness to experience, conscientiousness, extraversion, agreeableness, and neuroticism. This alignment with the basic differentiating characteristics in personality is why the leadership styles construct is both revealing and valid. The five major leadership styles are:

- *Authoritative*—forceful, decisive and competitive;
- *Persuasive*—sociable, sympathetic, optimistic and motivating;
- *Caretaker*—peace loving, patient, relaxed and seeks harmony;
- *Conservative*—accurate, precise, detail oriented, rule bound; and
- *Flexible*—adaptable, diplomatic, good negotiator.

All styles were represented fairly equally in both MBA and EMBA groups with two important exceptions. The number of those with flexible (adaptable) styles was lowest in all groups and the number of those with authoritative styles (domineering) was highest in EMBAs and dramatically higher among mainland Chinese across both EMBA and MBA groups. This should not be surprising as China was just opening up in the late 1990s and the most successful style in a single culture leadership is generally the authoritative style. The same was true of post-war United States when the military returned home to take up business positions. Trained in authoritarian styles, these former troops were among the most successful business leaders in their American single culture teams.

In China, it was the dominant leader with a strong mind and determined will that was successful over the years. Working in teams, listening and collaborating with others, was a distant concept in China in the years before and during the beginning of opening up. Mainland Chinese students reflected this. Fully 50% of our mainland Chinese students had authoritative styles. Most interestingly, this was not true of Chinese students from other parts of Asia, including Hong Kong.

My interpretation of this result was that in single or dominant culture organizations, the most aggressive person tends to make things happen. However, when multicultural activity dominates the leader's responsibility and his/her top team members are internationally and culturally diverse, team play becomes essential. When a culture opens up and grows to have multinational teams, the dominant local leader no longer knows best nor leads alone.

When I followed up on my EMBA alumni, 5–10 years after their graduate training, I found some dramatic changes in their self-reported styles. Most of the dominant autocratic leaders, including the mainland Chinese, had become more persuasive and flexible as their careers developed. No longer were they leading from the front but had taken a leadership position in the middle of their internationally diverse top management teams. They listened more and learned to make their positions known through persuasion instead of force. They became more flexible, adaptable, and open to input. Clearly they were learning from their global experiences and were showing considerable learning agility. Flexibility and persuasive styles illustrate some of the most valued characteristics of global leaders. My interest in Asian leadership has now become defined by a more general term: global leadership. The characteristics of the successful global leader work as well in Asia as in the West.

Now working in Russia at SKOLKOVO, I have gained an impression of Russian leadership where the most common successful leadership style is an authoritative one. Many organizations that I have come across have a dominant leader as the primary decision maker and the leadership teams are there to support their leader. This is very much what I saw 20 years ago in China and what was happening 75 years ago in the United States. As Russia opens up more, ventures out, and globalizes, Russian leaders will adopt a more open and flexible leadership style. Russian leaders, like their Chinese counterparts, will need to take advantage of the skills and knowledge held by their newly formed culturally diverse teams. Even within single culture teams operating globally, a flexible and collaborative style will have considerable benefits.

V 2

Seven Delusions of Russian Business Leaders

Money Likes Silence and Businesses Need a Brilliant Idea

Andrey Shapenko

Russian businesses have been operating in a free market environment for about 25 years, but few have achieved global success. Only a handful of Russian firms are listed in the top global rankings,[1] and these are mainly in the natural resources sector. This can partially be explained by the "lost decade" of 2004 to 2013 when the super-profits from the sales of raw materials and energy resources plunged the country into a chronic case of "Dutch disease." However, one must not forget the biased mind-sets and prejudices of Russian business people, which are equally responsible for the overall dire performance of their firms. Here are seven delusions that Russian business people must expunge from their minds.

The Life of Russian Business, pages 251–254

Delusion No. 1: Russia Is a Big Market

Russia is territorially the world's largest country, but the size of an economy is not determined by territory. No matter what the indicator, whether we measure Russia's global share of population, of GDP, of trade flow, or of world consumption, the figure never exceeds 2%. Economically speaking, Russia is a mid-sized country at the periphery of the global economy and with a rather poor logistics network. Entrepreneurs who wish to scale their business will have to go beyond Russia's borders and integrate into global markets and ecosystems.

Delusion No. 2: The More Resources, the Better

Russian firms usually grow through mergers and acquisitions. It is normal practice to build vertically integrated structures. However, efficiency does not necessarily correlate with size. Hence, one of the largest Russian oil companies—Rosneft—produces only half as much oil per employee as BP or Shell, while at the national leader in the automobile industry, AvtoVAZ, workers make five times fewer cars than those at General Motors.

Small- and medium-sized businesses in Russia are much more efficient in this respect. Most had to start on a very small scale and companies developed using their own funds, unable to rely on external investors. New businesses must learn from them and understand that technology, products, and clients are more important than large asset endowments, thousands of employees, or large capital infusions. Our firms must understand that while you can borrow money and assets you cannot borrow a good product or loyal clients.

Delusion No. 3: Business Needs a Brilliant Idea

Many early stage entrepreneurs exercise excessive self-restraint in Russia; they are held back by the belief that with the absence of a breakthrough idea their business will be marginal. And yet, in reality, most successful Russian companies do not have unique business ideas. Social networks such as Odnoklassniki and VK—commerce retailers like Ozon and KupiVIP, banks such as Tinkoff, classified advertisements companies like Avito, supermarket chains such as Magnit, and many others have just built a high-quality product, service or business model around a well-known market demand. We must understand that business value is not determined by a unique or brilliant idea but by the effectiveness of its implementation and the quality of the team.

Delusion No. 4: Trust No One

Global business is based on trust, and lack of trust immediately leads to increased costs. Public trust in Russia remains at moderate levels—possibly higher than in Bulgaria or Greece, but much lower than in most Western countries. It is a serious issue that Russians generally do not trust others, and both consumers and businesses have to pay for this. Russian online stores have to maintain a high level of working capital and build their own logistics capabilities, since consumers will pay only when they see (and touch) purchased goods (and no one trusts the postal service of Russia as a logistics operator).

Managerial paranoia vis a vis outsiders and striving to do everything internally, leads to Russian businesses accumulating non-core assets, which brings a loss of management focus and increased cost structures.

This vicious circle of mistrust can be broken, as can be seen in the examples of BP and Shell in Russia. They were the first to introduce "post-payment" options at their Russian gas stations, meaning that customers can pay after they have filled up their tanks. They calculated that the losses from drivers who just "forgot to pay" were small in comparison to increasing brand loyalty among consumers. This model has now been introduced in Moscow by almost every gas station chain and is a new standard of customer service.

Delusion No. 5: Money Likes Silence

Russian enterprises and entrepreneurs have always had difficulties with openness. After all, business was a banned activity in Soviet times. Then, in the 1990s, it became the domain of mafia-like organizations, while in the early 2000s a company could easily be taken away from their rightful owners. Caution was wise and widely advised. But today, with the growing prevalence of social networks, openness offers many more benefits than threats.

A good example of this new approach is Fedor Ovchinnikov's Dodo Pizza. The company demonstrated openness from the start: It publishes its business plans and reports online; finds investors through crowdfunding; and shows its clients how their pizza is cooked over a webcam. Coupled with a well thought out business model, this approach has yielded stellar results and Dodo has become the largest pizza chain in Russia in just over 5 years. By May 2017, the company and its franchisees had opened 193 pizzerias in nine countries, including in the very competitive U.S. and Chinese markets.

Delusion No. 6: You Don't Have to Go to School to Be a Businessperson

Successful mid-sized entrepreneurs do not usually hold a business degree or an MBA. A survey conducted by SKOLKOVO revealed that most founders of successful mid-sized businesses in Russia had an engineering degree and lacked a formal business education. It is only recently that businesspeople are realizing that a business education is of value if they are to manage large or complex organizations, or if they want to scale their firm up from a medium-sized to a larger operation.

Delusion No. 7: Business Is Only About Money

Increasingly, Russian companies understand the value of the environmental and social aspects of business. Sustainable development is important for Western top managers, while their Russian colleagues are just taking the first baby steps in this direction. Yet, some heart-warming stories illustrate this incipient trend.

Guzel Sanzhalova, an entrepreneur from Ekaterinburg, started to produce honey containing berries in order to restore a family bee yard (this was her main goal) and to help locals to earn money (the social aspect). She purchased equipment in Germany and raised funds four times at Boomstarter. She borrowed a brand for her new company from her previous bow-tie business, Cocco Bello. Now, her products fly off the shelves despite their high prices. The company provides jobs to almost half of the village of 50 residents, and Sanzhalova is contemplating expanding her production capacity.

Note

1. Overchenko, M. (2015). Российские компании в рейтинге Financial Times по рыночной капитализации вернулись на 10 лет назад [Russian Companies in FT Global 500 Are Now Back to Decade's Old Rankings], Vedomosti. Available at https://www.vedomosti.ru/economics/articles/2015/06/22/597310-rossiiskie-kompanii-v-reitinge-financial-times-po-rinochnoi-kapitalizatsii-vernulis-na-10-let-nazad

V 3

The Russian Inability to Communicate

How Culture and Hierarchies Interfere With Doing Business

Andrey Shapenko

In 1998, Jean-François Manzoni, the Dean of IMD business school, described an effect that he has called the "set-up-to-fail syndrome." This is the mutual distrust between a manager and a subordinate, which arises as a result of even minor failures at firms that do not have a well-run feedback system.

Non-constructive criticism or a total absence of criticism—or praise—makes the employee feel underestimated and left out of the work process. The manager who does not notice small local successes starts to think that the subordinate is fit for nothing. Such conflict dynamics may develop in different ways, but they often result in an employee's dismissal.

The Life of Russian Business, pages 255–257

Although Manzoni was describing Western companies, his analysis is extremely relevant in Russia, as certain national character traits exacerbate the problems of poor communication and a lack of feedback.

Many experts on intercultural communications, for instance, Geert Hofstede and Erin Meyer, have noticed that Russian companies are excessively hierarchical and characterized by a high power distance. It is hard to make yourself heard by the boss who is too distant to reach. At the same time, managers do not see much sense in giving feedback to a person they know practically nothing about.

At such organizations, information is normally provided from the top down, in the form of directives. Feedback, if any, boils down to criticism at moments of failure, including criticism for the purpose of reinforcing one's own superiority. There are many publicly available records of meetings conducted by senior executives in Russia or countries of the former USSR. Whether the meeting is held at a large industrial company or at a government department, it is always clear who is the boss in the room. Only a fool would dare question the wisdom and professionalism of their superiors.

Russia also has another problem: We are prone to conflicts, which is due to excessive emotional sensitivity. In Russia, people are not inclined to seek a consensus or to make a compromise. They would rather pick a fight instead. Moreover, they often go too far in conflict situations and get too personal. As a result, feedback is either not given at all ("What if he/she gets offended?") or, at the other end of the scale, is given in an emphatically negative manner that provokes an escalation of the conflict.

The third problem is in the very nature of communication between people in Russia. We tend to communicate indirectly, and this kind of communication normally has several levels. In addition to the message that lies on the surface, there is almost always something that needs to be read between the lines. Even if a conversation between the boss and the subordinate does take place, each party might draw completely different conclusions about the situation. Moreover, it will seem to both of them that what was communicated was absolutely straightforward and accurate.

Finally, we find it exceedingly difficult to trust others, when trust is a key cornerstone of all business relationships. Western business culture is far from being perfect, but trust is generally present and is simply created on the basis of participating in a joint activity or working in the same team. In Russia, a deeper, personal relationship is necessary for that. Following Hofstede's seminal cross-cultural analysis,[1,2] many researchers claim that Russia is a collectivist society, in which tightly woven groups exist where members are protected in return for loyalty to the group. At companies, this is manifested in the fact that managers often do not seek to establish feedback with employees who are not part of their immediate circle.

One of the few attempts to systemically describe the concept of the "Russian Management Model" was made by Alexander Prokhorov[3] in the book of the same name. According to Prokhorov, the key instrument for achieving breakthroughs in Russia is mobilization. That is, achieving the desired result by throwing massive resources at it, without regard to efficiency or even effectiveness. In this model, an employee is seen as a short-term resource of the manager. It is obvious that, in this scenario, there is no point in giving feedback to employees. Moreover, it can even be counterproductive.

The question then arises: Should we go against our national culture and try to change it somehow? History says that all countries that have successfully accomplished economic modernization have in some way or other gone through a cultural turn, introducing new standards and pivoting old ways of doing things around to their advantage.

Israelis have turned chutzpah (courage and bluntness, supreme self-confidence bordering on impudence) from being often destructive into a driver of innovation. Koreans have used the tendency towards nepotism to build chaebols, globally competitive industrial conglomerates. Singapore has defeated corruption through an authoritarian model and the principle of zero tolerance.

In Russia, managers could also learn to use cultural strengths, such as aspiration for self-realization, creativity, readiness for mobilization, and rapid breakthroughs. One key thing that is essential for Russian business, though, is to find a way to introduce the principles of feedback, since, as Peter Drucker said: "Organizational culture eats strategy for breakfast." The key to success is the commitment of the company's top executives and their personal example. History and experience teaches us that systems are usually impervious to extraneous influences. It is more effective to begin changing a system from the top and from the inside.

Notes

1. Hofstede, G. (1991). *Cultures and organizations: Software of the mind.* London, England: McGraw-Hill.
2. Hofstede, G. (2001). *Cultural Consequences: Comparing Values, Behaviors, Institutions, and Organizations Across Nations* (2nd ed.). Thousand Oaks, CA: SAGE.
3. Prokhorov, A. (2012). Русская модель управления [Russian Management Model], Artemi Lebedev Studio, Russia.

V 4

"I'm the Manager, You're the Fool"

Understanding Russian Leadership Through Proverbs

Virpi Outila

Russians are very fond of proverbs and use them extensively in everyday personal and business situations. Proverbs reflect the value system. The frequent use and reuse of proverbs in Russia shows how slowly traditional values change. In particular, the persistence of proverbs that date from the Soviet era reflects the immense impact of this period on Russian hearts and minds. These proverbs also reveal much about Russian leadership and business culture. In this article, we present some of the most prevalent proverbs in Russia and discuss their implications for contemporary Russian business.

Authoritarian leadership has long traditions in Russia. Russians are used to a ruling elite, whether the Orthodox Christian church, the Tsar, or the Communist Party. Even today, many managers and employees think that the most important task of a manager is to assign tasks to employees, and that an employee's role is to implement these tasks. The proverb, "I'm

The Life of Russian Business, pages 259–261

the manager, you're the fool" [я начальник, ты дурак], reflects the superior worldview of the manager as well as the expected obedience of the employee.

An inseparable part of the hierarchical leadership model is the manager's constant and intense control over employees. The relationship between trust and control in Russia differs from the Western understanding. Trust and control are not contradictory, but exist simultaneously and supplement each other. Although the manager trusts employees, he/she wants to control them. "Trust, but verify" [доверяй, но проверяй] is the well-known Russian proverb that illustrates this kind of thinking. The purpose of control is to ensure the implementation of tasks but also, as if it were a social contract, it is meant to support employees. Therefore, employees accept and expect a manager's control. Control is seen as needed in order to prevent mistakes.

Mistakes and punishment for mistakes play an important role in the Russian office or factory. Mistakes are usually analyzed thoroughly, because all "mistakes are different" [ошибка ошибке рознь], as the Russian proverb goes. It is also important to punish mistakes, because one must learn from mistakes and this learning takes place via the punishment. Managers believe that without punishment employees do not realize that they have made a mistake. Therefore, it is always important to find the person guilty of the mistake. Depending on the importance of the mistake, the consequences can be varied: a discussion, a warning, cancellation of a bonus, or even dismissal. By making punishments public it is ensured that all members of the working community learn from each others mistakes—and the consequences such mistakes can create.

Fear of mistakes and punishments has resulted in a reluctance to take risks or any sort of initiative. The proverb, "Taking the initiative is a punishable offence" [инициатива наказуема], was very popular in Soviet times and is still deeply rooted in the minds of Russians. In the USSR, it was not accepted that one should try to be better than others, nor to challenge the standard way of doing things. Even today, Russians have a hesitant attitude towards launching initiatives. Managers expect that initiatives need to be agreed upon with them in order to avoid undesirable mistakes and consequences, while employees think that if they suggest initiatives they should also be prepared to implement them, which would only lead to a larger workload.

The proverb, "You cannot put thank you on your bread" [спасибо на хлеб не намажешь], illustrates the importance of material rewards for Russians. Giving feedback is not typical in Russia. If feedback is given, it is mostly negative in nature. The proverb, "If you don't praise yourself, no one will praise you" [сам себя не похвалишь, никто не похвалит], reflects the view that positive feedback is rarely received.

Information sharing is uncharacteristic of Russian managers, as the proverb, "He who owns the information, owns the world" [кто владеет информацией, тот владеет миром], reflects. By controlling the sharing of data and information with employees, managers aim to prevent misinterpretation and speculation. Therefore, it is managers who inform employees about matters related to their work or the results of the company at a general level. But they will avoid disclosing exact figures such as financial information.

Proverbs offer an interesting way to understand the Russian culture and worldview and they may help to explain why many Western leadership practices may be difficult to implement in Russia. Through analyzing Russian proverbs, it becomes apparent that employees do not have very much say or leverage in the Russian workplace. Even though Russia has been a market economy for over 20 years, the country does not yet seem to be a fertile ground for Western participative leadership practices.

When working in Russia, Westerners are advised to take account of Russian culture. A good starting point is to understand these rather digestible Russian proverbs and their likely impact on the Russian business practices they will encounter.

V 5

Culture First

A Lawyer's View of Business Success in Russia

Karl Eckstein

As a Swiss lawyer practicing in Russia for over 35 years, I have learned that good personal relationships, especially those that one develops with local business partners and their friends, are far more important than any contracts or agreements you may have with clients. For instance, problems with the state administration are not resolved through filing complaints or going to the administrative courts. Rather, one scans one's own circle of acquaintances for someone who has a friendly relationship with the competent state official or—even better—with his or her superior. The intermediary does not even necessarily have to be a direct acquaintance; it could be a person in a long chain of friends. The person who represents your interests will meet with the relevant officer or his/her superior and will try to find a solution to the problem, one that is mutually acceptable to both parties.

The Life of Russian Business, pages 263–266

Many people will claim that working out a solution in such a manner amounts to bribery. From my experience, this is not the case. For instance, on one occasion, a government official was backtracking on his original decision to deny a planning application, but had a need to save face. It was of the utmost importance to the official in question to demonstrate a successful outcome, in this case a public good. Eventually, his initial refusal was reversed and the authorization finally granted. The previously rejected applicant had promised to gift a snow removal machine to the highway department of the local municipality.

Image Is Central

A Swiss client instructed his Swiss bank to transfer to a Russian bank a large amount of money for the purpose of purchasing raw materials. During the transfer, a mistake occurred and the funds were transferred to the wrong bank in Russia.

The Swiss bank informed the Russian bank and asked it to return the transferred funds. Despite repeated e-mails and registered letters there was silence from the Russian bank. Bearing in mind that the then prevailing interest rates were 18–25% it was, of course, very advantageous for the Russian bank to keep the funds for as long as possible and to lend them out. The Russian bank was undoubtedly interested in protracted proceedings and moving through all possible judicial channels. The earnings from the high Russian interest rates exceeded judicial costs, even in the event of a court judgment ordering the return of the remittance plus interest at the Swiss rate of 4%.

Finally, the Swiss bank instructed me, as its lawyer, to initiate judicial proceedings against the Russian bank. However, I was able to convince the client that in this case, one should not take legal action. Being familiar with the philosophy of the Russian elite, I knew the importance that regular trips abroad had in their lives. In Western Europe and the United States the privileged enjoy fantastic shopping escapades and vacations. The prestige associated with wealth is, after all, of paramount importance in Russia. Besides an expensive car and a luxury villa with its impressive façade, a regular series of foreign journeys are a must to boast to one's friends. So, having discounted the legal course, I wrote a letter to all board members of the bank stating that they were ultimately responsible for the due administration of business processes. The letter threatened them with the imposition of a visa ban for the Schengen area and the United States. That this was a bluff—and impossible for me to facilitate—was immaterial. Within a few days, the Swiss bank received back the mistakenly transferred amount in full.

Amending Contracts

A major Swiss industrial plant manufacturer concluded a contract with a Russian state-owned company for the delivery of a large production plant at a price in excess of CHF 100 million. The contract provided for large financial penalties in the event of delays in the staggered deliveries.

I had a good personal relationship with the responsible director of the Russian party. One day he called me by phone and told me to come to see him as soon as possible, ideally that very same day. Only once I arrived at his office did he explain why he had called me (Russians don't like discussing important matters over the phone because they are afraid of being bugged). The contract stipulated a partial delivery of plant materials in the next few days, but according to his employees' information, the Swiss party would only be ready to make the delivery weeks later. If the controlling body at his firm found out that there was a delay in delivery it would demand payment of the penalty.

To avoid penalties, we agreed to sign, still on the same day, an amendment according to the contract that stipulated that delivery would take place at a later date. The reason given for the amendment to the contract was that the Russian party was not ready to accept the delivery for technical reasons. The director of this state-owned company was far more interested in having a good relationship with me and the company I represented, than to enrich the state coffers with a penalty.

Big Is Beautiful

The Russians themselves make jokes about their passion for big things: "We have the largest minicomputer in the world." On the other hand, "small is beautiful" is not a very common expression in Russia.

A Russian acquaintance of mine asked me to find him a European service provider for a specific project. Having made a lengthy analysis I came to the conclusion that the best choice in that sector was company X, which I recommended. This company had been operating for 12 years already and had a pristine reputation. It was also a family enterprise with less than 10 employees.

My acquaintance thought that it was not possible to recommend to his superior such a small company as a business partner. We then decided on a white lie: We said that the company was secretly part of a large enterprise, and that this was concealed in order not to have any problems with antitrust legislation.

Company X has now been working successfully together with the Russian partner for several years, to the full satisfaction of all parties. If you represent a small foreign firm in Russia, you should make it appear slightly larger and more important than it actually may be—for instance, as an independent part of a conglomerate. At the very least, position your firm as the only supplier to a much larger group. In Russia, bigger is better.

V 6

Banya *Leadership*

Where the Master Is a Servant

Tomas Casas i Klett

"Nobody is a general in the *banya*." This seemed to me as a rather un-Russian statement, as we were changing into bathrobes. Two friends, Anton and Alexey, had taken me to a sauna bath in a regular Moscow neighborhood with the promise that it would be a tour into the Russian soul. As if to stress the paradoxical nature of the experience, they quickly added, "But there are masters."

The pig-iron oven had been accumulating heat overnight, and was turned off fully charged at 8:00 a.m. It now supplied the energy needs to provide extreme hotness and wetness across the two story heating room.[1] The heating room, "one of the best" in the city, was the inner sanctum of the bathhouse accessible only from the large shower area with its cool pools and the "cooking" table. The furnishings were clean, but not fancy; this was Moscow working class. Not much had changed there from Soviet times.

The Life of Russian Business, pages 267–269

We started the routine. We huddled around a table at the cooling space outside the shower area. Refreshments were served, and snacks brought from home by the *banya* regulars were offered. After half an hour of munching and talking we dispensed with the bathrobes and headed for the shower area. The ultimate destination was the optimally prepared heating room. The temperature—in some places it exceeds 80 degrees Celsius—begins to char the tip of one's hair—if not one's skin—despite the protective headwear. From early morning until lunch we made the short pilgrimage to the sauna proper at regular 30 to 40 minute intervals. During some rounds I managed to stay inside for three minutes, some rounds I skipped, and for others I barely lasted 1 minute. My mind raced and counted every second in the heating room.

Alexey explained the logic of going in and out of the heating room over the course of few hours using the analogy of traditional Chinese tea drinking. One enjoys the taste curve as the leaves are brewed repeatedly—up to seven brews for the prime teas. Fragrance transformation starts with the fresh opening and continues through to enrichment and maturation, which will eventually lead to alleviation. In the process, different tones and components of taste are revealed, just as at the *banya*. The bath's experience curve starts with an outright shock. But when repeated time after time, one's body stops defending itself. The system's response is intense circulation, relaxation, and finally very deep and pleasant exhaustion.

"Nobody issues orders, nobody is stressed." The *Banya* is not just physical; it is about the great conversations that happen between the rounds of wilting and dripping. It is a sense of community, emphasized by the lack of hierarchy. Sure, there are still social classes as there are differences both between and within a bathhouse, but there are no differences among guests that experience it together. "In a Russian *banya* everybody is equal."

After each round of strenuous heat dips we went back to the table and replenished our energy with delicacies like Siberian berry marmalade and amazing wild bee honeys. No alcohol. Everything revolved around stories, whose main condiment was humor. Literally, as when explaining the provenance of the marmalade's ingredients, "We pick bears and shoot berries."

I was told that there are "lots of rules" and everybody respects them. The "no women" rule "allows us to unwind" and "women have their own *banya* section and probably feel the same way in not having us men around." Again, "the first rule is to relax. Nobody is angry and if somebody gets angry he is asked to leave." The *banya* is an institution, self-run by the regulars and their norms. Where was the leadership structure?

Anton had been "cooking." The horseradish and dry herbs, which he had brought with him, were his main ingredients and lay spread on a table next to the cold pools. He smelled them with care, before smashing them into a concoction that would go into the water that humidified the heating room, lending their aroma to the experience. He had many fronts to manage and the preparation of the herbal potion was just a component of a larger process. He would check—or rather feel—temperature and dryness; make the air circulate in the heating room; and open the vents to let oxygen in at the right time. The master's manipulations also included the preparation of birch or oak brooms which he would flap or outright clap on our backs as a body massage. The skilled whipping was available to all ten or twelve of us in the heating room. This is probably the highest and the most admired qualification at the *banya.*

Throughout, Anton was alert, as if checking for the vital signs of the guests to ensure that nobody exceeded their physical endurance limits. At the end, the master got a round of applause from the parish as a sign of gratitude and respect.

In Russia, leadership comes in many forms. *Banya* leadership is when the master is a servant.

Note

1. Technically speaking the Russian *banya* stands in between the sauna and *hammam* or Turkish bath. Its temperature is set at about 70°C with 80–90% humidity. In a sauna the temperature reaches 100°C but at 15% humidity. In the Islamic *hammam* (not to be confused with the Victorian Turkish bath with its hot dry air), temperatures never rise above 50°C, but humidity is always at 100%.

7

Culture and Negotiations

Russian Style

Moty Cristal

There are dramatic differences in how various cultures negotiate. These differences are related to the prevailing mentalities and core values of each culture. In this article, we delve into the connection between Russia's cultural values and negotiation styles.

Russian Negotiation Culture

Russia is an empire: It perceives itself as an empire, it has an imperial history, and currently in geopolitical terms it sees itself as continuing to play the role of an empire. For this reason, most Russian negotiations, not only those undertaken by the Russian government, but also those conducted by Russian business people, come from a power perspective. Russians perceive negotiation as a "power game," as a "сила" (pronounced as 's′ila') or

The Life of Russian Business, pages 271–274

"force." They will typically present a very tough position at the beginning of a negotiation, and they will continue to offer strong responses to their counterparts even at the final stages of a negotiation. Although negotiation theorists speak about the overall opportunity, and finding "win–win" outcomes that can benefit both sides, Russians find it difficult to adapt to this negotiation approach. Indeed, the word "victory" itself in the Russian language means that the other side loses or leaves the game. The Russian negotiation mentality is typified by a very strong and rather inflexible approach that to some extent ignores the emotional and psychological considerations often discussed in negotiation theory.

Importance of Relationships

Russian negotiation culture is based on force, rooted in an empire mentality, and very formal. The fourth important element in Russian negotiation culture is what we call "отношения" (pronounced as "atnash′eniya"), that is, "relations." This can be loosely taken to mean "relationships," but "отношения" is something much more fundamental than what is perceived as "relationships" in the West.

To do business in Russia, entrepreneurs need to go through long periods of developing relationships, and only when they have gained entry into previously closed circles will they be able to conduct business. In the West, an alternative principle operates in place of the concept of "отношения," namely, the concept of trust. In the United States and Europe, many negotiations start with the assumption that a certain level of trust—in the sense of goodwill and good faith—can be imputed to the other side, even in cases where the negotiating parties have never met. In Russia, negotiators do not readily place such confidence in their counterparts. An entrepreneur will never be able to finalize a deal unless he or she has developed long-standing relationships.

Differences Between Russian and Western Approaches to Negotiation

When Russians negotiate outside of Russia, their approach often clashes with leading cultures in the West—notably those prevalent in the United States and Europe. The Western negotiation paradigm is based on sharing information; such disclosure is seen as a prerequisite for establishing an effective cooperative win–win process. In contrast, Russian negotiators do not want to volunteer or share any information. This behavior baffles

Westerners, who expect such information sharing in the spirit of both sides finding a satisfactory solution. Thus, Westerners will often ask Russians during negotiations: "Why are you behaving like this if you want to build a win–win outcome?"

While Westerners will often approach negotiations with a cooperative attitude, the Russian businessman or politician will come to the table with force and a confrontational mentality. This difference often prevents the two sides from reaching common ground during the negotiation process.

Russian and Eastern Negotiation Differences

The other cultural problem that Russians encounter is when they negotiate with what can be called "торговаться" (pronounced as "targav′atsa"), or "bargaining cultures." This broad description might apply to India, the Arab world, Latin Americans, and Mediterranean cultures such as the Italians. As the term implies, negotiations in these cultures often involve a bargaining process, which Russians are not good at because of the prevailing empire mentality. For Russians, bargaining can feel cheap, overly crass and commercial, unworthy of respect and lacking in dignity. From the Russian standpoint, in politics or business we do not bargain. We negotiate.

Given this difference, what should Russians do to successfully cooperate with "торговаться" cultures? One possibility is to include in the team a person familiar with Russian culture who also loves bargaining. For example, many Tadzhiks, Uzbeks, and Iranians are close to Russia but they also hail from "торговаться" cultures, and can effectively negotiate with Indians or Arabs from a bargaining perspective, and within their own language and culture.

Negotiating with China

The Russian negotiation style can also jar with Chinese negotiators. China is an entirely different culture from Russia, with a different mentality and a completely different way of operating. In Russia, alongside the described empire mentality, at least part of the mindset is a Western linear one. It is an analytical mindset. But China is characterized by systems thinking. In China, things often do not have a clear beginning or end; instead they involve a cycle. Given this circular mentality in China, without a start and a closure, it is common to reopen negotiations even after having signed an agreement.

In other words, a written agreement in China may not be final: From the Chinese standpoint, its terms could be revisited down the road. But this ambiguity is something completely unacceptable to the Russian mentality. Russians, coming from a formal culture, place importance on finality: After both sides have signed a contract, they must then implement it and abide by the rules. For the Chinese, the implementation stage is simply a continuation of the negotiation stage, while for Russians, reopening a negotiation after a deal has been signed is perceived to be a breach of the agreement. So Russians and Chinese may clash during the implementation of agreements.

In summary, the cultural context for negotiation is extremely important. More generally we propose five key rules that one would be well advised to adhere when conducting cross-cultural negotiation:

FIVE RULES FOR CROSS-CULTURAL NEGOTIATIONS

1. *Learn.* Learn all you can before negotiations begin. Learn about the situation; learn about the culture. There is no better way to learn about a culture and its mentality than to read relevant books, both nonfiction and fiction.
2. *Observe.* Observe the situation. Don't jump in and unconsciously apply your way of communicating and your attitude at the negotiation table. Look at what other people are doing.
3. *Suspend judgment.* If you want to be an effective cross-culture negotiator, you cannot say: "This culture is wrong, this culture is low, our culture is superior." You have to suspend judgment. There is no right and wrong. Everything is culturally sensitive.
4. *Respect.* As an immediate consequence of this suspension of judgment you have to respect the culture you are negotiating with. If you respect the other side, you respect the way of doing business in that culture. If you do not respect the culture, the other side will not enter into negotiations with you.
5. *Engage.* Engage, communicate, and reach out. Don't be afraid to ask questions in a polite, respectful manner.

V 8

Sales Leadership From an Israeli Russian

Four Cross-Cultural Stories, Each With a Moral[1]

Max Feldmann

Story I: Stalkers in the City of Osh Bishkek and Osh, Kyrgyzstan

At the Jerusalem branch of Net2Phone, an American telecommunications company, my responsibilities included business development in Eastern Europe, Russia, and the CIS. By 2003, Kyrgyzstan had become our primary market for promoting IP (Internet protocol) telephony services in Central Asia. Kyrgyztelecom—the national telecommunications incumbent—had just launched a large-scale project to modernise all telephone infrastructure in the country and expand broadband Internet coverage in major cities. To implement the project, the Kyrgyz government contracted Huawei, the leading Chinese telecom equipment vendor.

The Chinese worked very fast and Internet coverage in Bishkek and Osh improved weekly, yet international calling rates were still exorbitantly

The Life of Russian Business, pages 275–282

expensive. I was tasked with quickly deploying a dealership network in the two largest cities in Kyrgyzstan—Bishkek and Osh—before Russian IP telephony providers could flood the market with cheap solutions.

Since I didn't know anyone in Bishkek, I simply started going from one Internet cafe to another, talking to the owners. On the second day of doing the rounds, I met Emirbek—an entrepreneur who was a native of Bishkek. Emirbek owned a network of Internet cafes, and—I couldn't believe my luck—in a matter of days, he was about to get a license for IP telephony communication services. I knew we had to seize the opportunity and do business with my new acquaintance because this license could pave the way to important connections not only in the central telecom company, Kyrgyztelecom, but also in the national government.

We immediately struck a deal and Emirbek's Internet cafes soon had public telephone booths operating on my platform. The business took off. In just a few weeks nearly all of the Internet cafes in Bishkek were our dealers.

People in Israel say: "Don't put all your eggs in one basket," therefore, when Emirbek began negotiating exclusive rights for all of Kyrgyzstan, my American-Israeli boss, Uri, was dead set against it. He was willing to sign an exclusive contract only on the condition that Emirbek would make tough commitments and provide guarantees on the volumes of traffic to be purchased. Emirbek wouldn't give in; he didn't want to commit to anything. He even blackmailed us, knowing that we could not manage without him in Bishkek because he owned most of the Internet cafes and was the only one with the precious license.

The objective of my next trip to the city of Osh was to look for another partner. This is the second largest city in Kyrgyzstan and turned out to be the perfect place for me because there were several large merchandise markets staffed by students from Pakistan, Vietnam, and China who all wanted an inexpensive way to call home often.

In a cafeteria at Osh Technological University, I met Massoud—a fifth-year student from Pakistan—who spoke excellent English and barely understood a word of Russian or Kyrgyz. I made Massoud an offer to become my reseller in Osh. With his command of English, he could easily communicate with my technical support staff. I also realized that Chinese and Vietnamese customers might not want to buy phone cards from one another, but they would probably get along with a Pakistani.

We shook hands and signed a two-page dealership contract in the university library. I gave Massoud some training, provided him with a bunch of test accounts to access our platform, and taught him how to send money transfers to the company's account in the United States.

I was as happy as a clam—feeling that I had gained an upper hand over Emirbek. With two distributors in two major Kyrgyz cities, I would soon have full coverage of the country. Satisfied, I bought a few bottles of koumiss, a local delicacy made from fermented mare's milk, and flew home to Jerusalem.

There is one more thing worth mentioning: The entire week of my stay in Osh, I felt like I was being followed. It seemed odd how I kept running into same people over and over again as I went around my business in the city. Being focused on my task I didn't give this much thought at the time.

A few days later, Massoud called and happily announced that six representatives of various ethnic communities were ready to become his dealers, and they needed servers. Sales come first, so we agreed on a one-day training for all the new dealers together with my Moscow technician. I packed several servers into a large suitcase and flew out to Kyrgyzstan again.

The next morning, I went down to the hotel restaurant and what I saw stopped me dead in my tracks: There, sitting together around a table, was Massoud, six worried-looking and obviously non-local guys, and who else? Emirbek!

So, the stalking had been real, after all. Emirbek had people following me and was aware of everything I was doing.

We had an extremely unpleasant talk, including him threatening to switch the whole business to my competitors' platform. The foreign students, who were working for Massoud illegally, were completely intimidated, and me—a regional sales manager from Israel—felt embarrassed like never before.

A month later, Emirbek received exclusive rights on his terms. Now, Massoud and all the other dealers in Osh worked for him. The sales were great and Kyrgyzstan soon became my top country in Central Asia.

I worked with Emirbek for 2 years, until another incident with him came up. But this is a story for another time.

Moral of the story: Don't play games with more experienced entrepreneurs on their turf.

Story 2: Bibles, Not Satellite Dishes Khujand, Tajikistan

When I started my own company in Moscow, an important business was supplying satellite equipment to Tajikistan. I knew this country quite well and learned to negotiate with the Tajiks. They happen to be the most professional but difficult negotiators I have ever met.

With over a million Tajik migrants in Russia, the volume of telephone traffic between the two countries is large. Satellite communication was at that time the only solution for the non-state owned telecom carriers—especially in the North of the country—to get a share of this telephone traffic.

My customer in the city of Khujand had a satellite communications station, which he had wanted to expand for a long time. Prior to New Year's Eve of 2009, and the expected peak loads on the telephone network, they had an urgent need for a large satellite dish—the kind that we supplied from an American manufacturer via Germany.

We received a 100% prepayment, rushed to arrange the logistics, and managed to deliver the order by December 25.

Early the next morning, I received a call from Azamjon, the CEO, who shouted into the phone, "Are you out of your minds? Is this some kind of practical joke? Why did you send us Bibles?!"

It turned out that somebody at the logistics chain had mixed up cargoes and sent a batch of American Bibles to Tajikistan instead of the much-needed satellite dish, which had instead been delivered to Minsk, Belarus.

What could we do? We had no idea how to salvage our good relationship with the customer.

It took us several days of tearful apologies and a trip by my engineer to Khujand to help the customer reconfigure and temporarily expand the existing communications center.

A few months later, I received a parcel from Azamjon on my birthday. It was a beautiful box containing . . . a deluxe edition of the Quran!

Moral of the story: It's human to make mistakes. Some mistakes, however, may be offensive to customers. If you get into a situation in this region where you cannot remedy a mistake you have made, put all your focus on maintaining the good relationship with the customer.

Story 3: A Jewish Issue in a Ukrainian *Banya* (Sauna) Lviv, Ukraine

I had several distributors in Ukraine, each with exclusive rights to his or her city. One of the tasks assigned to local partners was to create a dealership network for the sale of phone cards for long-distance and international calls through our American IP telephony platform. I had recently found a partner in the city of Lviv. Andrey organised the operations very well and the traffic was steadily growing. At some point, I decided to personally inspect this first dealership network in Western Ukraine, especially since I had never been there before.

To be perfectly honest, I was a little wary of going there. Back in my childhood, I had heard about anti-Semitic sentiments in the region. Of course, I did not know of any real-life stories, but I was ready for anything, just in case.

When I met Andrey and his partner—both hospitable, amiable, and open-minded men in their thirties—I immediately liked them. On the first day, I inspected their sales system and we discussed plans to take over the market. In the evening, I was treated to a traditional Ukrainian dinner in a *banya,* to which Andrey had also invited a dozen of his friends.

Andrey's guests arrived one by one. One of them was a restaurant owner, another worked for the city council, and a third was in logistics. Most of them had business connections with Poland. While everyone was chatting, a lavish table was being set in the main hall and I couldn't wait to sit down for dinner. I was told, however, that we were waiting for someone named Bogdan, and that he was about to be here any minute now.

Finally, a pot-bellied short man turned up and began to apologise for being late.

"This is Bogdan, my friend. He owns a big factory," Andrey said, introducing the man to me. "And this is Maxim from Israel, my telephony provider."

Bogdan was amazed, "Wow, from Israel!" Then he added, "It's been ages since I saw a real Jew!" He used the Russian word "Жид" (pronounced as "zh'yt"), whose English equivalent is sometimes translated as "kike."

I grew up in an educated Moscow family, but nevertheless, my father believed that there were certain situations when a man has to fight. "If I ever find out that someone called you a 'kike' and you didn't punch him in the face, I won't let you into my home," he told me when I was still a young boy. When I was a teenager, I heard this word several times, and I always followed my father's advice. Perhaps it was the force of my genes, or perhaps I did it out of respect for my father or for fear of being locked out on the street—I am still not sure.

This time, my reflexes nearly took the upper hand over my finer breeding. Seeing my angered face and sensing danger, Andrey moved closer to me in a flash and quickly said, "Max, it's all right… This word is completely acceptable here. He didn't mean to insult you. Bogdan likes Jewish people, he really does…"

"But indeed," I heard the voice of my grandmother, a well-known Soviet linguist, in my head, "the word 'kike' is quite a normative ethnonym in the Old Slavonic and Ukrainian languages . . . " I came to my senses and overcame my reflexes.

Andrey was right—Bogdan turned out to be a nice man. All evening long he asked me questions about Israel, its history, hi-tech, the army, attractions, and, of course, about Israeli women. All in all, the get-together was great fun.

Moral of the story: A true salesman must have good knowledge of different cultures. This will help him or her to keep a warm heart, a cool head, and nerves of steel.

Story 4: Give It a Few Days, *or* How My Competitors Ended Up in Jail Tel-Aviv, Israel And Rostov-On-Don, Russia

At the turn of the century, calling-card platforms were one of the best ways to sell IP telephony services in the regions of Russia. This story begins when I placed one such card platform to a new dealer in the city of Rostov-on-Don.

Technically speaking, it was a special server that was connected to both regular telephone lines and broadband Internet. A user would buy a card, activate it, and then he or she could make cheap phone calls to any place in the world.

The Rostov platform was used for calls exclusively to China and Vietnam, which meant that my new dealer was selling cards to the respective ethnic communities in his city. Phone calls to Vietnam were expensive, the mark-up was high, and I really needed to understand how my Rostov agents were managing to double the traffic to Vietnam every month—we wanted to learn how to replicate this success in other cities.

There was one more thing I needed to look into: The figures in the reports received from Stanislav, the Rostov dealer, had showed odd shifts in traffic. Once every 2 or 3 weeks, the traffic would stop almost completely, only to resume a few days later and then rapidly grow again. Soon after, the whole cycle would repeat itself. Such issues would sometimes happen when my dealers did not transfer their payments in time, or if they experienced technical problems. Stanislav, however, never had any financial or technical problems. When asked what happened with the traffic he would always reassure me, "Give it a few days and everything will be fine."

All things considered, I really needed to fly out to Rostov.

I arrived late at night. Stanislav put me up in his house on Lenin Street. I ate dinner and went to bed. The next morning, right after breakfast, we went to the city centre to meet with Stanislav's partner. I was looking forward to this because every time we spoke on the phone Stanislav would mysteriously pronounce, "I will have to ask my partner," or "I don't know if my partner will agree to this." So I knew there was a partner, but I had no idea who it was.

We pulled up to the building of the Rostov Police and climbed the stairs to the top floor. Stanislav's partner turned out to be one of the highest-ranking police officers in Rostov-on-Don.

I was starting to gain some clarity on what was happening. At our meeting, we discussed the threat of terrorists penetrating the central part of the country and the fact that Rostov-on-Don is the southern gateway through which they could sneak in. We drank some Kalashnikov vodka. We took photos. We drank vodka again. We hugged like good old friends. In a word, we did everything Russians do at get-togethers.

Then we left the beautiful white police building to visit the "points of sale"—the merchandise markets where my Rostov partners sold phone cards to representatives of the immigrant communities. There was a police station at the entrance to one of the markets. We went inside. "I've seen too many police for one day," I thought to myself as Stanislav began greeting everyone there. "Look! It's our competitors over there, damn them," he uttered through his teeth, with a toss of his head towards the police cell. I saw a few sad-looking young Vietnamese behind the bars.

It suddenly dawned on me what caused the ups and downs in the Rostov traffic! These guys had been selling our competitors' phone cards at the market. For this, they were arrested and jailed for a few days, as other competing sellers had been many times before, and probably would be again in the future. A pattern repeated every two or three weeks: When customers used up the phone cards sold by competitors, they bought new ones from us again, the "official" suppliers.

We continued working with Stanislav until I got a job with another company. The profits were excellent and we had a friendly relationship. But every time I saw zeros in the reports on traffic from Rostov, I knew that someone had been jailed.

Moral of the story: Administrative resources combined with "creativity" equal good sales!

Note

1. The original stories first appeared on Max Feldman's Facebook page between October and December of 2016 and the on his website; http://maximfeldman.com

V 9

Leadership Development

A Challenge for Russia

Konstantin Korotov

Professional human resources management (HRM) is a relatively new phenomenon in Russia. It first appeared through the activities of multinational companies entering the Russian market after the collapse of the Soviet Union. Rapid economic development created an unprecedented situation where young leaders were asked to take over senior positions in management.[1] That meant bypassing several rungs of the corporate ladder, with talented young employees at large organizations grasping positions of responsibility that their peers in the West could only dream about.[2]

The need for a new breed of leaders in post-Soviet Russia emerged primarily at Western multinationals—as did the demand for leadership development interventions. With the absence of local providers of quality business education at the time, English-speaking Russian managers chose to enroll in the management education courses of high-profile Western

The Life of Russian Business, pages 283–285

business schools. Their choice was often driven by the reputation and prestige of the school rather than by content or the relevance of the program, often making the experience akin to educational tourism, rather than to meaningful learning.

Today, although professional business education has become increasingly common among Russian corporate leaders, leadership practices still lag behind the West. There are only a handful of cases of exemplary management practices among Russian leaders, while most of the examples of successful leadership in Russia are found at Western-invested companies. It is even more infrequent to see best leadership practice in the lower echelons of the firm.

The reality of management in Russia is high uncertainty and relatedly frequent job changes. Ironically, employees who change their positions often find themselves in situations where they are again sent to a leadership program with content similar to the one taken at previous firms. If leadership development is HRM's responsibility, should not HRM in Russia address the issue of measuring learning outcomes from leadership programs across one's career?

A second issue is that management education aims primarily at filling labor market gaps, rather than at developing and growing managerial talent. Despite Russian executives filling leadership programs at top global business schools, and Russia having become a favorite destination for the people in the "leadership industry,"[3] many essential tools have only recently been made available to Russian leaders-in-making. What is still missing are the more personal aspects involving management of the emotional aspects of leadership. Likewise absent is the taking of personal responsibility for one's leadership development.

Beyond being provided with new leadership theories from the West, what Russia leaders sorely need are opportunities to explore the deeper-seated issues of their own motivation to lead, as well as to engage managers in challenging conversations about the leadership at their institutions. This work cannot be done without the involvement of the top management echelons at organizations. While HRM has historically been responsible for bringing leadership development to the organizational agenda in Russia, it is time for HRM to step down from its spearheading role and defer this critical task to top management and boards.

Notes

1. Korotov, K. (2008). Citius, Altius, Fortius: Challenges of Accelerated Development of Leadership Talent in the Russian Context. *Organizational Dynamics, 37*(3), 277–287.
2. Korotov, K., Khapova, S. N., and Arthur, M. B. (2011) Career Entrepreneurship. *Organizational Dynamics*, 40 (2), 127–135
3. Pfeffer, J. (2015). *Leadership BS: Fixing Workplaces and Careers One Truth at a Time.* HarperCollins.

V 10

Developing a New Generation of Leaders for Russia

Not Without an "Emerging Market Leadership Mindset"[1]

From an Interview With Andrei Sharonov

Alexey Kalinin, Andrey Shapenko, Vladimir Korovkin, Natalia Zaitseva, Oleg Remyga, Kamila Novak, and Bryane Michael

The term "global challenge," which has become such a buzzword in political and economic circles, is not really applicable to emerging markets. Despite the popular notion that the world is becoming flatter and more interconnected, what we actually see is ever-growing fragmentation. Successful solutions in one region of the world may fail in another. Different parts of the globe do not reflect a unified whole, and if there are any similarities between them, they do not always contribute to a sense of global community.

The Life of Russian Business, pages 287–288

Any challenge carries both threats and opportunities. Success or failure depends on the response of an actor to the challenge—an actor who might be a human being, or an organization driven by a leader. The more ambitious the goal is, the greater the challenge, and the higher the demand for integrity, strategy, resources, and strong leadership. Thus, talent development greatly depends on the context where leaders operate, and each emerging market has its own unique set of challenges requiring specific behaviors and responses.

Of course, despite this fragmentation, all emerging markets share some key similarities. The major one is that, along with rapid economic growth, emerging countries have to fight for non-economic goals like equitable development and the preservation of their environments. The aim is long-term sustainable development and for a type of growth that benefits all members of the population. Yet unlike the "old" developed economies, emerging markets often lack the experienced institutions anchored in civil society that ensure this balanced development. So, the responsibility on the shoulders of businesses and businesspeople is all the larger.

We believe that business leaders in emerging markets should follow specific codes of ethical values, and uphold behaviors that enable them to generate growth along with accepting broader responsibilities for advancing social development and environmental consciousness. These added responsibilities are what ought to become the "emerging market leadership mindset."

One of the major issues for us today is the development of the next generation of leaders that can shoulder these responsibilities. This won't be easy, because on the one hand, most successful Russian entrepreneurs started up in the 1990s; they are driven visionaries whose main challenge now is handing over their businesses to a new generation. On the other hand, the massive cohort of managers now in their 30s and 40s learned to lead in a very different business environment: The severe transformational crisis of the 1990s and the steady 15-year growth in the early 21st century cannot be compared to today. The existing generation of business leaders has a very special set of "growth" competencies and skills. These alone will not help them lead change and effectively perform broader social responsibilities.

Note

1. This contribution has been derived from an interview with Andrey Sharonov published in the report *"Emerging markets decoded: the four domains of development for growth"* by Kalinin, A., Shapenko, A., Korovkin, V., Zaitseva, N., Remyga, O., Novak, K., & Michael, B. (2016) SKOLKOVO IEMS.

About the Contributors

We would like to acknowledge the diversity of perspectives presented in the book and recognize the input of each of the authors by introducing our contributors.

Given the centrality of Russian management and business perspectives, and consistent with the research resources and access provided for the realization of this work, an important part of contributors have an affiliation with SKOLKOVO.

About SKOLKOVO

SKOLKOVO is one of the leading business schools in Russia and the CIS with a strong international orientation. It was established in 2006 by a group of founding partners comprising eight Russian and multinational firms and 11 individuals. The mission of the school is to: (a) empower and support leaders for their success, and (b) inspire the transformation of the region and the world. SKOLKOVO delivers a wide range of cutting-edge international business education programs based on internally developed methodologies effectively blending together theoretical and practical insights. SKOLKOVO has also been developing an academic partnership with HKUST and in the Fall 2018 the two schools launched a joint executive EMBA program with a focus on Eurasia, innovation, and leadership.

The Life of Russian Business, pages 289–298

About the Authors

Marat Atnashev is dean of the Moscow School of Management SKOLKOVO, and has been associate professor of the Faculty of Economics at the Higher School of Economics since 2006. Formally a vice president at EVRAZ, he supervised multiple major projects in the coal and mining industries. He graduated from the Energy Department of the State University of Management (SUM) in 2003, where he subsequently obtained his PhD. He has an MBA from INSEAD, is a graduate of the BP Academy of Major Projects and Engineering at MIT, and was awarded an MPA (Master in Public Administration) at Harvard Kennedy School.

Anastasia Belostotskaya is an analyst at Moscow School of Management SKOLKOVO. She is responsible for the sustainable agriculture research area within SKOLKOVO Sustainable Business Center. She has broad operational and project management experience across commercial and government projects. She holds a BSc in Sport Dancing and an MBA from IE Business School.

Tomas Casas i Klett is an assistant professor at the University of St. Gallen's Research Institute for International Management (FIM-HSG), specializing in international business, Asia, and top teams. As a director of the HSG China Competence Center, he works on various research streams including the Sino-Swiss Free Trade Agreement, the Belt and Road Initiative (BRI), and China entrepreneurship and innovation. He is visiting professor at SKOLKOVO and a member of its academic council, where he is developing research initiatives on the Sino-Russian trade and investment relationship and future perspectives on Russian innovation. He graduated from the Wharton School of Business at the University of Pennsylvania, later earning a Master of Science in Management at Fudan University in Shanghai, followed by a PhD (Doctor Oeconomiae) at the University of St. Gallen in Switzerland.

Steven DeKrey is currently serving as associate dean for the Hong Kong University of Science and Technology Business School, a school he joined in 1996. His assignment includes overseeing the Financial Times Global #1 Kellogg HKUST EMBA Program of which he was founding director and running the MBA Program HKUST offers in Saudi Arabia. He is the HKUST partnership representative to the Moscow School of Management SKOLKOVO where he serves as the chair of the academic council. Since January 2017, he has traveled to Moscow on a monthly basis. He is a professor of leadership, an area in which he has edited three books, developed and taught five graduate leadership courses and has over 30 years' experience as a senior academic leader at five culturally different schools including a recent term as president of the Asian Institute of Management.

Walter Denz, grew up in Zurich, Switzerland. In 1989, he graduated from the University of St. Gallen (HSG) with a degree in international relations. He subsequently moved to London for a MSc in Political Theory at the London School of Economics and Political Science. In early 1992 he went to post-communist Russia and set up Liden & Denz Language Centre, one of the first private institutions teaching Russian as a foreign language. He lives together with his family in Saint Petersburg, Russia.

Maria Cristina Di Vito has worked as analyst in energy specialized in renewable energy, sustainable cities, and M&As in European utilities. Much of her work has focused on the development of renewable energy regulation in BRIC nations and other emerging markets. She holds a Master of Public Management from SDA Bocconi, Italy and a BA in Business Communications from the University of Montreal and McGill University, Canada.

Moty Cristal is professor of professional practice in negotiation dynamics of the Moscow School of Management SKOLKOVO. He also lectures on negotiations and civil crisis management at Tel Aviv University, the Lauder School of Government, Diplomacy, and Strategy and the Arison Business School (Israel). He graduated from Bar-Ilan Law School (Israel) and Harvard Kennedy School of Government. He is currently completing his PhD at the London School of Economics. He is the founder and CEO of NEST Consulting and one of the leading Israeli experts in negotiations. He served as Deputy Head of the Negotiation Management Centre at former Israeli Prime Minister Ehud Barak's office.

Karl Eckstein is a Swiss lawyer who has been living and working in Russia for over 35 years. His Moscow law office represents the interests of foreign companies, primarily from the German speaking countries. On the back of his practical experience, he emphasizes that the key aspects of a successful commercial relationship are not statutory or contractual provisions. Rather, the most important success factors in Russia are to understand the cultural background of Russians; how they think and how they feel.

Maxim Feldman grew up in Moscow and studied history at the LOMONOSOV State University. He started his career as an evangelist and preacher and then spent over 15 years working abroad in the high-tech industries of Israel and the United States. He founded his own technology businesses in Israel, Russia, and the CIS and then pursued an Executive MBA degree at the SKOLKOVO Moscow School of Management where today he heads SKOLKOVO's MBA and EMBA programs and teaches sales management to entrepreneurs. An experienced diver, a fan of fishing, and devout student of philosophy, he is the "proud father of three great kids."

Carl Fey is a professor of international business at Aalto University (Finland) and a visiting professor at the Chinese University of Hong Kong. From 2011–2015, he was dean of Nottingham University Business School China. His research focuses on what management practices work best in China and Russia. He has over 50 publications in leading international management journals. In 2013 he was a recipient of the *Journal of International Business Studies* Decade Award. He is a highly sought-after executive educator and consultant.

Keith Goodall is senior faculty member at University of Cambridge Judge Business School and a visiting professor at SKOLKOVO School of Management and China Europe International Business School where he has taught in a number of executive education courses. He obtained his doctorate from the University of Cambridge. His research has been published in a number of leading academic outlets including *Journal of General Management* and *Journal of World Business.*

Herman Gref is the CEO and Chairman of the largest state Russian bank, Sberbank. He is a board member of several Russian listed corporations. Prior to his appointment at Sberbank, Herman Gref held several positions in Russia's state administration. Between 2000 and 2007 he served as Minister of Economic Development and Trade of the Russian Federation.

Irina Ivashkovskaya is full professor and head of the Finance School at the National Research University "Higher School of Economics" (NRU HSE). She also leads the Corporate Finance Research Center, which she launched in 2006. Irina founded the *Journal of Corporate Finance Studies* at NRU HSE which is now included in the international Web of Science 1000 index. At the Finance School she is responsible for the development and implementation of corporate finance research strategies.

Dmitri Melkumov lives and works in Helsinki. With an academic background in economics and marketing, he graduated with a PhD (Econ.) from the Hanken School of Economics in 2011. His research interests include international business, corporate governance, boards of directors, and their tasks and directors' identification. He currently works as a business development manager in the field of industrial sales and project management at Oy Listech Ltd, a private enterprise based in Helsinki.

Mikhail Mishchenko was born in Kursk, Western Russia, where he studied agricultural engineering, completing his education in Germany and earning an EMBA from the University of St.Gallen (HSG). An entrepreneur for over a decade he has been running his own business importing agricultural equipment from Germany, the United States, and Switzerland into Russia.

Yuri Mitin is the head of SKOLKOVO Startup Academy. He is also a partner in Universe Ventures seed investment fund, the founder of the MSU business incubator and the director of SKOLKOVO EMBA alumni association. He holds a PhD in innovation and entrepreneurship from Moscow State University. He is a co-author of several books on entrepreneurship and a host of Business FM, Russia's leading business radio station.

Elena Korotkova is the director of KB Strelka Department of Urban Economics and a land law expert. In 2015–2016 she was a senior analyst at the SKOLKOVO Centre for Urban Studies and has work and teaching experience at Russian and international universities and organizations such as MIT, Harvard University, Cambridge University, Technion—Israel Institute of Technology, UNHabitat and Jones Lang LaSalle. She holds a degree in Urban Studies and Planning from Massachusetts Institute of Technology (MIT).

Konstnatin Korotov is a full professor and dean of executive education at ESMT European School of Management and Technology. He is also the director of the ESMT Center for Leadership Development Research. He obtained his PhD from INSEAD. Apart from his academic achievements he has over 20 years of professional experience in management consulting services.

Vladimir Korovkin is the head of innovations and digital research at Moscow School of Management SKOLKOVO. He is an expert in IT-management and Internet communication platforms with a focus on organizational development and psychology as well as on data management. He holds a degree in engineering from Moscow State Technical University and a diploma in International Business from the All-Russia Academy for Foreign Trade.

Irina Kulikova is a professional in communication and strategic planning with more than 20 years of experience in leading international communication agencies including BBDO, Leo Burnett, Lowe, and DDB. She has also worked with large multinationals including Mars, McDonald's, VW, Tele 2, Coca-Cola, Unilever, Pepsico, Ebay, and others. She holds an MBA in Marketing from Plekhanov Russian University of Economics together with London Guildhall University. She also participated in programs on strategic communications planning at the Kellogg Business School at Northwestern University.

Jiatao (J.T.) Li is Chair Professor of Management, Lee Quo Wei Professor of Business, and Director of Center for Business Strategy and Innovation, Hong Kong University of Science and Technology (HKUST). Professor Li is an expert on global business strategy. His research work has been published regularly in premier management journals such as *Academy of Management Journal, Academy of Management Review, Organization Science, Strategic Management Journal, Journal of Management,* and the *Journal of International Business Studies,* and several of which have won best paper awards. Professor Li is also the academic director of the HKUST-SKOLKOVO dual degree EMBA.

Ekaterina Molchanova is a project leader and the head of Global Strategy Studies Lab at SKOLKOVO Institute of Emerging Markets. She has extensive experience in marketing and management consulting as well as applied research in the area of human capital and higher education. She holds a BSc in International Business and an MSc in Marketing Management from Rotterdam School of Management—Erasmus University.

Kamila Novak is the senior research fellow in Moscow School of Management SKOLKOVO. She provides analytical support to the Sustainable Business Center in the research streams of sustainable development, corporate sustainability and impact investment. Her past professional affiliations include such international organizations, as World Wide Fund for Nature (WWF), UNICEF, OSCE, and Korea Trade-Investment Promotion Agency (KOTRA). She was awarded with a Master of Public Management from SDA Bocconi, Italy, and a BSc (Honors) in Investment and Financial Risk Management from Cass Business School, U.K.

Virpi Outila is a postdoctoral researcher at Aalto University School of Business. Her doctoral dissertation on employee empowerment in Russia was based on Russian proverbs used by her interviewees. Prior joining academia she worked as a business executive in HRM with special focus on Russia.

Egor Pereverzev holds a PhD in Philosophy from Belgorod University and MBA from Washington University in St. Louis. Having spent most of his professional life in China working on operations at international firms, he is now managing director of the China subsidiary of a global electric equipment distributor. He has recently been appointed professor of practice at the SKOLKOVO Moscow School of Management and is an opinion leader in Russia on topics related to Chinese business, contributing to several magazines including *Forbes* Russian edition.

Vitaly Polekhin has a PhD in philosophy from Magnitogorisk State University and an Executive MBA from SKOLKOVO School of Management. In addition, he has completed several executive education programs at leading business schools including Berkley, Harvard, and MIT Sloan. He is the president of the National Business Angels Association and the Head of SKOLKOVO Investors Club. He is also a co-founder and a managing partner at Angel Investors, a shareholder, and a member of the board at several business ventures. In 2015 he was the winner of the Angel Investor of the Year category in Venture Awards Russia 2015.

Yuliya Ponomareva is a lecturer in the Department of Strategy and General Management at ESADE Business School (Barcelona, Spain) and a research associate at SKOLKOVO Moscow School of Management (Russia). She holds a PhD in Business Administration from Linnaeus University (Sweden). She has been teaching at Toulouse Business School (Barcelona), Uppsala University, Linnaeus University, and Kristianstad University (Sweden). She has also been a visiting scholar at Arizona State University. Her research focuses on corporate governance. She studies executive leaders, boards of directors, and ownership structure with a focus on strategic decision-making.

Oleg Remyga is an oriental studies specialist responsible for monitoring and analyzing structural reforms in China. He has a background in banking and international relations with a focus on the Chinese financial system. He graduated from Lomonosov Moscow State University, Institute of Asian and African Studies, and Peking University, Department of Economics.

Andrey Shapenko is the project leader and the head of academic platform at Moscow School of Management SKOLKOVO. He is responsible for strengthening SKOLKOVO's educational offering by integrating IEMS research into existing and new programmes, building international academic partnerships and providing advice on strategic thinking and economics. He is an experienced professional in strategy, project management and people development with a track record in leading Russian and international industrial corporations. He holds an MBA from IMD and a PhD in economics and master's in project management from the Russian State University of Oil and Gas.

Andrei Sharonov is the president of the Moscow School of Management SKOLKOVO. He joined the SKOLKOVO team in September 2013. Prior to this, he served as deputy mayor in the Moscow government for economic policy. In 2013, he was appointed dean of SKOLKOVO Business School and in September 2016, he was elected president of the Business School. He was born in Ufa in 1964. He graduated from Ufa State Aviation Technical University and the Russian Academy of Public Administration under the President of the Russian Federation and holds a PhD in Sociological Science. He is a chairman of the board of NefteTransService LLC, member of the management board of such companies as PAO Sofkomflot, OAO NOVATEK, PAO PhosAgro, and a member of the supervisory council of PAO VTB Bank. He is also a deputy head of the executive committee of the Moscow Urban Forum.

Stanislav Shekshnia is a senior affiliate professor of entrepreneurship and family business at INSEAD (France) and a senior partner at Ward Howell. His research interests include leadership and governance practices in emerging markets. He is an author of seven books and numerous articles. From 1991–2002 he held senior management positions in various Russian and foreign organizations.

Dmitri Sinitsin has degrees in Southeast Asian studies (Moscow State University) and simultaneous interpretation (Moscow State Linguistic University). He is the voice of all Moscow-based Tech Crunch events and numerous SKOLKOVO School of Management programs. He has for nearly two decades been active in bridging Russia with the world by translating ideas and intentions.

Irina Skvortsova graduated from the National Research University "Higher School of Economics" (NRU HSE), with a master's degree in finance. She participates in M&A research projects at the Corporate Finance Research Center at NRU HSE. She is currently project director at the Department of International Business of the State Atomic Energy Corporation Rosatom where she is responsible for economic analysis and control of Rosatom's global construction projects.

Marianna Slutskaya is program manager at SKOLKOVO Wealth Transformation Centre where she focuses on research, lecturing, and educational program design. She graduated from Chinese University of Hong Kong with an MA in Global Communication. She holds a BA in Politics and International Studies from the University of Warwick. Her prime area of research and teaching is private philanthropy.

Ksenia Sokolova is responsible for research in the area of management models of companies from emerging markets and their strategies in going global. Her background is in international supply chain operations and regional cluster development projects. She graduated from the World Economy and Finance Department of Astrakhan State University and attended

IBUS-module in KH Kempen University College, Belgium. Her fields of professional interests include global market niches, family business, international supply networks, and value chains.

Segei Stepanov is a vice president and head of the Coal Division of EVRAZ. Prior to this he worked as an executive in several large companies in the gold and coal mining industries. From 2003–2005 he worked as a consultant in the Boston Consulting Group. He holds a masters degree in finance from Lomonosov Moscow State University and a bachelor's diploma in economics.

Zeljko Tekic is an assistant professor at the SKOLKOVO Institute of Science and Technology (Skoltech) in Moscow, Russia. Before becoming a member of Skoltech's Center for Entrepreneurship and Innovation, he was an assistant professor at the University of Novi Sad, Serbia and a postdoctoral scholar at the Freie Universität Berlin, Germany.

Timurs Umans is an associate professor at Kristianstad University (Sweden). He received his PhD from Lund University (Sweden). He studies cultural diversity in teams and how diversity influences performance outcomes. He is an associate editor of the *Baltic Journal of Management*, and also a reviewer for several top journals in the fields of corporate governance and international business.

Ekaterina Vainberg is head of entrepreneurship programs at the Center for Entrepreneurship (Former U.S.-Russia Foundation), co-founder of Singularity University Moscow Chapter, and an independent journalist for *Inc Russia* and *Snob*.

Ruben Vardanyan is a prominent businessman, social entrepreneur, and impact investor. Between 1992 and 2012 he was the CEO and Chairman of the Board of Troika Dialog, one of the largest investment banks in Russia. He serves on various boards of commercial companies, non-governmental organizations, educational institutions, and public and professional bodies. A founding partner of SKOLKOVO business school, he was its first president between and 2006 and 2011. Together with his family and partners, Vardanyan invested about US$ 600 million in projects in Armenia, developing a commercial approach that relies on blended financing to find solutions to social problems. In 2015, Vardanyan co-founded the Aurora Humanitarian Initiative, on behalf of the survivors of the Armenian Genocide and in gratitude to their saviors. He spends a significant amount of his time on projects related to the development and professionalization of charity infrastructure in Russia and the questions of wealth and legacy curation.

Lorenz Widmer is director of Swiss Business Hub (SBH) Russia, the Moscow-based representative of the official international trade and investment promotion agency, Switzerland Global Enterprise (S-GE), responsible for implementing Swiss export strategies in Russia and for promoting Switzerland as a business location. For over 15 years, SBH Russia has been supporting small and medium-sized enterprises from Switzerland and Lichtenstein starting or expanding their market presence in Russia.

Kelvin Willoughby is professor of innovation and intellectual property at the SKOLKOVO Institute of Science and Technology, in Moscow. He is an expert on the management of intellectual property, technology-based entrepreneurship, and strategic planning for technology-based industry development. He holds doctorates in both strategic management and technology studies, and a master's degree in intellectual property law. He has extensive international experience as an educator, researcher and industry consultant, and has occupied academic positions at universities in the United States, Europe, Asia, Australia, and Russia.

Ruslan Yusufov is a director for private client services at cybersecurity start-up, Group-IB, one of the global leaders in preventing and investigating high-tech crimes and online fraud. He focuses on providing effective cybersecurity solutions for wealth possessors, entrepreneurial families, and family offices. Prior to joining Group IB, he conducted research on the state of private wealth in Russia and the CIS at SKOLKOVO Wealth Transformation Centre.

Natalia Zaitseva is the head of SKOLKOVO Sustainable Business Center. Natalia has extensive experience in strategic planning, business development, and international and government relations with a track record in energy and innovation. She holds an MSc in Political Science from Moscow State Institute of International Relations and a BSc in Management from Lomonosov Moscow State University.

Max von Zedtwitz is a professor at Kaunas University of Technology, and director of GLORAD, the Center for Global R&D and Innovation with offices in Shanghai, Silicon Valley, Sao Paulo, Kaunas, Heilbronn, and St. Gallen. He is an expert in global innovation, R&D and product development, especially with respect to emerging markets such as China. He was previously on the faculties of Tsinghua and Beijing University in China, SKOLKOVO Institute of Science and Technology (Skoltech) in Moscow, and IMD in Switzerland. He holds PhD and MBA degrees from the University of St. Gallen, and a MSc in Computer Science from ETH Zurich, and completed a post-doctoral fellowship at Harvard University.

Printed and bound by CPI Group (UK) Ltd, Croydon, CR0 4YY

15/09/2026

14962335-0004